W9-ACE-076

The Culture of the School
and the Problem of Change

The Culture of the School and the Problem of Change

Seymour B. Sarason
Yale University

Allyn and Bacon, Inc.   Boston

To my wife, Esther, and dear friends Murray Levine and Anita Miller for their help and support, particularly during the first two years of the Psycho-Educational Clinic when it was not at all clear whether we would make it.

Library of Congress Catalog Card Number: 70-116572

Printed in the United States of America

Third printing . . . April, 1972

～ Contents ～

v

Contents

⌣ Preface ⌢

The ten years I spent planning and directing the Yale Psycho-Educational Clinic was the most exciting, interesting, and instructive period of my life. Whatever contributions this clinic has made are in large measure due to a group of staff colleagues, each of whom played a unique role in my own development as well as that of the clinic. In different ways some part of them and their work is in this book. It is with great pleasure that I note my thanks and debt to the late Dennis Cherlin, Ira Goldenberg, Frances Kaplan, Kate McGraw, and Dick Reppucci. As for Esther Sarason, Murray Levine, and Anita Miller, the dedication speaks for itself. I am quite aware that the many graduate students and interns who worked at the Clinic from Yale and elsewhere were a remarkable group, intellectually and personally. They kept us going and on our toes. This past decade has taught me well that indeed life is with people.

In writing a book I have always found it helpful and necessary early in the process to decide what I was not going to include. This was a particularly difficult decision to make with this book, as one might expect when one is writing about schools. I finally decided that it would be best for me and the reader to give priority to an attempt to make sense out of what I have experienced in schools. Although this has narrowed the scope of the book in terms of problems and literature that are covered, I hope that what I do describe and discuss will be helpful to future, more ambitious attempts to understand the culture of the school and the problem of change.

S.B.S.

∽ 1 ∾

The Plan of the Book

It is not possible for one person to describe the culture of *the* school. In our urban centers particularly, there are different kinds of schools (elementary, junior, senior high, technical, and "special"), each of which is an entity with distinctive characteristics and yet bearing the stamp of the larger system of which it is a part. The types of schools are finite, but that is not the impression one receives when one talks of programs which seem to multiply by some exponential factor. The categories of personnel are numerous and they include more traditional as well as newer types of position. This complexity is more than one person can grasp and experience, especially if one's goal is to do more than deal with organizational charts, job descriptions, and written accounts of what school personnel say they do. To complicate further the problem of understanding the school culture are three other considerations: the school culture reflects and is a part of a larger society; like the larger society, and because of it, it is far from static; and its present characteristics have a history. Finally, the conceptual complexity of the problem is not made any easier by a literature which is staggering in its size and range of quality.

For reasons that are taken up elsewhere (Sarason, Levine, Goldenberg, Cherlin, and Bennett, 1966) and briefly discussed in Chapter 8 of this book, I concluded that my attempt to study and understand the school culture should be based on my being in a helping relationship to schools, and that decision was one of several reasons for starting the Yale Psycho-Educational Clinic. What one learns via the helping relationship is hard, if not impossible, to learn by other means. I was also impressed by the fact that practically all of the literature bearing on the school culture was written by people who were not in a working or service relationship to the school setting. I am not saying that what one learns about the school culture via the helping relationship is superior to what one learns in other ways; it is different, and the nature of the difference fills in or rounds out the emerging picture. The work of any one individual, based as it is on the particular perspective from which he views the problem, hopefully alters the perspective of others, regardless of the particular methodology they may choose to adopt.

Choosing to experience the school culture via the helping relationship determined the way this book was planned and organized. Nowhere is this more true than in the first several chapters, which in diverse ways take up the issue of how the outsider's subculture (for example, the university) inevitably affects and distorts the way he looks at the school culture. This issue is interesting and important because the critical outsider is often intent on changing something in the schools.

Rare indeed is the individual who does not consider himself expert about some aspect of our schools. There is a surprising degree of similarity in the thinking of the outsider who wants to change the schools and the insider who has a similar goal: both the insider and outsider show an amazing degree of ignorance about the culture of the school, and (equally as fateful) both seem to have no theory of the change process.

The more things change the more they remain the same — that is a recurring statement in this book, which in part is devoted to trying to understand why this is so. If any statement is, unfortunately, unassailable in these chapters it is that about the unavailability of adequate descriptions of the modal process of change in the school culture. I discuss this problem in terms of the new math, which was introduced a number of years ago into a school system in which we happened to be conducting research. My opinion, based on a fair amount of experience in a variety of schools, is that it is quintessentially representative of how change takes place in the school culture, and how the outsider and insider unwittingly cooperate in self-defeating efforts.

In Chapters 6 and 7 I take up the problem of how one ascertains the overt behavior and programmatic regularities in the school. An overt behavioral regularity, for example, would be the rate at which teachers ask questions or the rate at which children ask questions. An example of a programmatic regularity is the fact that for every school day from first grade through high school a child is expected to do something with, or learn something about, numbers. Once these kinds of regularities have been discerned one can ask two questions: How is the regularity justified? and From what universe of alternatives of action was this particular regularity chosen?

What then emerges from this discussion is a point which I consider of utmost importance: *any attempt to introduce a change into the school involves some existing regularity, behavioral or programmatic.* These regularities are in the nature of intended outcomes. It is a characteristic of the modal process of change in the school culture that the intended outcome (the change in the regularity) is rarely stated clearly, and if it is stated clearly, by the end of the change process it has managed to get lost. It certainly was not an intended outcome of the introduction of the new math that it should be taught precisely the way the old math was taught. But that has been the outcome, and it would be surprising if it were otherwise.

Discerning overt behavioral or programmatic regularities requires that one look at the school culture from a non-judgmental, non-interpretive stance, a requirement that is not natural to us. We are so used to thinking about what other people are thinking that we pay little attention to what is there to see. I hope the reader will find helpful in these chapters my use of the man from outer space who is parked on his space platform above a school, incapable of comprehending written or oral language, capable of seeing everything that goes on, and (of course) possessed of the most advanced computers, which allow him to discern any and all kinds of behavioral and programmatic regularities. The regularities he discerns permit us to ask why they exist and what alternative ways of thinking would give rise to different regularities. The man from outer space has taught me much about the school culture.

Beginning in Chapter 8 I focus on school personnel, particularly the teacher and the principal, from a perspective rather different from that employed in earlier chapters, although from time to time I revert to the man-from-outer-space approach. In these chapters I draw heavily from the personal experience of my colleagues and myself with teachers and principals, in order to emphasize several things.

The first point emphasized is the *complexity of each role* — its demands, built-in conflicts, relationship to other types of roles, and relationship to the overall system. Attention to this point is independent of considerations of personality, which, although of obvious importance, too often obscure the nature of the role. Once one understands the role of the teacher and principal the importance of personality factors becomes more clear.

The second point of emphasis is the crucial importance of the principal in determining the fate of the change process. As I point out in Chapter 9, at the time this book was written (1969) the two jobs in this country in which there had been a dramatic increase in turnover rate, and for which it was by no means easy to recruit, were the jobs of college presidents and school principals. It is all too easy (because the idea contains an element of truth) to understand this situation in terms of the characteristics of individuals — a superficial understanding that, when it serves as a basis for action, makes it likely that the more things change the more they will remain the same.

The third point stressed is the need to adopt the set of understanding each role, controlling the tendency to criticize. There is a place for criticism, but uncontrolled by a conscious effort to understand (to see the world the way the other person sees it), it too often results in polarization between the "good guys and the bad guys." This type of polarization may be permissible at football games where personal expression and victory are the ends sought. However, I have too frequently witnessed the *consequences* of such polarizations in the school culture, so I am not really able to distinguish the good from the bad guys. If the quality of life in the classroom (the regularities which are modal in it) is an important criterion, the football game has ended in a tie, which is where it began.

Some readers will conclude that I am one of the bad guys because I do not describe the thinking and actions of the modal teacher and principal as adequate either to the possibilities of their roles or to the problems that those in the roles inevitably face. I can only say that much of what I say represents not only what I have observed and thought about but, more important, what teachers and principals have told me after we had come to know each other. One of the definite advantages of a sustained helping relationship is that once one gets past the initial stages of a mutual "casing the joint," the barriers of role are lessened and straight talk begins (with the inevitable ups and downs, of course). It is certainly not a peculiarity of school personnel that what they will say in public will not always square with what they think privately, particularly if they know what that particular public expects them to say — a lesson, incidentally, which anthropologists learned the hard way. It is difficult to learn from the experiences of others.

In Chapter 12, I attempt to summarize one of the most comprehensive descriptions of a school that we have available. It is an account by Mayhew and Edwards (1966) of the school which John Dewey started and for which he was basically the principal. My summary of this school comes where it does because it permits a comparison between its behavioral and programmatic regularities and those in the modal school discussed in previous chapters. The differences in regularities, of course, brings to the fore the role of the principal, the differences in theory and thinking, and issues surrounding the applicability of Dewey's thinking and accomplishments to our present day schools.

The problem of applicability brings us back again, in Chapter 13, to the processes of change, which are discussed in light of the fact that *Dewey's task was not to change a school but to create one.* While these tasks are not completely different, their differences have profound consequences for the change process. I attribute the failure of the spirit of the Dewey school to take hold in the public schools primarily to the fact that this distinction between creating a social organization and changing an ongoing one was not drawn and examined.

What I have tried to do in this book is to describe and to understand certain aspects of the culture of the school, from a certain perspective and on the basis of my experience with and in schools. I have not dealt with all aspects of the problem but I believe that what I have dealt with is important and has significances for these other aspects.

This book could have been planned and organized differently. I am told that one of the characteristics of authors is that they dearly believe that their books could only be written in a certain way, that is, the way they did it. Whatever the validity of that assertion may be, it contains an assumption which is central to this particular book: there is no one way of looking at and understanding the school culture. There is a universe of alternative approaches or ways of thinking. What I present in the following chapters is one of the ways one can think about the culture of the school.

❧ 2 ❧

The School and the Outsider

There are few, if any, major social problems for which explanations and solutions do not in some way involve the public school — involvement that may be direct or indirect, relevant or irrelevant, small or large. After all, the argument usually runs, the school is a reflection of our society as well as the principal vehicle by which its young are socialized or prepared for life in adult society. Therefore, it should not be surprising that discussion of any major social problem — be it violence, drug addiction, sex, illegitimacy, malnutrition, unemployability, smoking, or racial discrimination — quickly centers on what schools are and what they should be. The initial response seems to be what the federal government should or could do, and the government, in turn, usually takes actions which in one way or another impinge on the school setting. Since we do not lack major social problems, and because the scope of federal responsibility has changed so dramatically, primarily as a consequence of the depression in the thirties, we are now in an era when more people spend more time than ever before planning and executing educational programs and changes. And those who neither plan nor implement spend a portion of their leisure time criticizing those who do.

I do not offer these introductory comments as criticism but simply as recognition of several factors, ordinarily too lightly passed over, that account for many of the failures that come back to haunt us. The first of these factors is that many people having

7

a role in, or concern for, educational planning and change possess no intimate knowledge of the culture of the setting they wish to influence and change. I do not mean that the criticisms giving rise to the plans and changes are necessarily wrong or that the goals are without merit. What I do mean is that many of the people involved have little or no basis, either in theory or experience, for understanding the social structure of the school, its traditions, and its usual ways of accommodating to change.

One could write a fascinating but discouraging history of man illustrating the point that the possession of "truth," or power, or a mandate for change, or the pursuit of justice is far from enough for achieving intended purposes. I should hasten to add that when I say "many people" I am not referring only to those who have not had a sustained experience in the schools, because many individuals have spent years in schools without having a clear conception of their workings, that is, a conception that would mirror both their social complexity and behavioral regularities.

As we shall see later, the first step one takes on the road to describing and conceptualizing the school culture is the clear recognition of where one is in relation to that setting. The superintendent of schools, a regular classroom teacher, the custodian, the principal's secretary, the school nurse, the members of the Board of Education — how these individuals view the school is determined by where they are in relation to it, and their failure to recognize this limits the possibility that one will ever see the larger picture or comprehend another's reality.

Another factor too lightly passed over by those involved in planning and change is that many of those who comprise the school culture do not seek change or react enthusiastically to it. There are those among the "change agents" whose ways of thinking are uncluttered by the possibility that others see the world differently than they do. In my experience, the number of these individuals is far exceeded by those, in and out of school systems, who know that their plans and intended changes will not be viewed with glee but who seem to assume that either by prayer, magic, sheer display of authority, or benevolence, the letter and the spirit of the changes will not be isolated from each other. Far more often than not, of course, letter and spirit are unrelated in practice if for no other reason than that in the thinking of planners the relation between means and ends was glossed over, if it was considered at all.

In some ways it is most unfortunate that our language has two words like "means" and "ends" because they facilitate acceptance of the fallacy that they are related only in a temporal sense; that is, means come before ends, or means are a way of getting to ends. In reality, of course, ends come before means and determine (or should determine) each aspect of means, which in turn is in some way a determinant of what ends will look like. By conceptualizing the process as consisting of means *and* ends, one simplifies thinking and action at the risk of failure, partial or complete.

There is nothing unusual in the fact that many of those who comprise the school culture do not seek change or react enthusiastically to it. In this respect school people are no different than those who make up any culturally distinct organization. The significance of the fact resides in the sources and nature of resistance and how these affect the means-ends problem. To relate the sources and nature of resistance to the means-ends problem is, perhaps, the most difficult and important problem, which may be why it is glossed over. Accepting this relationship, as I shall endeavor to show later, is far more encouraging than what I believe is most often the case: the problem is not seen as a problem.

Assuming that I am correct that those who are responsible for introducing change into the school culture tend to have no clear conception of the complexity of the process — no organized set of principles that explicitly takes account of the complexity of the setting in its social psychological and sociological aspects; its usual ways of functioning and changing; and its verbalized and unverbalized traditions and values — one may ask, How come? It is fashionable, and no end elevating of self-esteem, to answer the question (or to explain any educational failure and nonsense) by derogating the intelligence or personal capabilities of individuals. But the answer, which is neither simple nor clear, is not in the characteristics of individuals. Such explanations, in the present instance, would effectively distract one from recognizing that what is at issue is the absence of formulated and testable theories of how the school works, the conditions wherein it changes, and the processes whereby the changes occur.

When the issue is stated this way, three things become clear. First, the issue is but an instance of a much more general problem: How does change occur in *any* complicated, highly organized setting? Second, those fields (political science, sociology, anthropology, history) that have been most interested in the general issue have concerned themselves only minimally, if at all, with the school setting. Third, it is by no means clear that what these fields have come up with is applicable to the problem of change and the school culture.

What is missing in the educational scene is recognition and study of a very basic problem, and its absence is symptomatic of the isolation of education from the social and behavioral sciences, an isolation that stems historically from the snobbish traditions of academia (Sarason, Davidson, Blatt, 1962). But if what is missing is recognition and study of a very basic problem — a problem which transcends the educational setting and about which our level of sophistication is no cause for satisfaction or enthusiasm — one should be somewhat cautious about assigning blame for failure of educational change to the intellectual and personality characteristics of individuals. If only the problem were understandable in such simple terms!

A GLIMPSE OF THE PROBLEM

For introductory purposes I shall describe some situations and experiences that may give the reader a glimpse of the problem I have discussed.

Numerous people from a variety of fields, previously unconnected with schools, have approached a school or school system to do a study requiring the cooperation of children, teachers or both. Far fewer people have approached the schools with the specific aim of rendering some kind of service within the schools, requiring that in some way they become part of the school. In either case, one of the most frequent reactions they come away with is that the school is a "closed" place that views with marked suspicion any outsider who "wants in" in some way. The outsider feels he is viewed as some kind of intelligence agent whose aims, if not nefarious, are other than what he states. The adjectives that the puzzled outsider applies most frequently to school personnel are *insecure, uncoop-*

erative, paranoid, and *rigid.* The adjectives vary, depending on how far beyond the principal's or superintendent's office the outsider gets.

Now let us ask this question: What permits the outsider to apply these characterizations? One factor is his inability to consider the possibility that the response of the school *may* be based on a realistic and statistical appraisal of past experience. In the past the school (particularly the urban one) has "learned" that if a stranger comes into the school the odds are very high that when he leaves, or after he leaves, he will have some very unkind things to say. If this is the case, one could argue that the response of the school, rather than being pathological in any sense, indicates some good reality testing.

A second factor is the unquestioned assumption that the response of the school person is understandable only or primarily in terms of *that* individual's personality — the pejorative adjectives reflect an individual psychology. It rarely occurs to the outsider that the response of the school person reflects in some measure the fact that he is in a role that is characterized by duties and responsibilities and is defined by a complicated set of personal and professional relationships with many other people in the setting. The school principal, for example, no less than the outsider, is part of a social-professional structure that places constraints upon him independent of his personality.[1] In short, the outsider responds as if his own knowledge about himself and his role in his own complicated setting have no bearing on how he understands and approaches the school.

There is a third factor that permits the outsider to respond in the way I have indicated, a factor that, when recognized, would make for a less personal response at the same time that it would facilitate an appreciation of the complexity with which one is dealing. I refer here to the fact that the response of the school person to the outsider is a frequent one to others *within the school culture.* The response of the school person to the outsider is not unique to outsiders but occurs frequently to those who represent other parts of the school system and who wish in some way to introduce a change of some sort into particular

[1]A situation illustrating the identical principle is one in which the beginning undergraduate or graduate student blithely assumes that a full professor is a law unto himself, operating under no constraints, and perfectly capable, if he but willed to do so, to accede to any student request.

schools. Many school supervisory and administrative personnel talk about their experiences the way outsiders do about their experiences. The icing on this cake of vexation is that principals talk similarly about some of their teachers into whose classroom they may try to introduce some change.

Finally, of course, teachers frequently talk about their principals, supervisors, and administrators as uncomprehending, rigid, and uncooperative in matters of change. The outsider is unaware of the degree of his kinship to those within the schools!

But why is the outsider unaware of this state of affairs? In my opinion the primary reason is that so many of us are intellectually reared on a psychology of the individual; that is, we learn, formally or informally, to think and act in terms of what goes on inside the heads of individuals. In the process it becomes increasingly difficult to become aware that individuals operate in various social settings that have a structure not comprehensible by our existing theories of individual personality. In fact, in many situations it is likely that one can predict an individual's behavior far better on the basis of knowledge of the social structure and his position in it than one can on the basis of his personal dynamics.

All that I am saying at this point is that when we say a setting is "organized," or that cultures differ from each other, we mean, among other things, that there is a distinct structure or pattern that, so to speak, governs roles and interrelationships within that setting. What is implied, in addition, is that structure antedates any one individual and will continue in the absence of the individual. It may well be that it is precisely because one cannot *see* structure in the same way that one sees an individual that we have trouble grasping and acting in terms of its existence.

One aspect of structure will loom large in later discussion. What I have suggested up to now is that existing structure of a setting or culture defines the permissible ways in which goals and problems will be approached. Not so obvious, particularly to those who comprise the structure, is that existing structure is but one of many alternative structures possible in that setting and that the existing one is a barrier to recognition and experimentation with alternative ones. In fact, as Garner (1966) has so well shown and discussed in relation to visual and auditory patterns or structures, the response to any one pattern cannot be understood without considering the matrix of possible patterns from which the particular one was taken. Analogously, the significance of the structure of a setting has to be viewed in light of alternative structure. The ability to generate alternative structures, and the capacity to evaluate each alternative dispassionately in terms of the stated purposes of the setting, pose an extraordinarily difficult theoretical problem. For practical purposes it is a near-impossible one for most people because it confronts them with the necessity of changing their thinking, then changing their actions, and, finally, changing the overall structure of the setting. If the theoretician, in the quiet of his thoughts and office, finds this a complex task, one should be tolerant of those within the school setting who struggle successfully against change.

Let me briefly illustrate this point here because it is so central to what comes later in this book. On numerous occasions I have said the following to a variety of educators:

Beginning in the first grade and continuing throughout the elementary and secondary school years, every child on every school day receives instruction and drill in the use of numbers. This is an amazing regularity within the school culture. I confess to not understanding why this is so. Why *must* first grade children be exposed to such instruction and drill? Why *must* arithmetic and mathematics be taught every year? For the child, teacher, and arithmetic supervisor (among others) arithmetic is a part of a highly structured day. I am tempted to say that it is an involuntary activity of each day but that would be quite wrong, because to everyone concerned that is the way it is and that is the way it should be. But are there no alternative ways of looking at arithmetic in terms of when or how often it should be taught?

The most frequent and prepotent response to these comments is to justify the existing regularity and to avoid anything resembling a dispassionate consideration of possible alternatives. In fact, my comments are not viewed as an intellectual task but as criticism of the existing school culture and its formal workings. The way things are is the way things should be because alternative ways of structuring school life are seen, clearly or dimly, as requiring changes within individuals and within the structure.

A number of educators asked, "If I didn't teach arithmetic for a whole year, what would I teach instead?" That is an extremely important question because it implies that there is an existing "order" and alternatives to that order, but that the existing order is not explicitly understood or justified in light of the universe of alternatives in which the existing regularity characterizing the teaching of arithmetic is but one possibility.

The important point is that we can never understand the significance of existing regularities apart from the response to alternative ones. Because I consider this so crucial to the understanding of the school culture I have endeavored throughout this book, as I have in my work in schools, to seek response to a standard question: What are the alternative ways one might think about this particular aspect or regularity? The response to this type of question is as revealing of the school culture as a description of the aspect or existing regularity. We will have more to say about this in later chapters. But before getting to such a discussion in relation to the school culture we must try to become more clear about why it is so difficult to recognize, state, and study the issues.

ᴄ3ᴏ

University
and School Cultures

The attempt to gain perspective on the structural characteristics of the school culture, particularly as they have bearing on the processes and problems of change, runs headlong into the problem that the observer is not neutral. By virtue of the fact that the observer is himself part of a structure — be it in the school culture or in one outside of it — his perception and thinking are in various ways incomplete, selective, and distorted. In the normal course of living we do not deliberately adopt a stance that permits us to see clearly how our thinking and behavior are determined by the characteristics of the structure of which we are a part; that is, we do not see the characteristics of the structure independent of our particular place in it. Variants of this problem were the basis of some of the enduring contributions of Darwin, Marx, Freud, and Einstein. The position of an observer in relation to events is a problem that any theory or interpretation of those events must deal with explicitly. But as we shall now see, this is not something of which observers of the school culture have been willing or able to be aware.

THE OBSERVER FROM THE UNIVERSITY

In recent years some of the most vocal critics of the school culture have been found in our universities, particularly in the arts and sciences departments. It is unlikely that any aspect of what goes on in schools has escaped criticism. A partial list of such criticisms follows:

1. Textbooks and curricula tend to be dull and out of date.
2. Teachers are not well grounded in their subject matter.
3. Teachers do not make the learning experience stimulating and exciting.
4. Teaching is primarily a "pouring in" of knowledge rather than a "getting out" of interests, curiosity, and motivations. Put in another way, children learn for extrinsic rather than intrinsic reasons and rewards.
5. Teachers are too conforming, intellectually and personally, and resist new ideas and the need to change.
6. There are selective factors at work determining who goes into teaching. One of the consequences is that those who go into teaching tend, on the average, not to be as bright as those who go into many other professions.
7. Schools are over-organized settings, top heavy with supervisors and administrators who are barriers to the individual teacher's initiative and creativity and not responsive to the needs of individual children.

What this list does not convey, what words can only inadequately reflect, are the disdain, heat, and emotion with which these criticisms are offered and surrounded — characteristics that, in other contexts, the university critic would say do not suggest the neutral observer or the quest for understanding. (The reader, of course, should recognize that although strong emotion may be conducive to "weak" thinking, it does not necessarily invalidate the content of criticism.) There is one characteristic of these criticisms that is a more secure basis than emotion for suggesting that they may not be the consequences of dispassionate observation. I refer to the *shoulds* and *oughts* that are contained or implied in these criticisms. There is nothing inherently wrong in making value judgments. Difficulty arises when, as is usually the case, there is no explicit, objective statement of criteria by which to decide whether things are the way they ought to be, or whether the consequences of actions are consistent with the values to which they are supposed to be related. In the absence of such objective criteria the university critic, like those he criticizes, remains in a realm of discourse conducive to passion rather than to clarification, to the defense of values rather than to what constitutes their manifestation in behavior.

But we cannot get to the heart of the matter — in fact, we effectively obscure its recognition — by looking at the university critic as *an* individual who happens to hold to certain values and to think in certain ways. To look at him in this way — in terms of a psychology of the individual — would be identical to the way he looks at a school person like a teacher, principal, or supervisor; that is, as if the individual's behavior could be comprehended without considering his place in a structure of a particular sub-culture. Let us approach this problem by presenting a partial list of frequently expressed criticisms of the university culture:

1. College teachers have no training for teaching and are not very much interested in teaching (as compared with research). Their hiring and promotion have little or nothing to do with the quality of their teaching or the opinions of their students.

2. Most courses are dull rather than exciting affairs in which the student, usually in large classes, "takes in and down" what the instructor says and gives it back to him on examinations.

3. The needs, interests, and curiosities of individual students seem not to be the primary concern of the university, in part reflected in small amount of contact between student and faculty member.

4. College life is unrelated to "real life" and is an inadequate preparation for it. In addition, universities are unresponsive to the needs of the surrounding community.

5. The university has been amazingly successful in resisting change that might represent a break, small or large, with its traditions and accustomed style of functioning.

6. Universities are hierarchically and elaborately organized within both the faculty and the administration, so that several consequences are frequent: change is slow and diluted, bureaucratic struggle is ever present and exhausting, and "deviant" proposals and individuals tend to be screened out.

The reader, particularly if he is *not* a member of a university faculty, will have noted some marked similarity between this and the previous list. If he is a member of a university faculty, he may maintain that the similarities are only superficial and divert one from the obvious differences between the university and the public school culture, by which is meant the superiority of the university as an educational institution. What is so noteworthy is that for many university people it is difficult, if not impossible, even to think seriously about possible similarities. As one colleague remarked, "You are comparing apples and oranges." *My colleague seemed unaware that from certain ways of looking at nature, apples and oranges are indeed comparable.* But it requires that one go beyond one's individual or personal relation to apples and oranges.

In his inability to face the issue, and in his subsequent resistance to the possibility of some marked similarities, the university critic unwittingly concedes the argument that his particular setting is organized and has a tradition, a structure, and vehicles for the attainment of goals. He assumes that his setting is not comprehensible in individual terms. When, however, he rejects the possibility of similarities between his and the school culture, he is, of course, confusing opinion, on the one hand, with the world of reality, on the other hand. As he so well knows, hypotheses should require validation, particularly when the hypothesis is, or will be, basis for social action and change.

I wish to make three rather simple points. First, the university critic is himself part of a very complicated social system that, in diverse ways, determines his view of himself and that system. Second, how he views or observes the school culture will in large part be influenced by his implicit and explicit conceptions of his own setting and his place in it. Third, the university critic, like the rest of humanity, has extraordinary difficulty in viewing his culture independent of his place in it (it is hard to "see" one's mother or father independent of the fact that one is their child). As a consequence of these points, when the university critic goes to the school culture he ₁is very much like the traveller to foreign lands who begins by taking for granted that life elsewhere is truly different than in his own country and ends up proving it. That the "proofs" may in part be valid allows their selectivity to go unchallenged and unnoticed.

One other factor has to be mentioned. It has to do with the critic's desire to change the school culture. On the basis of whatever observations he makes he ends up with *shoulds* and *oughts*. The important problem here is that any suggestion for change implies two related considerations: first, that one has an explicit theory of change, and second, that this theory is appropriate to the setting in which the desired change will be affected. As I have already suggested, we have no firm basis for enthusiasm about the university critic's knowledge of the school culture or his own. I would maintain that the same is true about theories of change, which may be a good part of the explanation of why a number of people feel that in the university and school cultures the more things change the more they remain the same. To illustrate the point:

Elsewhere (Sarason and Sarason, 1969) we have discussed in detail some observations on the teaching of new math. As the reader may know, for some time before the first Russian Sputnik in 1957 there was a good deal of dissatisfaction with the teaching of mathematics in the public schools. The leadership of this dissatisfaction was primarily in the universities, and the content of the criticism took different forms. But on at least one point there was complete agreement — the way children were being taught math was an unmitigated bore and disaster that very few children could survive either in the sense that they experienced the joy of the world of numbers or pursued mathematics as a career. The Russian Sputnik catalyzed the effort to change the teaching of math, and various new maths were developed in university centers and introduced into the schools. After several years of the new math we observed the teaching of the new math in a number of classrooms in several school systems. As we pointed out, joy is the last word in the English language that one could apply to the children in those classrooms. We have also been told that the hoped for increase in math majors, proportional to the increase in the college population, has not occurred.

The new math was introduced into those schools without taking into account their structural and cultural characteristics, and without any discernible theory of how change was to be effected and the criteria by which its effects were to be evaluated — and we shall not dignify change by reason of faith, good intentions and administrative fiat as constituting a theory of change.

THE CRITIC FROM THE SCHOOLS

It is not necessary to emphasize that whatever makes it difficult for the university critic to be a dispassionate observer of the school settings operates in identical fashion with school personnel. What is ordinarily not recognized by the university critic, however, is that the schools are, and have been in the past, far from devoid of critics from their own ranks, that the contents of some of their criticisms are very similar to those of the university critics, and that these school critics often have been in position of leadership and power. Why, then, have so many of their efforts been unsuccessful? and Why has their morale been so poor? Why do so many of their efforts appear to others within the system to be as effective as shadow-boxing?

The fact is that we simply do not have adequate descriptive data on the ways in which change is conceived, formulated, and executed within a school system. Obviously, there are many different ways in which it comes about, with differing degrees of success and failure, but it has hardly been studied. We are frequently, therefore, in a position analogous to that of interpreting the data from an experiment without any clear idea of the procedures employed. *We lack adequate knowledge of the natural history of change processes within the school culture.* But this lack of knowledge is less serious than the lack of recognition of the problem, because it is this lack of recognition that, in my experience, has contributed to the continued failure of the critic from the school. I have known many such critics who were extremely clear about the changes they wished to effect — changes that many university critics would heartily applaud — but whose clarity vanished when faced with the problem of implementation. Too often the result is that the "good guys" and the "bad guys" within the system go about their ways in similar fashion with similar results, in addition to which each ends up confirming his original assessment of the other.

What I have just said could be interpreted as suggesting that the critic from the schools does not have an understanding of the school culture adequate to his efforts to change some aspect of it. That is to say, by virtue of his immersion in, and relation to, the school culture he is ordinarily prevented from perceiving those characteristics fateful for the processes of change. Although I would agree with this, I am stressing another and more general point: the theory or problem of change is not in the focus of their thinking and *they would think and go about the change process as they did regardless of whether they were in the school or some other culture*. It is not that these people are antitheoretical or untheoretical, because many of them are quite sophisticated as to the theoretical bases for what should or ought to be. What their theories fail to do is to face the problem of how one gets to one's goals. That is something with which reality confronts them but for which the theories are not adequate. As I suggested in the previous chapter, this is far from being a "practical" problem (in the sense of how one "engineers" change) but rather we are dealing with a theoretical problem involving not means *and* ends, but a continuous process. That reality stubbornly refuses to conform to our theories and categories of thought is what has caused so much grief.

It is interesting that within the school culture there is at least one group that agrees with what I have been saying about the critic from the schools who is in a position to effect change. The classroom teacher, who so often is viewed as if he or she is a mechanical transmitter of change, can frequently be heard to say about the critic that he has "good" ideas but "bad" or impractical methods of implementation. Basically, the complaint of the teacher is that the critic really does not know the system to the degree that he is aware of obstacles and can adopt the means to deal with them. To the teacher, the school critic is impractical — he does not "know" enough in the sense of sheer knowledge or information. But in voicing this complaint the teacher unwittingly is underlying the significance of what is behind this impracticality: a theory that permits the separation of means and ends.

In focusing in the way I have on the critic from the schools I may well have diverted the reader's attention from what I consider to be a major barrier to our understanding of the school culture: the lack of systematic, comprehensive, and objective description of the natural history of the change process in the school. We have loads of anecdotes, and even more opinions, about the change process, but nothing resembling adequate description. What is troublesome is that what we do have is frequently misleading. For example, Lauter (1968) begins his description of his view of the Adams-Morgan Community School Project in this way:

> On May 18, 1967, the District of Columbia Board of Education approved a memorandum prepared by the then Superintendent, Carl Hansen, which turned effective control of the Morgan Elementary School over to Antioch College. The memorandum pro-

vided that Antioch, with the advice of a "Parents' Advisory Board," would be able to select staff, determine curriculum, and allocate resources within normal budget allotments; a final staffing pattern and budget were to be worked out and approved at a later meeting. The memorandum did not accurately reflect the real agreement that had been made, neither in terms of its history nor the intentions of the parties to it. Another memorandum, prepared by the Vice-President of Antioch, Morris Keeton, and representatives of the Adams-Morgan Community Council, but never finally ratified by any body, spelled out somewhat more of the project's character. This document made clear that there were three parties to the agreement: schools, College, *and* Community Council; that decision-making power — within the general framework established by the law and the District of Columbia Board — was to be exercised by College and community somehow working "within a policy of consensus"; and that all parties contemplated launching a whole set of quite radical experiments over and above that of community participation.

The rather different pictures these documents convey reflect one of the fundamental problems of the Adams-Morgan Project: people with very disparate views and interests agreed to certain words on a page without revealing, or perhaps recognizing, that they assigned various meanings to the words. The general feeling seemed to be, "Let's get started, and we'll find out just what we're doing as we go along." The submerged differences and the haste were rooted in the history of the project and the structure of the neighborhood, but, I would suggest, the history of Adams-Morgan is indicative of the currents in urban education generally.[1]

Lauter then proceeds, in a refreshingly candid manner, to detail some of the problems encountered in a never-ending obstacle course. Lauter's description does more than demonstrate that his description and those of others are far from identical. For example,

> . . . . the impetus for obtaining a "community-controlled" school lay with the whites from the first meeting on. Subsequent planning hardly involved the population "served" by Morgan school. Negro people in the neighborhood were told they might have a chance to run their school; but what, exactly that might mean beyond, presumably, an end to overcrowding and abuse of the children, no one could be very clear. No real program of community discussion

[1] P. Lauter, "The Short, Happy Life of the Adams-Morgan Community School Project. *Harvard Educational Review*, XXXVIII, 1968, p. 236.

or education was conducted; there were, to be sure, large general meetings and a campaign for petition signatures. But there was no sustained opportunity for people to discuss and compare their educational ideas and aspirations, to look at new programs, to talk about how children learn and what they might want from a school. Thus, people from different backgrounds proceeded with very different expectations, linked only by an overwhelming urgency to put the project into operation immediately or sooner. Suggestions for a year of planning or even for beginning with a small experimental unit were quickly rejected. People would lose interest, it was said, and would be disappointed in the promises of the Council. Begin now at Morgan, some people whose children went to Adams said, and if things work out, expand to Adams next year. It was, unfortunately, such personal and political motives that established the context in which the school project was to operate.

It was not only the parents of most of the Morgan children who were excluded from the development of the program; so was most of the school administration. Negotiations were carried on, for the most part, with the Superintendent and one or two Board members in a semi-private fashion, but backed by the threat of the community's general anger at the schools. Plans were not considered by the Elementary and Research offices. (Indeed, the Superintendent called in his assistants only when the agreement had been reached.) This procedure might have been necessary to avoid bogging down in the school bureaucracy. On the other hand, it meant that many of the school officials felt absolutely no stake in the project; in fact, they harbored a good deal of resentment for it, at worst, and were very confused by its status, at best. Their tendency was not to bother the project if it didn't bother them, which provided a large degree of freedom, but also a great let-down of normal services.[2]

Let us assume that Lauter is correct, that at its inception there was not a meeting of minds as to the details of what was to be done or what was agreed upon. And now let us ask the following questions of his description: Were the disagreements explicit at the inception? If so, what were the contents of the disagreements? What was done to deal with the disagreements? What consideration was given, and by whom, to alternative ways of dealing with disagreements? What were the explicit ground rules for dealing with disagreements? or Was the problem of ground rules never discussed and formulated? These questions are not answerable by

[2]Ibid, p. 238.

Lauter's description. Without data relevant to these questions one is left with the strong impression that this was an ill-fated project that from the beginning was doomed to failure. One of the major values of an adequate description of what was done is that it would provide us with a basis for deciding what could have been done, and until one faces the fact that there are many alternatives the significance of what was done for future action is drastically reduced.

The problems involved in obtaining adequate descriptions in the natural setting are enormous, and the reader should disabuse himself of the notion that all that is involved is looking, recording, and reporting. I shall have more to say about this in later chapters. The point I would stress here is that until we have more comprehensive and dispassionate descriptions of the processes of change in the school culture — which, of course, would be revealing of the formal and informal structure of the school — any effort to introduce change maximizes the role of ignorance with its all too familiar consequences. In this respect my experience has not permitted me to distinguish between the critic from the university and the critic from the school.

THE UNTESTABLE ABSTRACTION

Thus far I have discussed three major barriers to our observing and understanding the school culture: (1) We put undue reliance on a psychology of individuals that, as C. Wright Mills (1959) has so clearly pointed out, is no adequate basis for studying structural characteristics of a society or one of its important parts. (2) Observers are not neutral, and what they observe about their own or someone else's setting is to an undetermined extent biased by the structure, traditions, and ideology of their own setting. (3) Particularly in relation to the school culture, our ignorance about how change occurs is vast. and this at a time when programs for changing the school are being proposed and implemented at a fantastic rate. Another barrier to which we now must come is what I shall call the well-intentioned but untestable abstraction. These are the "should be" and "ought to be" types of statements that refer to virtue and sin without any specification to the listener about criteria he can use to determine if actions based on these statements are consistent with them or not.

The classroom should not be a dull and uninteresting place but one which brings out the *creativity* in children.

The *potential* of children is not being *realized.* The classroom should be a place where self-actualization is constantly occurring.

School systems in general, and classrooms in particular, are authoritarian settings. The *democratic spirit* must become more pervasive.

Schools have become encapsulated settings within our society and unresponsive to it. They must become more *open.*

Teachers are inadequately prepared for understanding ghetto children and culture. *Their training must be broadened if they are to become knowledgeable about and sensitive to these disadvantaged children.*

These types of statements can be multiplied interminably without exhausting the supply. Most people would probably nod assent upon reading or hearing them. What such ready assent obscures is that these types of statements are rarely elaborated in a way that tells one what observable consequences (in behavior, practices, or relationships) must be obtained in order to decide whether intent and action are consistent with each other. The problem, of course, is a very general one, by no means restricted to statements about the school culture. Sidney Hook (1966) has discussed the problem incisively in his essay "Abstractions in Social Inquiry."

What then is the difference between analyzable and unanalyzable abstractions? To begin with we must observe that all meaningful terms are employed in sentences or propositions or statements. Indeed, it is only when a sentence or a proposition or a statement (I shall use these terms interchangeably) taken as a whole is meaningful, that its terms can be said to have meaning. When are sentences meaningful? Briefly, a sentence is meaningful if we know how to go about testing it, and what would constitute evidence tending to confirm it or refute it. If we know what would be evidence one way or another for our proposition, then we know what kind of situation to look for or construct (as the case may be). We then would know whether our proposition is probably true or probably false, or, when judgment has to be suspended, what kind of possible situation would be relevant to our inquiry. Every statement, then, which purports to be a true account of what is so or isn't, enables us by the use of certain rules or inference to derive other statements that direct us to do certain things and to make certain observations.

How, then, do we recognize that a sentence contains abstractions that are unanalyzable? Not by any special terms employed but, roughly speaking, by the inability of the speaker or writer to state at some point the conditions or situations in which certain observations can be carried out to test it. Let us consider a few illustrations:

(1) We often hear such expressions as "The will of the people is sovereign in the United States." This seems to have a meaning, for it is often affirmed or denied with some heat. Now as soon as we inquire what evidence can be advanced for this statement, perhaps someone will point to the fact that at certain periodic intervals municipal, state and national elections are held; that the results are more or less carefully tabulated; and that depending upon their outcome, one group of men or another is invested with certain powers of office. But now we observe an interesting and characteristic thing. If this were the state of affairs which we would be prepared to accept as indicating that the sentence "the will of the people is sovereign" is true, there could hardly be any dispute about it for any protracted period of time. But the dispute continues even when there is no question about the existence of elections. It turns out that those who assert this proposition maintain that they mean something *other* than this or *more* than this. What is this other or additional meaning? Is it something of the same kind as election procedures, i.e., something about which by making experiments and observations we can come to a decision? Or is it something concerning which no statement of an empirical kind will be accepted as adequately expressing its meaning? In the first case, we are dealing with a legitimate abstraction, i.e., one which promotes intelligent discourse and makes possible the acquisition of knowledge. In the second, we are dealing with an unanalyzable abstraction, with nothing except a sound that has certain causes and effects.[3]

And now let us look at some "recommendations requiring action" from Conant's "The Education of American Teachers" (1963).

Public school systems that enter contracts with a college or university for practice teaching should designate, as classroom teachers working with practice teaching, only those persons in

[3]Sidney Hook, *Reason, Social Myths and Democracy* (New York: Humanities Press, Inc., 1966), pp. 14-16.

whose competence as teachers, leaders, and evaluators they have the highest confidence, and should give such persons encouragement by reducing their work loads and raising their salaries.[4]

Some of the consequences of this "should be" type of statement are quite clear: there should be a contract between two agencies, the school system will designate the practice teacher, work loads will be reduced, and salaries will be raised. Quite clear. But what about the statement that the teachers to be designated ought to be "only those persons in whose competence as teachers, leaders, and evaluators they have the highest confidence?" How are we to decide if those chosen are those of whom Conant would approve? Would he be satisfied, as the statement requires him to be, with choices meeting the sole criterion that "they" (who are *they*?) say they have the highest confidence in the competence of the person designated? Are we to assume that Conant and those who will make the choices agree on a definition of competence?

Let us take another of Conant's recommendations:

> If the institution is engaged in educating teachers, the lay board of trustees should ask the faculty or faculties whether in fact there is a continuing and effective all-university (or interdepartmental) approach to the education of teachers; and if not, why not?[5]

What is indisputably clear is that one group will ask a question of another group — a point that is quite testable; that is, one group asks or does not ask a question of another group. But what does Conant mean — what does he want a lay board of trustees to mean — by an *effective* all-university approach? I do not know of anyone who would oppose an effective approach, just as I know of nobody who is in favor of starvation. One must know what Conant believes are the defining characteristics of an "effective" approach, so that one can decide whether or not one agrees with the characteristics and so that, *regardless of agreement,* one knows how to test for the presence or absence of these characteristics. It is the case with many of Conant's recommendations that he is

[4] J. B. Conant, *The Education of American Teachers*, pp. 212, 213, 214. Copyright 1963 by McGraw-Hill Book Company, New York. Reprinted by permission of the publisher.

[5] Ibid, p. 214.

most clear about unimportant matters and most vague about the important ones. One more example:

> To insure that the teachers are up to date, particularly in a period of rapid change (as in mathematics and physics), a school board should contract with an educational institution to provide short term seminars (often called workshops) during the school year so that *all* the teachers, without cost to them, may benefit from the instruction. Such seminars or workshops might also study the particular educational problems of a given school or school district. (No credit toward salary increases would be given.)[6]

With one exception this is a clear statement of what Conant thinks should happen. The one exception is the phrase "may benefit from instruction." How are we to decide when and in what ways teachers benefit from the instruction? How are we to determine that teachers may not be benefitting at all? How are we to know when they are being adversely affected? Conant would probably be the last person to defend the statement that the mere presence of a child in a classroom benefits that child. Are the issues any different when the pupil is a classroom teacher in a seminar taught by a member of a college faculty? As long as "benefit" remains undefined, or defined in a way which defies testability, we indulge our good intentions at the expense of clarity.

The problems of the observer and critic that we have discussed are neither new nor subtle. The significance of these problems resides in two related but separate issues. The first of these, which we shall be taking up in chapter 6, is a methodological issue that can be put in the form of a question: To what extent is it both possible and productive to observe the school in ways that minimize, if not eliminate, the observer's values, biases, and expectations? The second issue, which we shall take up in Chapter 7, concerns the actions the observer and critic take when they get into the processes of change. We shall not be interested, at this point at least, in whether the goals of change are good or bad. What is the natural history of, or the modal way in which people go about introducing a change in the school?

[6]Ibid, p. 213.

4

The Modal Process of Change: a Case Report

There are several reasons for inquiring into the usual, or modal, way in which change is introduced and effected in the school culture.

1. If one happens to be in a position to introduce or effect the change, one's subsequent experience and ultimate effectiveness will be found to have been determined in part by one's initial knowledge of the modal way in which change occurs in the setting.

2. Unless one understands the modal way in which the change process occurs, one cannot understand and benefit from the failure of others' or one's own efforts.

3. An understandable but unfortunate way of thinking confuses the power (in a legal or organizational-chart sense) to effect change with the processes of change. That a board of education, a superintendent, or a principal has the power to effect certain changes is but one aspect of the change process and its outcomes.

4. If it is true, as I think it is, that in the school culture the more things change the more they remain the same, we must begin to try to understand why this may be so.

5. The response to the need or demand for change brings to the fore some of the most important structural and social psychological characteristics of the school culture.

AGAIN THE UNIVERSITY CRITIC

Before developing the central theme of this chapter further, I feel it necessary to caution the reader against the tendency to interpret our discussion as being concerned with a set of questions and problems unique to the school culture. This caution stems in no way from a desire to be fair or tolerant but rather from the fact that it is all too easy for us to fail to see underlying similarity because of surface dissimilarity — a failure that prevents our being aware of what we know, transferring the knowledge from the realm of the specific to that of the general, and utilizing it appropriately in judging actions. An example of what I mean:

At lunch with a highly respected university colleague from another field I had to listen for some time to a polemic against school personnel because of their resistant attitude toward the introduction of so-called non-professional individuals in the classroom. Although education was far from his own field of professional interest and research, he was vitally interested in the public schools and served on various community committees concerned with improving ghetto schools. Apparently he had talked with many teachers and came away with the impression that a majority of them felt strongly that only trained teachers should engage in the teaching process — that there were many chores that a non-professional person could do in or around the classroom but teaching was not one of them. The important point is that my colleague described school personnel as being too guild-conscious, professionally precious, and obstacles to much needed change.

I confess (shamefacedly) to listening sympathetically to my colleague's polemic, *until it suddenly dawned on me that he was one of the most vociferous opponents in the university to the idea that someone who did not do research or publish deserved faculty status — the quality of the individual's teaching was irrelevant.* After some discussion we both agreed, with differing degrees of reluctance, that the schools and the university were rather similar in their response to the possibility of changing or breaking with tradition.

As important as the insight into the similarity of the two cultures was the recognition that introducing change into an ongoing system, particularly when that change involved a long standing tradition, had to be a complex process. As my colleague plaintively stated, "Why should we expect that the schools should be less successful in upholding tradition than we have been here at Yale?"

THE LACK OF DESCRIPTIVE DATA

In a previous chapter I indicated that descriptions of the change process in the school setting were very hard to come by. By description I mean a presentation that, among other things, tells the reader the following:

> Specific conditions giving rise to the need for change.
>
> Individuals and groups associated with those conditions.
>
> Who (individuals and/or groups) formulated and initiated the need for change.
>
> The action that was considered.
>
> The basis for choosing the course of action.
>
> The degree to which problems were anticipated and vehicles developed for their prevention or amelioration.
>
> The ways in which the changers were themselves affected by the process of change.
>
> The clarity of and transformations in the criteria by which the changers and others judged the effort.

This list should be enough to indicate that we are dealing with a problem of staggering complexity, not at all surprising to anyone who has seriously thought about, let alone attempted to study, a complicated, ever changing social setting. The situation is not unlike that of an individual who, having become aware for the first time that there are billions of stars in the heavens, sets for himself the problem of understanding their relationship. He becomes aware that his "subjects" move; that he cannot always be in a position to see them; that even when they are available to him he is faced with the limitation that a single brain has limits as to what and how much it can see and record; that he will have to develop indirect criteria for the presence or absence of things; that he is faced not only with the task of constructing conceptions of what is, but literally reconstructing what was or might have been the past, and even predicting the future as history. Collapsing the history of astronomy into the life of one individual gives one a fair idea of what will be involved in trying to describe and understand a natural, complicated, truly dynamic (non-static) social setting. It is no wonder that field research, to the laboratory researcher at least, is usually viewed as a messy business. Indeed it is, should be, and will be for a long time.

As will become apparent later in this chapter, the complexity of the problem is not methodological in the sense that the first order of business is to develop procedures or techniques for observing and gathering data. It is rather in the fact that we do not possess the security of the feeling that we have experienced the problem to the extent that we are formulating the problem well. By "experiencing the problem" I mean initiating and engaging in the change process in the school setting, using one's own experience as an object of change, or being in a position to observe the change efforts of others. I can, perhaps, make the point more clearly by turning to the field of psychotherapy. Our understanding of psychotherapy — the ways in which we now can conceptualize the process and those involved in it — has come from three types of experience: as a patient, as a therapist, and as an observer. It may well be that those who contributed most to our understanding had all three types of experience. In any event, the reader should understand that when I talk about what might be required for an "adequate description of the change process in the school setting," I am merely suggesting what we ought to be thinking about and experiencing in order to avoid the understandable but self-defeating tendency to flee from complexity at the expense of relevance.

It may well be that one of the reasons we lack adequate description of the change process in the school setting has been the recognition of the complexity of the problem (and let us not forget that the university culture does not make it easy for graduate students and ambitious young faculty members to work on messy problems in the field). But recognition of complexity is probably quite secondary to the fact that the problem has not been seen as a problem; therefore, there has been no good or compelling reason for focusing on the description of the change process.

For example, over the past twenty-five years hundreds of researchers have devoted a lot of time, effort, and thought to the problem of describing what goes on in the therapeutic situation. From the standpoint of theory it was desirable, and from the technical or mechanical standpoint it was feasible. But this was also true and possible before Carl Rogers and his students forced the field to see the importance of describing what really goes on; that is, it was possible to record mechanically the verbal behavior of therapist and client, as it was possible to film the process. But it was Rogers and his students who helped make the field conscious of the problem of describing at least the overt aspects and contents of the interactions.

I am quite aware that far more goes on in a psychotherapeutic interaction than is given by recordings of any kind. The point is that whatever else we think goes on is related to or stems from the assumption that we validly know the overt behavior or aspects of the interaction. As the work of Friedman (1967) and Rosenthal (1966) so well demonstrates, this assumption cannot be blithely made for psychologists who do experiments with humans, let alone for psychotherapists.

In the remainder of this chapter I shall attempt to describe the change process in the school setting. At the very least this attempt will make several things clear to the reader: the nature of the inadequacies of our own descriptions, the relations between conceptualization and description, and, ultimately of greatest importance, the need for a theory or way of thinking that would prevent us from thinking in our usual self-defeating, "practical" way (thinking of ends and means as if they were two different things or processes).

To illustrate the change process we have chosen the introduction of the new math, because it involved a large part of a particular school system — all elementary schools and all teachers and children in grades 4 to 6. This was not a small undertaking and one can question whether our description can be generalized to more modest efforts at change, for example, a change involving one child, one classroom, one school, or a small number of teachers or children. We shall return to this question later in the chapter not only because it is an important and legitimate one in terms of understanding the school culture, but also because the answer to the question is fateful for determining the course of future action.

THE BEGINNING CONTEXT:
THE LARGER SOCIETY

To the reader who was not an adult in 1957 it will be difficult to convey what a "narcissistic wound" the American pride experienced when Russia successfully launched its first sputnik. The reactions were diverse and pervasive. One of these reactions was the opinion that our educational system was not training enough scientists and, perhaps more important, that its teaching techniques and curricula were effectively extinguishing students' interest in science and scientific careers. Even before the first sputnik, a number of individuals and groups had voiced dissatisfaction with the teaching of mathematics in the public schools, and some had been working to develop new curricula, the contents and goals of which would prevent the student from being bored by numbers.

The most vocal critics, as well as those who were developing new curricula, were not indigenous to the school culture; they were mostly university people. The significance of this fact can be put in the form of two statements and one question:

1. One of the most important groups calling for change was part of the university culture.
2. There was nothing like a clamor for change from those within the school culture.
3. How did those in the university group understand this lack of clamor? Put more generally, to what extent was there explicit awareness that people in one subculture in our society wanted to introduce a change in another subculture?

The question, obviously, suggests that we are dealing with a problem that in principle has nothing to do with mathematics. As best as I can determine there was no realization on the part of the "change agents" that changing the content and techniques of teaching math may have involved them in the problem of institutional change. I may be guilty of slight oversimplification when I say that far from such a realization was the "engineering" way of thinking that seemed to characterize the formulation of the problem: a curriculum is developed, tried out, and revised; teacher's manuals undergo a similar process; and training and retraining institutes for teachers and other school personnel are developed. There is nothing wrong with this "delivery of curriculum" approach as long as one can assume that there are no characteristic features of the school culture that can adversely interfere with stated objectives. Let me be concrete at this point by asking the reader to perform a *tentative* act of faith and assume that the following statements are correct:

1. The relation between teacher and pupil is characteristically one in which the pupil asks very few questions.

2. The relation between teacher and pupil is characteristically one in which teachers ask questions and the pupil gives an answer.

3. It is extremely difficult for a child in school to state that he does not know something without such a statement being viewed by him and others as stupidity.

4. It is extremely difficult for a teacher to state to the principal, other teachers, or supervisors that she does not understand something or that in certain respects her teaching is not getting over to the pupils.

5. The contact between teacher and supervisor (e.g., supervisor of math, or of social studies) is infrequent, rarely involves any sustained and direct observation of the teacher, and is usually unsatisfactory.

6. One of the most frequent complaints of teachers is that the school culture forces them to adhere to a curriculum from which they do not feel free to deviate, and, as a result, they do not feel they can, as one teacher said, "use [their] own heads."

7. One of the most frequent complaints of supervisors or principals is that too many teachers are not creative or innovative but adhere slavishly to the curriculum despite pleas emphasizing freedom.

If one assumes that these are some characteristics of the school culture, it becomes clear that introducing a new curriculum should involve one in more than its development and delivery. It should confront one with problems that stem from the fact that the school is, in a social and professional sense, highly structured and differentiated — a fact that is related to attitudes, conceptions, and regularities of *all* who are in the setting. Teaching *any* subject matter, from this viewpoint, is in part determined by structural or system characteristics having no intrinsic relationship to the particular subject matter. If this assertion is even partly correct, any attempt to change a curriculum independent of changing some characteristic institutional feature runs the risk of partial or complete failure.[1]

But we are running ahead by talking of outcome. At this point the reader is asked to bear three things in mind about the beginning context: (1) the stimulus for change came primarily from outside the school culture; (2) there was little or no attention to the characteristic regularities of the institutional culture and their possible social and psychological correlates; and (3) there seemed to be the unverbalized assumption that the goals of change could be achieved independent of any change in these regularities.

THE BEGINNING CONTEXT:
THE SMALLER SOCIETY

Within the school system the impetus for change came from personnel with supervisory responsibilities for the mathematics curriculum and from those members of the board of education who had university affiliations. There are no grounds for assuming that any aspect of the impetus for change came from teachers, parents, or children. The teachers were not "hurting" because of the existing curriculum. In addition, at the point at which a decision to change was made there had been no formal attempt to inform or otherwise involve teachers. But the teachers did know two things: that a change was being discussed and contemplated, and that they, the teachers, were in on nothing.

To a number of teachers this situation caused no particular upset or concern, not only because "that is the way things are," but also because "that is the way it ought to be." It did not occur to those teachers to question the process — to question the relation between the process and its possible consequences — and

---

[1] The issue here is identical to one that has been raised in relation to the so-called "war-on-poverty," that is, that certain aspects of the problem were a consequence of how certain institutions (e.g., the welfare system) viewed and serviced poverty groups, and that the expectation that these institutions could do a better job without some fundamental changes in their structure and culture doomed their "new" efforts to failure.

only a few of them raised an issue in terms of "courtesy." In a fundamental sense the teachers were not questioning their relationship to the process. Both the administrative personnel and the teachers seemed to agree on where decision-making should and did reside. They also agreed that bringing the teachers into the process would be a (desirable) matter of form rather than of substance.

Another group of teachers, albeit not clearly, questioned the wisdom of a process in which the knowledge and opinions of the classroom teacher were not utilized or solicited. Here, too, one did not get the feeling that the validity of the process was being questioned but rather that the judgment of their administrative superiors was not held in high regard. I had the impression that if these teachers could have put different people into the decision-making role they would have been content, because those people would possess better judgment. The teachers were questioning the judgment of individuals and their relationship to the process. By and large, they accepted the nature of the system and its decision-making processes.

Needless to say, the mathematics supervisors also accepted the nature of the system and its decision-making processes. What is not clear is why they were so eager for a change. The teachers were not dissatisfied or clamoring for a change. Nor was there pressure from above to change the curriculum. Several factors seemed to be at work: the supervisors had various kinds of contacts with university settings where new curricula were being developed or the inadequacies of the old curriculum were under discussion; they were dissatisfied with the attitudes of children to math and their difficulties with the subject matter; and they very much wanted "to do good."

What I think deserves emphasis is that the supervisors, far more than teachers, knew more about and identified with the activities and values of the university culture. When one remembers that supervisors were once classroom teachers, that they sought to "rise above" that position, that in order to do so they had to return to the college or university for advanced graduate work, that, in effect, promotion was determined by performance outside the school setting — when one bears these factors in mind it is reasonable to assume that supervisors may identify with the activities, attitudes, and values of the university culture.

If this is true, as my experience indicates, it further suggests that supervisors will tend to view teachers as so many university people do: teachers as a group tend to be mediocre intellects, uninspired and unimaginative, and more often than not obstacles to, rather than facilitators of, progress. This hypothesis goes a fair way to our understanding the lack of relationship of teachers to the decision-making processes. It is not only that supervisors have more decision-making power than teachers, or that they are higher up in the organizational chart, but that they tend to have values that, as they see it, come from sources different from those from which the values of teachers come. It is these values, as much as conflict arising from differing roles, that are frequently (and silently) at work.[2]

In trying to understand why teachers were not at all involved in the decision to change the math curriculum I have referred to some possible relationships among role, values, and attitudes. But now let us look at the question from a different but related viewpoint, i.e., the nature of the diagnosis of the condition requiring change.

THE NATURE OF THE DIAGNOSIS

I am not aware that anyone at any time viewed the problem in terms of the following: a diagnostic process requiring a description of "symptoms;" the differing significances that can be attached to any one symptom or a combination of symptoms; possible alternative explanations (differential diagnosis); the consequences of any explanation for remedial tactics; and the investigative pro-

---

[2] My observations in a variety of school systems suggest the hypothesis that the greater the discrepancy between the values of the teachers and those of the supervisors the greater the conflict between them, or the poorer the morale of teachers, or the less they talk to each other. I have seen instances when the supervisors, far from sharing the values of the university, had an anti-university stance and experienced little or no conflict with teachers. I am quite aware that the issue is far more complicated than I have stated, and, of course, I am not suggesting that the presence or absence of conflict is inherently good or bad. My comments are intended not for the purposes of convincing the reader or proving a hypothesis but rather to suggest that in the school culture the change process and its outcomes cannot be understood only in terms of differing roles and responsibilities but in terms of values and attitudes and their sources. I also want to emphasize that values are not intrinsically related to roles, but they frequently have their source in roles characteristic of settings other than the school.

cedures to gain new information that would support the diagnostic formulation on which one will act. Diagnosis is problemsolving, decision-making, and action-producing based on processes subsumed under such terms as calculation, reflection, and conceptualization. But what is often taken for granted and, therefore, left unsaid is that diagnosis requires the awareness that one is engaged in processes that are intellectually demanding precisely because of man's capacity to think and do foolish things.

The decision to change the curriculum did not reflect this awareness of these processes. The diagnosis went something like this:

The present curriculum is antiquated and does not reflect newer or different ways of thinking about or using numbers. It erroneously assumes that young children are not capable of learning important mathematical concepts. It works against understanding by virtue of its emphasis on drill and rote memory. It tends not only to extinguish interest in mathematics but also to produce negative attitudes toward the subject matter. Because mathematics is so basic to understanding of, and performance in, all the sciences, and is increasingly important in vocational adaptation in the modern world of science and technology, the negative aspects of the present curriculum have consequences beyond a particular subject matter.

I should emphasize to the reader that we are not concerned here with the validity of the diagnostic formulation. The significance of the formulation resides in two interchangeable words: *it* and *curriculum*. It is not a diagnostic formulation that says something about teachers or the teaching process. In no explicit way does it say teachers are related to the condition requiring change. What the formulation states is that "it" must be changed; "it" is the etiological agent without which the condition would not exist; and if "it" changes, the condition would be ameliorated, if not cured. My point is a simple one: there is nothing in the formulation that would *require* involving teachers for the purposes either of getting new or more information before a decision is made, or of discussing the contribution of teachers to the presenting symptoms.

As I indicated earlier, teachers could have been involved on the basis of courtesy, a word reflecting considerations of tact, style, ethics, and morality. That basis for involvement is quite different from one that demands involvement by virtue of the way the problem is formulated.

The point I am making is identical to a problem of which researchers in recent years have become aware. If, in *thinking* about a psychological experiment with humans, one never realizes that the attitudes of the subjects to the experiment and the experimenter will in some way be related to the results, one cannot take steps that will protect one against over-interpretation of results or simply getting results that are not explainable. If one is aware of the problem — if it is part of one's way of conceptualizing problems — one takes certain actions, because the way the problem is formulated *demands* them. This is quite a different basis for action than if one thinks in terms of courtesy toward the human subject, the obligations of the experimenter, or the rights of the subject.

However, in the particular case I am attempting to describe, the diagnosis that was made public did not contain a factor that was contained in the private diagnosis of some of those pushing for change, and we now turn to a discussion of that factor. As so frequently happens in the communication of clinical diagnoses to patients and their families, there was much that deliberately was not said aloud.

THE NON-PUBLIC ASPECT OF THE PROBLEM

At least some of those pushing for change were of the opinion that not all of the inadequacies of the old math resided in the old math *as such* but also reflected inadequacies of many teachers.[3] The least insulting opinion was that the inadequacies were consequences of teacher training — they were not given the appropriate attitudes toward, and conceptualizations of, productive learning and the goals of the educative process. The more insulting opinion was that selective factors work against the "best" people going into public school teaching. I use the word *insulting* because those who held either or both of these views knew that if they were expressed, teachers would understandably feel insulted. *The important point is that this non-public aspect of the formulation of the problem put into different perspective what could be expected to be accomplished by substituting one curriculum for another.*

[3]This view was not peculiar to the individuals in this particular system. It was also the view of many university people, who viewed the general and specific training programs for teachers as an unmitigated disaster (Sarason, Blatt, and Davidson, 1962).

There were, of course, those who seemed to believe that the problem was the curriculum and that changing it would have all kinds of desirable consequences. But even these people recognized that going from an old to a new curriculum — involving in this case subject matter that would be new to teachers — would require some retraining of teachers. One can change the curriculum in American history drastically, but the teacher is still dealing with familiar facts and concepts (e.g., Civil War, Constitutional Convention, etc.). The proposed change in the math curriculum was qualitatively of a somewhat different order because for many teachers what they had to learn and then teach was truly new.

All were agreed that teachers would for a time become pupils again and learn the new math. No one formulated the problem as one requiring teachers to *unlearn and learn* — to give up highly overlearned ways of thinking at the same time that they were required to learn new procedures and new ways of conceptualizing. To state the problem in this way would require, at the very least, the acute awareness that one must make explicit and examine the degree to which one's theory of change takes account of the important social and psychological dimensions that characterize the setting. Such awareness was clearly not present.

THE CURRICULUM AND
THE TRAINING WORKSHOPS

Once the decision to change the curriculum was made, a series of meetings was held to decide which of several curricula should be adopted, and the time and length of the training workshops for teachers. At this point some classroom teachers became part of the working groups. I do not know how those teachers were chosen. But in formal and informal ways all teachers came to know that the curriculum was to be changed beginning the following September, approximately seven calendar months from the time the decision was made.

Teachers seemed to react in one of two ways, sometimes in both ways. On the one hand, they were caught up in the enthusiasm surrounding the change and looked forward to the stim-

ulation expected from what was intellectually novel and pres-
tigeful; on the other hand, they became increasingly anxious as it
became increasingly clear that the new math was indeed new (to
most of them), that learning it to a criterion of security was not
going to be easy, and that summer workshops of five weeks duration might expose their insecurity and, in the case of some, their
inadequacy.

The summer workshop took place in an atmosphere of tension and pressure. One might characterize what went on by saying
that the teachers were taught (by supervisors and outside experts)
in precisely the same ways that teachers had been criticized for
in their teaching of children. There was little sensitivity to the
plight of the teachers — they were being asked to learn procedures,
vocabulary, and concepts that were not only new but likely to
conflict with highly overlearned attitudes and ways of thinking.
Many of the teachers were unable to voice their uncertainties and
lack of understanding. *The pressure and tension stemmed not
only from being in a group learning situation with peers but
also from the scary knowledge that in several weeks they would
have to teach the new math to their pupils.*

The energy output of the teachers, at the workshop meetings
and at home, was somewhat awesome. The more anxious they
became the harder they worked to try to master the material, all
the time asking themselves that if *they* were having difficulty what
would their pupils experience?

But the content and depth of feelings could only indirectly
reach the surface in workshop activities for two major reasons:
(1) the teachers perceived themselves as pupils whose job it was
to learn what the teacher was presenting, and (2) the workshop
teachers perceived themselves as imparters of knowledge and over-
seers of skill training. In short, both teachers and pupils in the
workshop implicitly agreed that personal attitudes and feelings,
as well as the nature of the relationship between pupil and
teacher, was not an inevitable part of the educative process and,
therefore, had little or no claim to workshop time — despite the
fact that these factors were impeding productive learning. What
was going on in the workshop also characterized the relation
between these people outside the classroom, as well as the relation between the classroom teacher and her children.

At this point I am not suggesting anything concrete about the workshop — what might have been done, how it might have been conducted, etc. The sole point I am making is that within the workshop or the classroom, or in other types of relationships within the school culture, there is a conception of learning that makes it next to impossible to take account of factors *that are always present*. One might wish that they were not present or would go away, or hope that they were not important, or hope that they had facilitating effects (as they sometimes do). Hopes and wishes aside, they are inevitably there, and to fail to take them into account is to avoid reality, which many of us in education apparently do rather well.

THE SCHOOL YEAR AND THE PROBLEM
OF SUPERVISION

It had been expected that teachers would need help and support once the school year began, and these were to be provided through individual meetings with the math supervisors, as well as group meetings. Two things became clear to the supervisors after the close of the workshops. First, the number of supervisors was inadequate to meet the individual needs and problems of the teachers. Second, the supervisors had seriously underestimated the difficulty teachers would have learning the new material to a degree of mastery comparable to that they had attained with the old curriculum.

Even with the old curriculum, individual help to, or observation of, the classroom was virtually impossible. As in most suburban school systems there was one supervisor and perhaps one or two persons part of whose duties was to assist the supervisor. When one remembers that in the case we are describing there were eleven elementary schools, it is clear that individual supervision was and would be a rare occurrence.

It is worth emphasis that in the school culture supervision rarely means observing and working with the classroom teacher. But, one may ask, is not this type of supervision the responsibility of the principal of the school? We shall take up this question later. At this point in our discussion I wish to point out that even if one assumes that individual supervision was primarily the responsibility of the principal, he was not, in the case of the new math curriculum, competent to perform the task; that is, the principals of the schools were no more knowledgeable about the new curriculum than were their teachers. If, as we have discussed elsewhere (Sarason, Levine, Goldenberg, Cherlin, and Bennett, 1966), teaching is a lonely profession, it became even more so with the introduction of the new math curriculum.

For the purposes of this chapter it is not necessary to describe in detail what happened during the year. Teachers generally were anxious, angry, and frustrated; many children were confused and many parents began to raise questions about what was going on and about their own inability to be of help to their children; parent workshops were organized. It was an unsettling year for practically everyone involved.

It was inevitable that all of those who participated in, or were affected by, the unfolding social drama would, at some point, "explain" what happened or was happening, a polite way of saying that blame assignment would be an important issue and topic of conversation. Of all the participants (administrators, supervisors, principals, children, parents, and teachers) the teachers were in the center of the stage. In a real sense, they were the actors and the rest were audience. It is not surprising, therefore, that the teachers were the chief recipients of blame. No one viewed the situation as the consequence of processes taking place in and characterizing a particular social organization, or as reflecting conceptions (implicit or explicit) about the nature and structure of the settings that determine how the change process will be effected.[4] Some teachers were dimly aware of what had happened and was happening, but even among them one sensed that they were interpreting the situation as reflecting some inadequacy on their part. Put in another way: *many teachers agreed*

[4]An analogous situation would be one in which one would go about trying to understand strange behavior in a child as if it existed in him independent of the most important settings (e.g., home, school) in which he lives. In other words, one would view the child as if he was not part of highly structured settings that in different ways are related to his behavior, both in the past and present. In addition, if one held such a view and one wished to change this behavior, one's actions would be quite different than if one viewed the behavior as reflecting something about the child *and* the structured settings of which he is part.

with the diagnosis that indeed they were largely to blame. It is not surprising that teachers should have tended to view themselves as they thought other people viewed them.

SOME OUTCOMES

Approximately ten years after the new math was introduced into American schools, and by virtue of our rather intimate involvement in classrooms in a variety of school systems during that period, an informal observational study of the teaching of the new math was done (E. K. Sarason and S. B. Sarason, 1969). "Over a period of six weeks we observed six classrooms, two in each of three school systems, during those hours in which math was taught. Only sixth grade classrooms were chosen. In each of the three schools there were two sixth grade classrooms. Each classroom was observed at least three times a week. Principals and teachers rearranged schedules so that the two classrooms in each school could be observed on the same day. In two schools the School Mathematics Study Group (SMSG) program was used while in the third school they were using the Addison-Wesley program. In all schools the SMSG program had been used in the previous grades." All three school systems were suburban and the intelligence level of the pupils was well above national norms.

It will be recalled from an earlier section of this chapter that one of the bothersome features of the old curriculum was that children did not *enjoy* the world of numbers; they found it dull, unstimulating, and a chore. To use more modern parlance: rather than being turned on to, the children were turned off from, mathematics. And now we turn to the most dominant impression of the observers of the new curriculum:

> . . . . The two observers came away with the impression that enjoyment was one of the last words they would use to characterize their impressions of the feelings of the children. Struggle was certainly one way of characterizing what was going on but it was not that kind of intellectual struggle which generates its own sources of internal reinforcement or elicits such reinforcements from others — in this case the teacher. At no time in our discussions did any of the six teachers say anything which disconfirmed our opinion that neither

children nor teachers enjoyed what they were doing in the sense of feeling intellectual excitement, a desire to persist, and a joy of learning. One had the overwhelming impression of a task having to be done not because children desired to do it but because that is the way life is. Using the "joy of learning" as a criterion there appears to be no difference between new and old math.[5]

In light of the observations made in this study the authors conclude that the goal of attracting more students to mathematics as a career would not likely be achieved:

> It is fair, we think, to say that one of the major aims of the new math concerned not only schools and children but our entire society in the sense that the new math was viewed as one important way of helping to produce more and better mathematicians and scientists because that is what our society was viewed as needing. If our observations and those of others have validity and generality, one would have to predict that the goal of more and better mathematicians and scientists (relative to the total population) — or the number of college students majoring in math and physics — will not be met. If so, we will have another sad example of how the more things change the more they remain the same.[6]

It is perhaps too charitable to conclude that "the more things change the more they remain the same," if only because so many people continue to be unaware that basically nothing has changed; in addition, and perhaps more to the point, many of those who are aware that intended outcomes have not been achieved have no clear understanding of the factors contributing to failure. It is unlikely that in the future we will be spared the development of newer curricula, that is, new programs, attractively bound, surrounded by evangelism and the spirit of reform, and unrelated to the realities of the school culture.[7]

---

[5] E. K. Sarason and S. B. Sarason, "Some Observations on the Teaching of the New Math." In *The Yale Psycho-Educational Clinic: Collected Papers and Studies,* S. B. Sarason and F. Kaplan, eds., Monograph Series (Boston: Massachusetts State Department of Mental Health, 1969), p. 99.

[6] Ibid, p. 107.

[7] There have been some rather scathing criticisms of new curricula in the different subject matters, in terms of both their underlying conceptions and their outcomes (e.g., Fehr, 1966; Ausubel, 1967; Weinberg, 1965; Greenberg, 1967 (pages 38-39). My own position is very similar to that expressed by Epstein (1964).

Alfred North Whitehead (1929), in his 1916 presidential address to the Mathematical Association of England, said of curriculum change:

> This question of the degeneration of algebra into gibberish, both in word and in fact, affords a pathetic instance of the uselessness of reforming educational schedules without a clear conception of the attributes which you wish to evoke in the living minds of the children. A few years ago there was an outcry that school algebra was in need of reform, but there was a general agreement that graphs would put everything right. So all sorts of things were extruded, and graphs were introduced. So far as I can see, with no sort of idea behind them, but just graphs. Now every examination paper has one or two questions on graphs. Personally, I am an enthusiastic adherent of graphs. But I wonder whether as yet we have gained very much. You cannot put life into any schedule of general education unless you succeed in exhibiting its relation to some essential characteristic of all intelligent or emotional perception. It is a hard saying, but it is true; and I do not see how to make it any easier.[8]

In this chapter I have endeavored to describe and discuss the modal way in which changes are introduced into the school culture. In characterizing the process as "modal" I am quite aware that I am expressing an opinion; that is, the characterization is not derived from a number of descriptions (mine and others) that are compellingly similar. I would also not argue with the criticism that the description I have presented is neither complete nor systematic. As I indicated earlier, I am less concerned with the absence of relevant description than I am with the failure to recognize and state the problem.

Obviously, we cannot have relevant descriptions and studies until we recognize that the description of the change process involves, or is based on, the most fundamental (and unchallenged, if not unverbalized) assumptions determining three general types of social relationships: those among the professionals within the school setting, those among the professionals and pupils, and those among the professionals and the different parts of the larger society. Any proposed change — be it the new math, the new physics, busing, decentralization, etc. — affects and will be affected by all of these types of social relationships, and that is precisely

---

[8] Alfred North Whitehead, *The Aims of Education*, (New York: Mentor, 1929), p. 19. Reprinted by permission of The Macmillan Company.

what is neither stated nor faced in the modal process of change in the school culture.

The goals of change, the outcomes sought, surely are not to see if it is possible to substitute one set of books for another, change the racial composition of a class or a school, or have children read or listen to black or Mexican history — those possibilities are relatively easy to realize, and I have seen them realized in precisely the same way as in the case of new math, with precisely the same outcome: the more things change the more they remain the same.

Realizing these types of possibilities simply begs the question of their *intended consequences,* and in these as well as in other instances the intended consequences — the basic goals and outcomes — always intended a change in the relationships among those who are in or related to the school setting. But these intended consequences are rarely stated clearly, if at all, and as a result, a means to a goal becomes the goal itself, or it becomes the misleading criterion for judging change. Thus, we have the new math, but we do not have those changes in how teachers and children relate to each other that are necessary if both are to enjoy, persist in, and productively utilize intellectual and interpersonal experience — and if these are not among the intended consequences, then we must conclude that the curriculum reformers have been quite successful in achieving their goal of substituting one set of books for another.

ᢙ5ᢚ

The Modal Process of Change: an Example from the University

Why has it been so easy for intended consequences to be stated, when they are stated at all, in vague and untestable language? Why do so many efforts at change unknowingly proclaim abysmal ignorance of the social structure within classrooms and schools? Is it possible to effect a significant educational change in a classroom or school without changing regularities therein? To what extent do the most vociferous and powerful-prestigeful critics of our schools (and I include our curriculum reformers here) differ fundamentally from those they criticize? Is it an over-simplification to say that efforts at educational change have been based on an asocial theory of human behavior, just as American human psychology was based, for years, on rigorous, ingenious, systematic, "objective," sterile, and irrelevant studies of the Norway rat (Beach, 1950)?

The purpose of these questions is to focus attention on the thought content of those who view themselves (or find themselves) as agents of change, that is, their planning, anticipating, decision-making, problem-solving, and tactical behavior. But it would be unduly confining, and even misleading, if we were to focus on the agent of change only in relation to the public school setting because, as I pointed out in Chapter 3, it may very well be that his conception of the change process is to an important extent independent of his knowledge of the school setting. "They would think and go about the change process as they did regardless of whether they were in the school or some other culture."

If this is true, then one's knowledge and understanding of a particular setting or subculture (e.g., the public school), however important that is (and it *is* important), becomes somewhat less crucial than one's generalized conception of the change process. What then becomes more understandable is the frequency with which we find persons who possess a good deal of knowledge and understanding of the culture of a particular setting but who, when they try to change it in some important way, fail disastrously.

In previous chapters I stressed the importance of the degree of one's understanding of a particular culture for how one goes about introducing change. In this chapter, however, I stress a somewhat different, and more significant, point: depth of understanding or familiarity with a setting may have no intrinsic relationship to one's conception of the change process. That they may not be intrinsically related *in practice* reflects the fact that they are not related in theory even though they should be.

The point I am discussing is, I think, in principle related to one of Freud's most significant discoveries; that is, an individual may understand why he is what he is without being able to use this understanding for the purposes of change. But, as Freud found out about himself as a therapist, the depth of his understanding of a patient did not mean that the means he used to help the patient change was successful. It was the failure of his means of helping patients change that preoccupied him and led him to conceptions that changed his understanding as well as his techniques for effecting change. What he strove for and only partially achieved was a way of demonstrating the intrinsic relationship between the process of understanding and changing.

I shall try to illustrate my point by a concrete example in which the outside critics of the school culture attempted an educational innovation *in their own bailiwick:* the university culture, with which they had great familiarity.

AN EDUCATIONAL INNOVATION
IN A UNIVERSITY

Shortly after the first Russian sputnik — in the context of much national breast-beating, wounded pride, and fantasies of national decline — a major university (Yale) initiated a new program for the training of secondary school teachers. The major force behind this move was the president of the university, who had achieved attention on the national scene because of his criticisms of the usual teachers' college programs. His major criticisms were familiar ones: there was an excessive emphasis on so-called technique or "how to do it" courses; teachers did not have a deep enough grasp of the subject matter they had to teach; and the training of teachers tended not to take place in the context of the traditions of the liberal arts (i.e., the arts that "liberated" the mind of man from the shackles of old ideas, dogma, and static practices). It should be obvious that the specific criticisms of the old math discussed in the previous chapter were variants of these more general statements.

One criticism was never made as explicit as the degree of importance attached to it by the local and national university critics, namely, that the usual teacher training programs were stifling and technique-oriented and did not attract the best students. On the contrary, it was maintained, the best students were driven away from any consideration of a teaching career. A major goal of the proposed program at this university was to attract the best students from the best liberal arts colleges and universities, deepen their knowledge and intellectual horizons in the subject matter they wanted to teach, give them a bare minimum of the usual "how-to-teach-it-courses," and provide them with practice-teaching experiences under supervision.

As in the case of the new math, the faculty in no way clamored for this new program. *In fact, not too long before the new program was proposed the faculty had warmly approved the president's decision to eliminate the department of education because it was considered alien to the scholarly and research traditions of the university.*

There were two major reactions among the faculty to the proposed program when it was presented to them for discussion and vote. Some could not care less what happened as long as the university did not give education anything resembling an important status. Among those voicing this reaction, a significant number would have preferred that the university do nothing, but if a token gesture would keep the president happy (and it was recognized that he was strongly interested in education) they felt that their approval of the program was not a high price to pay. The second major reaction was more positive because people in that group saw the program as fulfilling an obligation of a university to the larger society in a manner consistent with its traditions *(including that of noblesse oblige)*; that is, the students would be of high quality, they would take the regular courses in the area of their special interests, and they would be treated and evaluated like any other student in the university.

As in the case of the new math those few people who took responsibility for the program concerned themselves almost exclusively with "organizational" issues. Unlike the new math there was not going to be a new curriculum; very little new was going to be taught or changed because the existing courses were considered to be precisely what prospective teachers needed. What existed, unlike the old math, was in principle what was to be protected. One might say that the content of these courses and the quality of relationship between student and instructor were the kinds of criteria the proponents of the new math would have liked to have seen met in the public school classroom.

The reader will recall that in the case of the new math no one anticipated that a process was being started that could engender hostility and resentment; that is, the conception of the process did not permit awareness that when people are asked or required to change, a part of them will resist changing, and if such resistance is then reacted to as incomprehensible human perversity, the level of hostility increases. In the case of the university the situation was different in that one had to be deaf, dumb, and blind (and in a fatal coma) not to know that the new program was being initiated in a setting very hostile to anything resembling the field of education, particularly the training of teachers. What conception of the change process did the proponents of the new program have, and how did that conception help them anticipate problems and take steps to prevent or minimize their occurrence and consequences?

Let us first note that they did nothing to handle the problem of a hostile atmosphere. I really cannot say what conception of change was in the minds of these people. But I have no evidence to contradict the statement that they neither faced the problem nor deliberately took steps to ameliorate it.

There is no reason to believe that their conception of change *required* that they develop vehicles for dealing with the problem.

Similarly, there is no evidence that they thought through the subtle and not so subtle ways in which the purposes of the program could be subverted. For example, since the students in the new program would be enrolled in existing courses, and since some of the instructors were likely to be among those who looked with disdain on education and educators, could this have untoward effects on the students? Would they be regarded as second-class citizens? Would they be differently evaluated? Would they be given similar opportunities to participate in courses? Prejudice, be it in relation to race, status, or occupation, does not operate differently in college teachers than among any other group.

Theory of the change process is helpful to the extent that it says not only what would happen but also what could happen under certain conditions. Theories are practical, particularly in relation to the change process, because they tell one what one has to think and do, and not what one would like to think and do. A theory of the change process is a form of control against the tendency for personal style, motivation, and denial of reality to define the problem and its possible solutions along lines requiring the least amount of personal conflict.

When we were describing the introduction of the new math we emphasized the inordinate significance attached to substituting one set of books for another. It would, perhaps, be more correct and fair to say that as the change process started, more and more hope and faith had to be placed in the new curriculum (a book with hard covers) as the major agent bringing about desired outcomes. In the case of the new university program there never seemed to be much doubt that the curriculum (a collection of courses) would have the desired outcomes: intellectual stimulation for the students, deeper grasp of subject matter, a greater feeling of confidence in the teaching situation, and, as a final consequence, models of what secondary school teachers should be. Put more briefly, the emphasis on subject matter courses would have a very positive transfer of training effect in the classroom situation.

I should warn the reader that as in the case of the description of the introduction of the new math, my description of the new teacher training program is undoubtedly far from complete as a description of a process. In the case of the new math my justification for attempting a description stemmed from the obvious failure of the change to achieve its intended outcomes — the simple idea that failure must have a history and in some ways reflect what people thought or did not (could not) think, what people did or did not do. And so the question: Is it possible that failure was in large part contained in the statement of the problem and conceptions about the processes of solution? Let us now turn to some data which are the justification for discussing the new university program.

SOME SERENDIPITOUS DATA ON OUTCOMES

In 1968 a study was done at Yale by A. G. Levine (1968) with the title "Marital and Occupational Plans of Women in Professional Schools: Law, Medicine, Nursing, Teaching." It was not a study conceived of or directed towards the issues and problems in this book. The study was sociological and its focus can be gleaned from the first paragraph of the report:

> The marital and occupational ambitions of women in four professional schools is the subject of this dissertation. The main body of the study will describe the women's plans and the way social class, mother's education and employment, and facets of the professional education are related to those plans. The study derives from the two obvious characteristics of well-educated women's work careers. First, like other working women, their careers are complicated by marital and familial responsibilities. Second, the majority of well-educated women enter but a few of the occupations requiring long years of educational preparation, despite widespread shortages of personnel.[1]

The women in the study were all enrolled in the four professional programs at Yale and, as one might expect, the bulk of them came from the highest socioeconomic classes (I and II). Each subject in the study was interviewed and filled out a variety of questionnaires. To the investigator's surprise the response of the women in the teaching program sharply differed from those in the other programs, particularly from those in medicine and law.

[1]A. G. Levine, "Marital and Occupational Plans of Women in Professional Schools: Law, Medicine, Nursing, Teaching" (Doctoral dissertation, Yale University, 1968).

The Law and Medical students are preparing for professions which have very high prestige in our society. At Yale, they are in professional schools respected both within the professions and within the university. The students, when they had complaints, expressed "gripes" which were focused around certain conditions whose correction could improve the educational process for everyone. However, they feel fully integrated into the professional training programs, they have the same access to the intellectual and material resources of the school that the men do, and they feel prepared to enter their professions, as neophytes to be sure, by the end of their programs.[2]

In the case of the nursing group Dr. Levine points out: "While their schools are accorded respect within the professions, their prestige within the university is not high relative to the other departments and schools." And now to the teachers in Yale's Master of Arts in Teaching (MAT) program, the object of our interest and discussion:

When the Teaching students were asked, "How has it been here for you? Has it been the way you thought it would be?" 14 of the 22 interviewed burst out vehemently that "it" had been "terrible," "bad and confusing," "a terrible disappointment," and the like. The reasons for their bitter discontent touched every phase of their program.

First, most of the students said that they found the core of education courses to be dull, almost completely irrelevant to classroom needs. They categorized these courses as appropriate to educational settings not as prestigious as those to which they had become accustomed. One Class I young woman pointed out, "I thought these courses would be different from a state teachers' college."

Second, they attend classes in their major areas in the appropriate departments of the University. This feature of the program attracted many of the women who want to teach but had dreaded the "intellectual insult of being undergraduate education majors."

However, as one student summed it up, "As good as it sounded in the catalog, that's how bad it is." For when they attend classes in the other departments, many of them are faced with unanticipated difficulties.* The courses are shaped to the needs of graduate students

---

[2] Ibid, p. 64.

*(We are not discussing the student's being able to keep up in the courses as far as required performance goes. They were all passing the courses, and no one complained of the intellectual difficulty of the work.)

who will be scholars in their fields, and whose interests are best served by exploring in depth the details of the subject matter.

> . . . . their idea of higher scholarships in this area [a language] cuts out all the lyricism, and concentrates on things that I don't like and cannot use . . . things like textual criticism. A little formalism is fine and helpful, but not when it is the whole thing.

The MAT students feel that they need broad coverage, and some question why some of the course requirements cannot be shaped for them to some extent. The few professors who take the MAT student's professional problems into consideration, (and there were some of these professors) were spoken of with warm gratitude.

These young women are made keenly aware in a variety of ways that in a social setting whose value hierarchy is based upon advanced scholarship, people who are going to be high school teachers command little respect. For example, analogous to the "last hired, first fired" phenomenon, they say that sometimes they must get special permission to enter courses, and if the section becomes crowded, they may be asked to leave. They spoke bitterly of being treated with scorn by graduate students and condescension by many professors.

> The professors are so condescending to the MAT students. The students are worse. I am planning to enter the doctoral program next year, in the —— department, so I can tell the difference. As an MAT I was talked down to. As a doctoral candidate, my intelligence has improved. The amusing thing about the —— department is that they use a special jargon, and the women are most prone to use it for they are so afraid of being mistaken for MAT students. It is maddening, because the MAT girls are just as bright and twice as lively.

The third part of the learning process for the MAT's is their practice teaching, which for most of the group has been concurrent with their course work. For a few the experience has been a good one, for they have had "good" classrooms, have found they like to teach, and enjoy their pupils. But most of the students complain that practice teaching is the discouraging counterpart to their own classroom experiences. The irrelevance of their education courses is brought home to them with dismal regularity.

> I'll tell you what I could use. I could use some sort of psychology of tough adolescents. I learned all about toilet training and weaning in my psych. course, and I am faced with a bunch of tough boys a few years younger than myself, and believe me, what they don't know about sex, drugs, gambling, and everything else isn't worth knowing. But the most elementary reading is beyond them.

Many students say that they lack supervision, and they feel that they have no one to turn to with their day by day practical problems. Many of them, like the young woman quoted above, have been assigned to difficult classes in urban schools. Such assignments compound the problems they face as neophytes. For women who come from protected, Class I-II surroundings, such confrontations are quite upsetting.

The effect of all these experiences is to make them doubt their own feeling of being capable *people* and of being able to perform as teachers.

> I feel dissatisfied with myself. I truly feel that if I had some guidance of a meaningful sort that I could feel more certain about what I'm doing and more interested in staying in teaching. As it is, I am hoping that I will stay in, but I have such self-doubts about achieving the standards that I have set for myself, that I don't know . . . . After all, a good teacher should be able to work in any situation by adapting her methods.

One girl summed up the feeling expressed by many.

> It is just so awful to see the girls lose heart and decide not to teach — to quit entirely, or to teach in some nice, quiet, private school or suburban school, because they aren't getting anything from the program.

Indeed many of the students said that they had originally felt very strongly that they should teach in city schools. The need is great, they point out. Many of them, aware of the good schools they had themselves attended, interested in "doing good," said that they had eagerly anticipated their first encounters with the real problems of the world. Now they feel that they simply do not have the ability to tackle such overwhelming tasks. These students have had few mentors to tell them which of their "failures" were inherent in the situation, and have had almost no one to turn to, to help them over the many rough places in the road.

Fully thirty percent expressed a "great deal of regret" about their choice of profession, and they plan to leave the field after graduating. Their responses were in marked contrast to the women in the other three school groups. We have noted before that in the process of randomly selecting MAT subjects for this study, we found that 5 of the students had already left the program. The reason they left is unknown, but of the other three school groups in this study, only 1 other (unmarried) young woman had quit the program since registering in the fall semester prior to this study.[3]

[3] Ibid, p. 65.

Dr. Levine's formal study coincides in all details with my own informal observations from afar. Further comment about the relationship between intended outcomes, the processes of change, and actual outcomes would seem to be superfluous.

It can be assumed that an attempt to introduce change into a setting with which one is relatively unfamiliar is likely to misfire. But what we have seen in this chapter is that familiarity with a setting is no guarantee against failure. What has emerged is the centrality of one's conception of the change process when one is dealing with a complicated social setting. To further our attempt at clarity as well as to see the dimensions of the problem better, I shall list and briefly discuss some characteristics of, or requirements for, a theory of change. At best this represents a small step toward the goal of engendering in others a greater awareness of the importance of the problem.

1.   An initial requirement of a theory of change is that it be appropriate to, and mirror the complexities of, social settings. It must explicitly recognize that settings are differentiated in a variety of ways (e.g., role, power, status) that make for groupings each of which may see itself differently in relation to the purposes and traditions of the larger setting and, therefore, perceive intended change in different ways. For example, a department of psychology is made up of psychologists, and there is the tendency on the part of outsiders gratuitously to assume that they have a great deal in common, which indeed they do. But the outsider only rarely acts on the basis of something he knows: that there are different kinds of psychologists or psychological fields, that there are different statuses (instructor, assistant professor, etc.) within the department and even within one of the specialties, that there is a chairman — that these and other dimensions produce groupings, formal and informal, that make a mockery of the outsider's assumption of communality among members of the department.

Few things bring this out as clearly as a proposal to make an important change in the department. Then, and usually only then, does one see how a group of individuals, possessing many formal characteristics in common, breaks down into small groupings each of which is acutely aware of how it differs from the others. A single department, only one of many making up that highly complex culture we call (so simply) a university, is inevitably a highly differentiated set of relationships. In a very formal sense a theory of change must contain statements that would force an agent of change to deal with or look for the relevant dimensions and relationships. In my experience, *in practice, most explicit and implicit conceptions of change derive from the language and vocabulary of an individual psychology that is in no way adequate to changing social settings. The fact that one can be the most knowledgeable and imaginative psychoanalytic, learning, or existentialist theoretician gives one no formal basis for conceptualizing the problem of change in social settings. The problem is simply not one to which these individual theories address themselves.*

2. It will be, I think, axiomatic in a theory of change that the introduction of an important change does not and cannot have the same significance for the different groupings comprising the setting and that one consequence is that there will be groups that will feel obligated to obstruct, divert, or defeat the proposed change. *Recognizing and dealing with this source of opposition is not a matter of choice, preference, or personal aesthetics. The chances of achieving intended outcomes become near zero when the sources of opposition are not faced, if only because it is tantamount to denial or avoidance of the reality of existing social forces and relationships in the particular setting.* When the problem is faced, and in what ways it could be dealt with, are tactical questions consequent to the more basic decision that the problem cannot be avoided. It can be avoided, of course, but that is why the natural history of innovations is not pleasant reading.

3. The history of the change process may be viewed as a series of decisions that increasingly involve or affect more and more groups in that setting. The decision making group is usually small and not representative of all those who will be affected by its decisions. How does one determine representativeness? Is it self-evidently desirable that decision-making groups should *always* be representative? If not, how does one determine when it should become representative? What might be the relationships between degree of representativeness, on the one hand, and outcomes, on the other hand? The assumption made by some that representativeness is a virtue second to no other may be justified by some scale of values, but its relation to outcome is by no means clear and will not be clarified by fiat or dogma. *The requirements*

*of leadership and the demand for representativeness are often in
conflict and not easy to reconcile in decision-making — their true
relationship is too frequently cloaked in the language of rhetoric
or public ritual.*

4. Any attempt to introduce change is accompanied, implicitly or explicitly, by a time perspective that, so to speak, tells one
when something should be done and when certain outcomes are
to be expected. A comprehensive conception of the change process must be formulated with at least two questions relevant to time
perspective in mind: Why is there frequently underestimation of
how long it takes to initiate the change process — an *underestimation* that can arouse such feelings of anger or discouragement
that it may result in aborting the process or in enveloping it in an
atmosphere inimical to the intended outcome; Why is the estima-
tion of time necessary to achieve intended outcomes usually *a
gross underestimation?*

I have had no intention of conveying the impression that it
is possible or desirable to formulate or conceptualize the change
process in cookbook style. My aims have been much more modest
and realistic. Initially, my major aim was to labor the obvious:
we do not possess adequate descriptions of the change process so
as to allow us to begin to understand the high frequency of failure
or the occasional successes. The second aim of the discussion
was to indicate that the relationship between knowledge of and
familiarity with a setting, on the one hand, and the conception
of how to introduce change into it, on the other hand, is by no
means a simple or self-evident one. As a consequence, what
emerged as a central problem was the conception of the change
process itself, not only in relation to concrete settings like the
school or university, but as a general problem arising whenever
there is an attempt to introduce change into complicated social
settings. In this connection I attempted in the present chapter to
suggest some of the ingredients that would comprise a general
statement of what is involved, or should be involved, in one's
formulation of the change process; the kind of general statement
that can act as a form of control over tendencies to oversimplify
and overpersonalize the nature of the process.

Underlying all of this discussion has been the assumption
that as more people become aware of the importance of the
problem and issues, and as more systematic efforts are made to-

ward a comprehensive general statement, those who initiate and engage in the processes of change will find it difficult to avoid recognizing and facing the complexity of what they are about. At the present time it is all too easy "to play it all by ear." Given the choice, I would much prefer a performance determined by a more reliable and structured vehicle. Even the possession of perfect pitch in no way insures an enjoyable musical outcome.

In this and the previous chapter I have emphasized the importance of the change process. In the next chapter I shall return to our earlier discussion of the school culture from the perspective of the following questions: How can one analyze and describe the school culture so as to provide clear criteria by which to judge whether an intended change in it has been achieved? Is it possible that criteria can be developed that will reduce, or even eliminate, the role of personal opinion in evaluating outcomes?

6

Programmatic and Behavioral Regularities

The attempt to introduce a change into the school setting makes at least two assumptions: the change is desirable according to some set of values, and the intended outcomes are clear. In this chapter we shall be concerned with the clarity of the intended outcomes.

The new math (Chapter 4) illustrates the problem of intended outcomes clearly. Was one of its intended outcomes to demonstrate that children could learn the new math to certain criterion levels? Was another outcome to show that children would enjoy the new math more than children enjoyed learning the old math? Was it an intended outcome that exposure to the new math would have some demonstrable effect on how children thought about other subject matter in school? Was it an intended outcome that the new math would affect the thinking and activities of children outside of school, more than the old math did? Was it an intended outcome to change in any way the nature of relationships between teacher and child? Was it an intended outcome to change the quantity and quality of questions that children asked about numbers and problem solving? Was it an intended outcome that children would learn that the principle that a particular thing (e.g., a number) can have different significances, is a principle equally applicable to other kinds of events, such as those they study in history?

Undoubtedly, one can ask about other possible intended outcomes. Neither in the specific case we described nor in the general literature is it clear what outcomes were intended, whether or not there was a priority among outcomes, and what the relationship is between any outcome and the processes of change leading to it. As a colleague remarked: "In a way this is a happy state of affairs. You don't have to think about important problems, you have little or nothing to evaluate, and faith and personal opinion carry the day." But more than the new math is at stake, and we cannot allow ourselves to be content with studying states of illusory happiness.

THE EXISTING REGULARITIES

Let us approach the general problem of outcomes by indulging in a fantasy. Imagine a being from outer space who finds himself and his invisible space platform directly above an elementary school. Being superior to earthly beings he is able to see everything that goes on in the school. But he does operate under certain restrictions: he does not comprehend the meaning of written or spoken language, and it can never occur to him that things go on inside of what we call heads. He can see and hear everything and, being an *avant garde* outer-spacer, he, of course, possesses a kind of computer that records and categorizes events on any number of dimensions, allowing him to discern what we shall call the existing regularities. (Let me anticipate the discussion of the latter part of this chapter by advancing the hypothesis that *any attempt to introduce change into the school setting requires, among other things, changing the existing regularities in some way. The intended outcomes involve changing an existing regularity, eliminating one or more of them, or producing new ones.*)

Let us start with one of the more obvious regularities. Our outer-spacer will discern (but not understand) that for five consecutive days the school is densely populated while for two consecutive days it is devoid of humans. That puzzles him. Why this 5-2 pattern? Why not a 4-3 or some other kind of pattern like 2-1-2-1-1?

What if the outer-spacer could talk to us and demanded an explanation for this existing regularity? Many of us earthlings would quickly become aware that we have a tendency to assume that the way things are is the way things should be. But our outer-spacer persists. Is this the way it has always been? Is this the way it is in other countries? Is it demonstrably the best pattern for achieving the purposes of schooling? Does the existing regularity reflect non-educational considerations like religion, work patterns, and leisure time? Is it possible that the existing regularity has no intrinsic relationship to learning and education?

The significance of an existing regularity is that it forces, or should force, one to ask two questions: *What is the rationale for the regularity? and What is the universe of alternatives that could be considered?* Put in another way: Can the existing regularity be understood without considering its relationship to the alternatives of which it is but one possibility?[1] I would suggest that if we could peruse this issue in the case of the 5-2 pattern we would become increasingly aware not only of the universe of alternatives but also of the degree to which the existing pattern reflects considerations that have little or nothing to do with the intended objectives of schooling.

Let us take another "population" regularity. After a period of time our outer-spacer notes that at regular intervals (what earthlings call once a month) a group of people come together at a particular time in the evening. No small people are there, only big people. With few exceptions, the big people tend not to have been seen in the school during the day. The exceptions are those who during the day are in rooms with small people.

At this meeting most of the people sit in orderly rows, very quietly, and rarely say anything. When someone in these rows says something it is most frequently preceded by the raising of his right hand. There are a few people who do most of the talking and they sit in front at a table.

---

[1] It is an interesting digression to suggest that one of the major sources of the conflict between generations is that the younger generation has the annoying ability not only to discern existing regularities but also to force the older generation to the awareness that there are alternative regularities. This, of course, the older generation finds difficult to accept because of the tendency to confuse the way things are with the way things should or could be. I remember as a child being puzzled and annoyed that no one could satisfactorily explain to me why one could not eat fried chicken for breakfast. It was obvious what the existing breakfast regularities were but I could not understand why the alternative of chicken aroused such strong feeling.

Several things puzzle the outer-spacer. For example, his computer tells him that there is no relationship between this meeting and any existing regularity during the day; that is, any existing regularity during the day is in no way affected by the occurrence of these meetings. This puzzles the outer-spacer because there are obvious similarities between the evening meeting and what goes on in the daytime. For example, at both times most people sit quietly in orderly rows — in the evening big people sit quietly, while during the day it is the little people who sit quietly. At both times it is the big people "in front" who do most of the talking — in the evening there is one big person who talks the most, while during the day it is the only big person in the room who does most of the talking. What complicates matters for the outer-spacer is that he has seen that in both instances as soon as the people leave their rooms they speak much more, and they have a much greater variety of facial expression.

How do we respond to our celestial friend when he learns English and demands explanations for these regularities and similarities? What do we say to him about why there is no apparent relationship between what goes on at a PTA meeting and anything else that goes on at the school? What do we say when he demands that we tell him the alternative ways that were considered for organizing a PTA meeting or classroom, and the basis used for making a choice?[2]

Earlier in this chapter I said that "any attempt to introduce change into the school setting requires, among other things, changing in some way the existing regularities." At this point I would further suggest that this statement should be preceded by the statement that *the attempt to introduce a change into the school*

---

[2] Most readers will be aware that a good part of the controversy surrounding large urban school systems arises precisely because some community groups are pushing for an alternative way of implementing "community control," a way that would presumably change, if not eliminate, some of the PTA and classroom regularities described above. I say "presumably" because I have neither seen nor heard nor read anything to indicate that aside from changing the curriculum (as in the case of new or old math) there is any intent to change the most significant existing regularities in the classroom, for example, the passivity of the learner or the teacher as talker and question-asker. My reservation may become more clear later in this chapter when we take up in detail some of the existing regularities in the classroom. The point I wish to emphasize here is that those who are in favor of "community control" state their intended outcomes for the classroom, when they state them at all, in terms so vague and virtuous that they would defy subsequent attempts at evaluation — quite in contrast to the specificity of intended outcomes as to the role of parents in decision-making.

setting usually (if not always) stems from the perception of a regularity that one does not like. We, like the outer-spacer, are set to see regularities, but unlike the inhabitant of the space platform we are not set either to observe the tremendous range of existing regularities or to inquire naively about the rationale for any one of them and the nature of the universe of alternatives of which the existing regularity is but one possibility.

Let us now leave both fantasy and heavenly friend and take up several existing regularities that not only illustrate the fruitfulness of this approach for understanding the school culture but also help clarify the problem of how to state intended outcomes in ways that are testable.

THE PHYSICAL EDUCATION PROGRAM

In most schools there is a place, usually large, where physical education programs are conducted. Those who conduct these programs are expected to have special training.

> What happens when, as I have done in numerous occasions, I say to groups of teachers that I simply do not comprehend why there should be physical education programs in the schools? As you might imagine, the most frequent response is staring disbelief followed by a request to reformulate the statement. Without going into the details of the discussion — which is usually quite heated — I shall indicate the significances I attribute to the initial response and the ensuing discussion. First, there is the implicit recognition both by the teachers and myself that we operate in different worlds, i.e., I perceive them and they perceive me as having different backgrounds and experiences. Second, it is inconceivable to the teachers that a school could or should be without a physical education program. They have a conception of a school which, if changed or challenged, they strongly defend. Far from being indifferent to the conception they defend it to a degree which illuminates how their sense of identity is related to their conception. Third, they justify the physical education program in terms of what they think children are and need. Put in another way, their justification is psychological and philosophical.[3]

[3]S. B. Sarason, "The School Culture and Processes of Change." In *The Yale Psycho-Educational Clinic: Collected Papers and Studies*, S. B. Sarason and F.

One of the most frequent responses to my question is that children need an opportunity "to get rid of all that energy which they have in them." This energy cannot be discharged by sitting and doing work in classrooms. (It is interesting to note that in the minds of teachers this response is much more applicable to boys than to girls.) This response seems to assume that at least three things are true: (1) the greater the amount of continuous time a child spends in a classroom the more restless he becomes; (2) much energy is discharged in gym activities, and (3) following the discharge of energy the child's restlessness in class is discernibly less than before gym.

As to the first assumption I am not aware that anyone has demonstrated that increased restlessness is a function merely of time. I have seen classrooms where I could discern no increase in restlessness, and I have seen other classrooms where the increase was predictably related to subject matter interacting either with teacher interest or adequacy, or with style. Teachers responding to my question in a group do not say what many have said to me when I have talked with them alone while their classes were in gym: *the gym period is one during which the teacher can recoup his or her energy losses, or get some paper work done.*

As to the second assumption, I do not doubt that there is much energy discharged in gym. But I do doubt, as do many teachers, the third assumption. *Observation rather compellingly suggests that following gym there is frequently an increase in restlessness and listlessness that interferes with class work. The intended outcome does not seem to occur; in fact the reverse of it may be the modal consequence.* In connection with outcomes my observations suggest that the level of class restlessness before gym is highly related to level of restlessness after gym.

The rationale for the regularity of gym frequently includes intended outcomes other than the ones given above. Increasing motor skill, teaching cooperation in group or team effort, and preparing children for productive use of leisure time are some intended outcomes advanced to justify gym programs. Although these are statements about intended outcomes they do not in any clear way tell me how existing behavioral regularities of children are changed or new ones are added.

Kaplan, eds, Monograph Series (Boston: Massachusetts State Department of Mental Health, 1969) p. 6.

For example, I know of several suburban school systems in which the major gym activities of girls during the fall and spring are field hockey and a variety of kickball games. If *one* of the intended outcomes of such activities is to influence leisure time behavioral regularities (types of physical activities, their frequency, etc.), I must report the fact that I have never seen girls engage in these activities outside of school. But, one can maintain, there are other and perhaps more important outcomes for out-of-school activities. Agreed; but without knowing the out-of-school behavioral regularities one cannot determine what effects, if any, gym activities have on them.

What *would* happen if gym programs ceased? This alternative would probably arouse reactions similar to those that surrounded the withdrawal of certain universities from intercollegiate football competition. But these universities have suffered no baleful effects.

Physical education personnel are not likely to believe that I have no strong feelings for or against their programs. My purpose in discussing these programs has been to make several points: first that they represent a programmatic regularity in the school culture; second, that any programmatic regularity, explicitly or implicitly, describes intended outcomes that involve either new behavioral regularities or the changing of old ones; third, that there are alternatives to the existing programmatic regularity; and, fourth, that any challenge to a programmatic regularity is more likely to engender feeling than reason. This last point is certainly not peculiar to the school culture.

It has not been my intention here, nor will it be in the later pages, to convey the impression that I am demanding proof or justification for the programmatic regularities that exist in the school culture. The absence of proof does not mean that the underlying rationale is invalid. Even where there is apparently disconfirming evidence we must be clear as to whether the rationale is being relevantly tested. My position in these pages is that the intended outcomes for programmatic regularities can and should be stated in terms of overt behavioral regularities that the dispassionate observer can record. To state intended outcomes in any other way increases the chances that we will be dealing with all the confusion and controversy produced by what Hook has called the unanalyzable abstraction (Chapter 3).

THE ARITHMETIC-MATHEMATICS PROGRAMMATIC REGULARITY

We turn to the arithmetic-mathematics regularity in order to help the reader see how easy it is to assume that the way things are is the way they should be, and to help him grasp how difficult it is to examine what I have called the universe of alternatives. In Chapter 4 I alluded to the following programmatic regularity: beginning in the first grade and on every school day thereafter until graduation from high school the child receives instruction and drill in the use and understanding of numbers. Like eating and sleeping that is quite a regularity, and one may assume that this degree of regularity reflects considerations vital to the development of children.

The naive person might ask several questions: Would academic and intellectual development be adversely affected if the exposure was for four days a week instead of five? Or three instead of five? What would happen if the exposure began in the second or third grade? What if the exposure was in alternate years? Obviously, one can generate many more questions, each of which suggests an alternative to the existing programmatic regularity. From this universe of alternatives how does one justify the existing regularity?

Before taking up this question we must first deal with the emotional reactions I have gotten when on numerous occasions I have asked different groups (e.g., educators, psychologists, and parents) questions that challenge what exists and implicitly suggest that there may be other ways of thinking and acting. I focus on the emotional reactions because they reveal the distinctive characteristics of the culture more than other ways of understanding the setting, particularly if one is or has been a member of that setting. Because we have spent so much of our own lives in schools, and watched our own children in school, we may never be aware of the process whereby we uncritically confuse what is with what might be. In fact, in diverse ways, one of the most significant effects of school on children is to get them to accept existing regularities as the best and only possible state of affairs, although frequently this is neither verbally stated nor consciously decided.

The first response to my statement of alternatives is essentially one of humor; that is, the listener assumes that I intended something akin to a joke and it was funny.[4] Having established myself as a comic, however, I usually persist and insist that I am quite serious. To keep the discussion going I then say the following:

Let me tell you the results of an informal poll I have been conducting among friends and colleagues, and I will take this opportunity to get your answers to this question: When you think back over the past few months, how many times have you used numbers other than to do *simple* addition, subtraction, multiplication, and division? The results of the poll are clear: highly educated, productive people very rarely use numbers other than in the most simple ways, leaving aside, of course, those individuals whose work requires more advanced number concepts (e.g., mathematicians). On what basis is it illegitimate to suggest that these results have no significance for the fact that a large part of what children learn in twelve years of arithmetic and mathematics is content other than the simple computations? Incidentally, I have also polled many far less educated individuals and, needless to say, the results contain no exception to the use only of simple computations.

And now the fur begins to fly. Among the more charitable accusations is the one that I am anti-intellectual. Among the least charitable reactions (for me) is simply an unwillingness to pursue the matter further. (On one occasion some individuals left the meeting in obvious disgust.) One can always count on some individuals asserting that mathematics "trains or disciplines the mind" and the more of it the better, much like Latin used to be justified as essential to the curriculum.[5]

---

[4]This reminds me of the suggestion that a former colleague, quite eminent, made in the course of a discussion about how a university could get rid of tenured professors who were "dead wood" (i.e., whatever contribution they made was a long time ago and there was no reason to believe that they served any function other than to stand in the way of younger men). His suggestion was that all beginning instructors be given tenure and as they get promoted (from assistant, to associate, to full professor) they have increasingly less tenure so that when they become full professors they have no tenure at all. The suggestion, of course, was treated as a joke and no one (including myself) considered for a moment that there *were* alternatives to the existing structure (the way things are is the only way things should be) even though no one had examined our thought through the universe of alternatives in terms of intended outcomes.

[5]It is important for an understanding of the school culture, although it certainly is not peculiar to it, that one not assume that the *public* positions taken by groups within that culture are those held *privately* by all or most individuals comprising those groups. Many within the school culture question many aspects

The fact is that whenever I have presented these thoughts I have been extremely careful to state them so that the words and sentences I employ do not contain any preference for any alternative, *simply because I have no adequate basis for choosing among the universe of alternatives* — and neither do the audiences. The intent of the thoughts is twofold: to indicate that there is always a universe of alternatives from which to choose, and to show that when any programmatic regularity is no longer viewed in terms of that universe of alternatives, rational thought and evaluation of intended outcomes are no longer in the picture, overwhelmed as they are by the power of faith, tradition and habit.

BEHAVIORAL REGULARITIES

Thus far in this chapter we have discussed two examples of regularities to which all within the school must adapt, since there is little or no element of individual choice. They are predetermined characteristics of the setting. Let us now turn to what might be termed behavioral regularities, which have to do with the frequency of overt behaviors. Laughing, crying, fighting, talking, concentrating, working, writing, question-asking, question-answering, test behavior and performance, stealing, cheating, unattending — these are *some* of the overt behaviors that occur with varying frequency among children in school. That they occur is important to, and expected by, school personnel.

---

of programmatic regularities and are willing to consider the universe of alternatives. However, several factors keep this seeking and questioning a private affair. First, there is the untested assumption that few others think in this way. As we have said elsewhere (Sarason, et. al., 1966) "teaching is a lonely profession" despite the fact that the school is densely populated. Second, existing vehicles for discussion and planning within the school (faculty meetings: teacher-principal contacts, teacher-supervisor contacts, etc.) are based on the principle of avoidance of controversy. Third, at all levels (teacher, principal, administrator) there is the feeling of individual impotence. Fourth, there is acceptance of another untested assumption: that the public will oppose any meaningful or drastic change in existing regularities. In short, these and other factors seem to allow almost everyone in the culture to act in terms of perceived group norms at the expense of the expression of "deviant" individual thoughts, a situation conducive neither to change nor to job satisfaction. It was only after I had worked intensively for months in schools, and had developed a relationship of mutual trust with school personnel, that I came to see that there was a difference between public statements and private positions.

But what is equally important is that they are expected to change over time. *Behavioral regularities and their changes represent some of the most important intended outcomes of programmatic regularities. Deliberate changes in programmatic regularities are intended to change the occurrence and frequency of behavioral regularities.*

In 1969, the time this chapter was being written, newspapers and other media daily reported how our schools and universities were changing programmatic regularities in an effort to change the overt behavioral regularities of students. That these reports reached us through public channels of communication reflects the fact that the programmatic changes were themselves a result of changes in the overt behavior of students; that is, the existing programmatic regularities were no longer achieving their intended outcomes. Changes due to open conflict are probably less numerous than changes (as in the case of new math) that were initiated by those at the administrative or supervisory levels. Although in both conflict and nonconflict situations of change, programmatic changes are intended to effect changes in behavioral regulations, there seems to be much greater clarity about intended outcomes in conditions of conflict than in the modal process of change. This should not be surprising because "revolutionary situations," almost by definition, are those in which issues and outcomes have become sharpened and polarized.

Some behavioral regularities are concerned with individual pupils while others reflect pupil-pupil interactions, such as boys with girls, older pupils with younger pupils, and black with white. As important as any of these are the behavioral regularities characterizing teacher-pupil interactions. We shall take up now a teacher-pupil behavioral regularity fateful for the intended outcome of any change in programmatic regularities.

QUESTION-ASKING:
A BEHAVIORAL REGULARITY

As in our discussion of programmatic regularities I shall not start with questions about assumptions, values, intended outcomes, or alternative patterns, but rather with the discernible regularity. It is, I think, only when one is confronted with a clear regularity that one stands a chance of clarifying the relationship between theory and practice, intention and outcome. Let us, therefore, start by asking two questions: At what rate do teachers ask questions in the classroom? At what rate do children ask questions of teachers?

From a theoretical and practical standpoint — by which I mean theories of child development, intellectual growth, educational and learning theory, techniques of teaching, presentation and discussion of subject matter — the importance of question-asking has always been emphasized. It is surprising, therefore, that there have been very few studies focusing on this type of behavior. Susskind (1969) recently did a comprehensive review of the literature. He expresses surprise that a type of behavior considered by everyone to be of great importance has hardly been investigated. However, he points out that although the few studies vary greatly in investigative sophistication, they present a remarkably similar state of affairs. But before we summarize the findings, the reader may wish to try to answer Susskind's question:

> Before exploring the research literature we suggest that the reader attempt to estimate the rates of two classroom behaviors. Imagine yourself in a fifth grade, social studies classroom in a predominantly white, middle-class school. During a half-hour lesson, in which the teacher and the class talk to each other (there is no silent work), how many questions are asked (a) by the teacher, (b) by the students? How do the two rates correlate?[6]

The first two questions are deceptively simple because, as Susskind has made clear, there are different types of questions, and there are problems as to how questions (and which questions) are to be counted. For example, if the teacher asks the same question of five children should it be counted once or five times? Susskind has developed a comprehensive, workable set of categories, and the interested reader is referred to his work. We will now summarize the answers to the above questions in light of existing studies, including the very recent ones by Susskind, whose findings are very similar to those from older studies.

[6] E. C. Susskind, "Questioning and Curiosity in the Elementary School Classroom" (Doctoral dissertation, Yale University, 1969), p. 38.

1.   Across the different studies the range of rate of teacher questions per half-hour is from 45-150.

2.   When asked, educators as well as other groups vastly underestimate the rate of teacher questions, the estimated range being 12-20 per half hour.

3.   From 67 to 95 percent of all teacher questions require "straight recall" from the student.

4.   Children ask *fewer* than two questions per half hour. That is to say, during this time period two questions by children will have been asked.

5.   The greater the tendency for a teacher to ask straight recall questions the fewer the questions initiated by children. This does not mean that children do not have time to ask questions. They do have time.

6.   The more a teacher asks "personally relevant" questions the higher the rate of questioning on the part of children.

7.   The rate of questions by children does not seem to vary with IQ level or with social-class background.

These statements derive from existing studies, but, as Susskind points out, scores of people have come to similar conclusions from informal observations.

We have here a clear behavioral regularity. How should we think about this? Is this behavioral regularity an intended outcome? Put in another way, this is the way things are; Is this the way things should be? I know of no psychological theory or theorist, particularly those who are or have been most influential on the educational scene, who would view this behavioral regularity as a desirable outcome, that is, as one kind of barometer indicating that an organized set of conceptions are being consistently implemented. In addition, I have never read of or spoken to curriculum specialists and reformers who would not view this behavioral regularity as evidence that their efforts were being neither understood nor implemented. Finally, the fact that teachers and other groups vastly underestimate the rate of teacher-questioning (in Susskind's study teachers were quite surprised when confronted with the rates obtained in *their* classrooms) suggests that this behavioral regularity is not an intended outcome according to some part of the thinking of teachers.[7]

---

[7]Children are the one group who realistically estimate or know the behavioral regularity. My informal poll of scores of children leaves no doubt in my mind that they view the classroom as a place where teachers ask questions and children provide answers.

We have, then, an outcome that practically nobody intends, a situation that would not be particularly upsetting were it not that practically everybody considers question asking on the part of teachers and children one of the most crucial means of maintaining interest, supporting curiosity, acquiring knowledge, and facilitating change and growth.

In Chapter 4, where we used the new math to illustrate the modal process of introducing change into the school culture, we emphasized the point that the curriculum reformers seemed quite aware that they wanted to do more than merely change textbooks; they realized that classrooms tended to be uninviting and uninspired places in which teachers were active and children passive. Their intended outcome was to change, among other things, behavioral regularities such as the one we are here discussing. But this intended outcome was never systematically discussed (or even written about) or stated as a criterion by which the new curriculum was to be judged. Certainly the teachers who underwent retraining could not focus on this issue, if only because they were in the same passive role that characterized, and would continue to characterize, their own students.

For our purposes here the generalization that requires emphasis is that *any change in a programmatic regularity has as one of its intended outcomes some kind of change in existing behavioral regularities, and these behavioral regularities are among the most important criteria for judging the degree to which intended outcomes are being achieved.* At this point I am not interested in whether or not one likes or agrees with the programmatic change but rather in the fact that these changes require changes in some kind or kinds of behavioral regularities. It is almost always true that changes in the behavioral regularities will be assumed to be effected or mediated by internal emotional and cognitive processes and states, but the behavioral regularities remain as our most secure, albeit not infallible, criterion for judging what we have achieved. In fact (and the question-asking regularity is a good example), behavioral regularities are probably our best means for inferring internal cognitive and emotional states.

It is the rare observer of classrooms who has not inferred from the overt behavior of children and teachers that the great majority of children seem "inside" to be neither strongly interested in, curious about, nor feeling satisfaction in regard to what they are doing or what is going on. They are, in short, not having a particularly good time. But, someone can say, this is an inference, and it may frequently be a wrong one, which of course, is true. To what behavioral regularities can we look that could serve as a kind of check on these inferences?

One of them, of course, requires asking children to respond to relevant questions about what they are feeling, but this will be regarded as either too obvious or naive because of the frequently held assumption that what people, particularly children, report about what they feel should not be given much weight. But what if we were to look at the behavior of children in the hall *immediately* after they leave one classroom to go to another, as is the case in junior and senior high? How does one account for the noise level, the animated talking, running, and formation of groups, and the absence of talk about the intellectual substance of what they had just experienced? *Why is it that one of the most trouble-producing (from the standpoint of school personnel) times in the school day is when students are in the halls going from one room to another?* When the behavioral regularities in the hall are ascertained, I have no doubt that they will be found to be related to regularities in the classroom in a way that confirms inferences made about the internal states of children in the classroom.

But we cannot understand the question-asking regularity without briefly trying to understand what aspects of the school culture contribute to a state of affairs that few, if anyone, feel is the way things should be.

1. *Teachers tend to teach the way in which they themselves were taught.* I am not only referring to the public schooling of teachers but to their college experiences as well — and I am not restricting myself to schools of education. In general, the question-asking regularity we have described does not, in my experience, differ markedly from what goes on in college classrooms. The culture of the school should be expected to reflect aspects of other types of educational cultures from which the teachers have come. As suggested in Chapter 3, the university critic of the public schools frequently is unable to see that his criticisms may well be true of his own educational culture. It would indeed be strange if teachers did not teach the way they had been taught.

2. *In their professional training (courses, practice teaching) teachers are minimally exposed to theories about question-asking and the technical problems of question-asking and question-producing behavior — the relationship between theory and prac-*

tice. To the reader who may be surprised at this, I would suggest he consult the most frequently used books in educational psychology, learning, or child development courses. Such a reader may conclude either that it is not an important question or that the obvious is being overlooked.[8]

3. *Whatever educational help or consultation is available to the teacher (principal, supervisors, workshops, etc.) does not concern itself directly with the question-asking regularity.* Particularly in the earliest months and years of teaching the primary concern of everyone is "law and order," and the possibility that discipline may be related to, or can be affected by, the question-asking regularity is rarely recognized. The anxiety of the beginning teacher about maintaining discipline too frequently interferes with his sensitivity to, and desire to accommodate to, the questions and interests of his pupils.

4. *The predetermined curriculum that suggests that teachers cover a certain amount of material within certain time intervals with the expectation that their pupils as a group will perform at certain levels at certain times is responded to by teachers in a way as to make for the fantastic discrepancy between the rate of teacher and student questions.* This factor touches on a very complicated state of affairs. From the standpoint of the teacher the curriculum is not a suggestion but a requirement, for if it is not met the principal and supervisors will consider the teaching inadequate. In addition, the teacher whom the pupils will have in the next year will consider them inadequately prepared. Therefore, the best and safest thing to do is to insure that the curriculum is covered, a view that reinforces the tendency to ask many "straight recall" questions.

From the administrator's standpoint the curriculum is only a guide, and the trouble arises because teachers are not "creative"; that is, the problem is not the curriculum but the teacher. As many administrative personnel have said, "We *tell* them to be creative but they still stick slavishly to the curriculum as if it

---

[8] How the obvious can be overlooked can be illustrated (Sarason, Blatt, Davidson, 1962), by looking at a function that all teachers perform, are expected to perform, and must perform — talking to parents. Yet, I know of no teacher-training program (some may exist) that gives the prospective teacher five minutes of training in this function, a situation that can be justified only by assuming that God singled out teachers to have the special gift of how to talk to parents meaningfully and productively. Reality, as we shall see later, does not support this assumption.

were a bible." To which teachers reply, "What they want to know at the end of the year, and what I will be judged by, are the achievement test scores of my children."

Although both sides *correctly* perceive each other's behavioral regularity, the administrator feels unable to change the state of affairs — that is, he is of no help to the teacher — and the teacher continues to feel unfree to depart from the curriculum. In short, we are back to a familiar situation in which no one sees the universe of alternatives to current practices.

There are, of course, alternatives. For example, as Susskind's studies show, there is variation among teachers in the question-asking regularity; some teachers can utilize a curriculum without being a question-asking machine and without requiring pupils to respond primarily to "straight recall" questions. In addition, and a source of encouragement, Susskind obtained data suggesting that when a group of teachers were confronted with the question-asking regularities in their classroom, and this was discussed in terms of theory and intended outcomes, the teachers as a group were able to change the regularity. *But here one runs smack into the obstacle of another characteristic of the school culture: there are no vehicles of discussion, communication, or observation that allow for this kind of variation to be raised and productively used for purposes of help and change.* Faculty meetings, as teachers are acutely aware, are not noted for either their intellectual content or their sensitivity to issues that may be controversial or interpersonally conflictful. (As our man from outer space could well have discerned, the classroom, the PTA meeting, and the faculty meeting, are amazingly similar in the question-asking regularity.) We shall have more to say on these issues in Chapter 8.

For our purposes here what is most important is not the particular behavioral regularity or the factors that may account for it, but the obvious fact that within the school culture these regularities, which are in the nature of intended outcomes, are not recognized, and it is not traditional to have means for their recognition. What is not recognized or verbalized cannot be dealt with, and if it is important and not recognized, efforts to introduce substantive change, particularly in the classroom, result in the illusion of change.

WHAT IS THE INTENDED OUTCOME?

We will now take up something that is not the usual behavioral or programmatic regularity, although it has features of both. It is a regularity that will not be found in all schools; in fact, it may be rather infrequent. The first justification for presenting it is that it illustrates well the fruitfulness of discerning regularities, using them to determine their intended outcomes, and squaring these outcomes with what actually happens. The second justification is that the data we possessed were surprising to all concerned. I should add that these data were gathered in relation to a study (Sarason, Hill, and Zimbardo, 1964; Hill and Sarason, 1966) tangential to the purposes of this book, and it was not until we experienced "surprise" at some findings that we examined the purposes of the regularities in terms of intended and actual outcomes.

In the two junior high schools of a suburban school system, when a student considered capable of good work is doing poorly in any subject, an "interim" is sent to his home indicating that he is in danger of failing the course. The student may be doing failing work or the level of his performance may be significantly below expectations. If the low or failing performance is considered a true indication of the student's intellectual capacity no interim is sent. Since the average IQ in these schools is discernibly above the national average (not surprising in light of the predominantly middle-class composition of the community), there are relatively few students who do not possess the capacity to get passing grades in their courses. In the bulk of instances when an interim is sent home the student is in danger of getting an F or a D for that marking period.

The study we were doing involved two large samples of children. We had been following one sample since they were in Grade 1; the other since they were in Grade 2. There was no reason to believe that each sample was not representative of all children in that particular class. One question in which we were interested was what happened to these children in their first year of junior high school?

One could say that we were dealing with a behavioral regularity in which the failing or near-failing performance of certain students gave rise to a certain action on the part of school personnel resulting in a standard written message being sent to the home. What was the intended outcome of the relationship between performance and school action? Was it merely *to inform* the home? If that were the sole intended outcome, then one could expect the parents to treat the information in much the same way as they would if they had been informed about the exact height of their children; there would be no intention that the parents act on the information. It is not violating the canons of reflective thinking to say that the intended outcome was to raise the level of the student's performance by actions that parents would take on the basis of the message from school. That, of course, is what school personnel explicitly expected.

Our surprise began when our data indicated that receiving interims was by no means infrequent. Forty-seven percent of the boys in one sample, about 49 percent in the other sample, received at least one interim during the four marking periods. For girls in the same samples the figures were 33 and 32 percent, respectively.

We then asked what happened to the student's grade in the subject in which he had received an interim — did his grade increase, decrease, or remain the same compared to the grade in the previous marking period? Since the previous grade was typically a D or F it was obvious that for many students they had only one direction in which to go, and that was up. *What the data clearly revealed was that in half the cases the grade remained the same, in 38 percent the grade went down, and in 12 percent the grade went up.* If the intended outcome of this procedure was to raise grades it clearly was not successful. School personnel were unaware of these actual outcomes, and when they were made aware of them they were surprised at the discrepancy between intended and actual outcomes.

We then asked the following question: in the three major courses (English, Social Studies, Mathematics) what was the frequency and pattern of interims over the four marking periods? We expected, as did the school personnel, that mathematics would have the highest frequency in each marking period. *To the surprise and consternation of everyone, social studies was far and away the subject matter in which the most interims were re-*

*ceived in each marking period, with English and mathematics
following in that order.*

NUMBER OF INTERIMS IN RELATION TO THE MARKING PERIOD
(ALL BOYS AND ALL GIRLS FROM THE TWO SAMPLES
IN THE TWO SCHOOLS)

| | Boys | | | | Girls | | | |
| | Marking Period | | | | Marking Period | | | |
	I	II	III	IV	I	II	III	IV
English	50	78	62	74	21	27	28	13
Social Studies	80	91	65	86	54	40	54	29
Math	40	66	72	64	23	20	20	19

One of the major advantages of viewing the school culture in terms of regularities and intended outcomes is that it requires one, at least temporarily, to suspend or control the role of opinion, values, or bias. As we shall see in later chapters, viewing the school culture in this fashion is but one way of understanding it, and I have been emphasizing and illustrating this way because so much of what is written about the school culture centers around issues of values and objectives without relating them to existing regularities or defining new regularities by which to judge the consistency between intent and outcome.

A second advantage of viewing the school culture in terms of existing regularities and intended outcomes is that one frequently comes up with unanticipated findings that further illuminate the existence of other kinds of regularities, and one's understanding of the setting deepens. For example, why should social studies have the greatest number of interims? Why is it apparently difficult for so many students in their first year of junior high school?

DISCONTINUITIES AND SOCIAL STUDIES

When so large a number of first year junior high school students in a middle-class, suburban community receives at least one interim in major subjects, and in very few instances can intelligence level be a factor, one is forced to speculate about possible explanations. Consistent with our approach in this chapter (the outer spaceman approach) we can begin by comparing the elementary and junior high school settings on the more obvious regularities.[9] For example, in contrast to the elementary schools the junior high schools are physically larger and contain more people. The students come from more than one neighborhood, they move more frequently from room to room, they have more teachers, and they have more freedom in that there is not one teacher who is *their* teacher and whose reponsibility it is to oversee them. In light of these and other differences there is a host of new rules and regulations that the students must observe. The students are like people who have spent their lives in a small town and suddenly find themselves in a large, unfamiliar city.

There are many discontinuities between elementary and junior high schools that require a good deal of unlearning and learning on the part of young people, and if one had to make any prediction it would be that many children would respond maladaptively. This expectation is reinforced by the fact that the usual orientation exercises are brief and ritualistic. I have sat through some of these exercises, and I have read the materials provided the children, and I can only conclude that the intended outcome was to impress on the new students that there was much to learn about socially navigating in this culture and most of that was what not to do.

But now let us ask some "regularities" questions. What information is provided the junior high about the new students? Who provides this information? What is done with the information? What we found out was that the elementary school record, including personality and academic evaluation by the student's last teacher, is sent ahead. We also found out that the teachers who made the evaluations were (a) resentful of the fact that junior high personnel never spoke to them or sought their advice, particularly in relation to children with one or another kind of prob-

[9]We are apparently in an era when the term junior high is somewhat in disrepute and the more fashionable term is "the middle school." In some communities the pupil comes to the middle school at a somewhat earlier age and remains there somewhat longer than was the case with the junior high. Typically, the building remains the same but the label changes. This is like the elementary school whose principal prided himself on the initiation of ungraded classes. I was impressed until I strolled through the halls and saw that each door contained grade signs (e.g., Grade 1, Grade 2). Observation in the classrooms provided no good evidence that they should be viewed as other than traditionally organized units.

blem; and (b) they were puzzled at the number of children who had not been any kind of problem in elementary school but who had various difficulties in junior high. As best as we could determine, the information sent on to the junior high was read and filed. It was the truly rare instance when junior high personnel (e.g., guidance counselors) acted on the information before the child showed up or shortly after. *Our study revealed that the single best predictor of the occurrence of academic or personality problems in the first year of junior high school was the evaluation of the last teacher the children had in elementary school.*[10]

If the intended outcome of this record keeping and its transmittal to the junior high was to *anticipate* problems with the aim of taking action to prevent their reoccurrence or to lessen their consequences, it clearly was not achieved. When this was discussed with junior high personnel it was pointed out to us that the size of the freshman class simply did not allow effective use of the information, a fact that concedes the argument that the major intended outcome was not achieved. Whatever the reason, the fact remains that these record-keeping regularities were not serving their intended purposes.

As I indicated earlier, discerning and examining regularities in relation to intended outcomes frequently lead one to questions, issues, or other observations that illuminate important aspects of the school culture. For example, in the process of doing this study — spending time in the elementary and junior high schools, talking to teachers, principals, and other administrative personnel — we became increasingly aware that junior high personnel view the new student in September rather differently than elementary school personnel did in the previous June. Whereas in June the elementary school viewed him as a *child*, in September the junior high viewed him as a *young adult*. These different views result in different expectations and are an important aspect of the discontinuity between the structure and organization

---

[10]In this study we were given the names of all first year junior high children who were referred to any administrator because of a problem, or who had received an interim. We were then able to see the relationship between what the child's last teacher in elementary school had said (and implicitly predicted) and how many and what kinds of problems were recorded in his folder. For two successive years the evaluation of the child's last teacher was the best predictor of the occurrence of problems in the first year of junior high school.

of the two settings. I am, of course, suggesting that meeting these different expectations is frequently difficult for some children, even for many who manifested no problems in elementary school. (Anyone who has any knowledge of, or experience with, college freshmen will not be surprised by this explanation.)

There is another aspect to this problem that is illuminating of the school culture: *the differences in the ways in which pupils are viewed by elementary and junior high personnel are reflections of the differences in the ways in which these personnel view each other.* Many (by no means all) junior high school teachers view themselves as "specialists" in a particular subject matter, while they view the elementary school teacher as a somewhat superficial generalist — much like the differences between the general practitioner and specialist in medicine. Put in another way, the junior high teacher tends to view himself as "higher" and, therefore, better than the elementary school teacher.[11] Although less true today than in previous decades, there is still a tendency for junior and senior high personnel to receive higher salaries than those in the elementary schools. The fact that there are far more men teachers in the junior high school than in the elementary school is undoubtedly a reflection of the view that the elementary school pupil is a child (taken care of by child-care kinds of teachers) while the junior high school pupil (who two months before was in elementary school) is a beginning young adult. These differences in views and expectations sharpen the discontinuities between the two settings.

But why should social studies (in these two junior high schools, at least) be so difficult in the first year? We looked into the curriculum manual and guide (a heavy and imposing document of two hundred or more pages), talked to teachers, and sat in classrooms. I do not pretend to know and understand all the factors that would comprise an answer, but I can point to two related factors that seemed important. The first of these factors is that the student was frequently required to engage in projects for which he had to read in different sources, use the library (school and community), and organize readings and materials.

[11]This is, of course, identical to the situation in universities where those who teach only graduate courses tend to view themselves as doing a more important, more worthy, or more difficult task than the instructor who only teaches undergraduates. In the public schools, as well as the universities, it is as if the worth of a teacher is determined in part by the age of his students.

Many of the pupils were simply not able to take on this kind of independent responsibility. The task was not made easier by the fact that the degree and content of direction given by the teacher seemed to assume an amount of previous experience with such a task that struck us as unrealistic.

Two years after the above observations I conducted a college senior seminar for the first time in my teaching life. Up to that time I had only taught graduate students. My attitude had been that parents who sent their sons to Yale had a right to expect that they would be given an excellent education, but it did not follow that I had to participate in that education. (Elementary school pupils = undergraduates; junior high school pupils = graduate students.) Midway through the seminar I was aware that I was frustrated and annoyed. Why do *they* know so little? Why is it that when I assign a paper, with a brief but commendably clear explanation of its purpose and scope, I get a barrage of questions (during and after class, in person and on the phone) about what I mean and want? Why are they so dependent and fearful of exercising independent judgment? Where have they been for three years? Who was spoon feeding them? The principle underlying these thoughts of a teacher is quite similar to that enunciated by Professor Higgins in *My Fair Lady* when he compares men and women and concludes "We are a marvelous sex!"

The second factor I can point to in regard to the social studies finding is that the pupils were required *to organize and write* papers and many of them clearly were inadequate to the task — and I must remind the reader that this population was discernibly above average in ability. This raised questions: In the last year (sixth grade) of elementary school how many times were pupils required to write a paper? How many times did a teacher sit down with a child and go over what he had written? My informal polling indicated that some teachers required as few as two "papers" and some required more than four.[12] Although I polled far more children than teachers, I did not hear of a single instance in which a teacher had sat down with a child to go over what he had written. When papers were returned to the children there were usually comments, pro and con, written on them, but the matter ended there.

At this point in our discussion it is not relevant to go into explanations of this state of affairs or to explore the universe of

[12]When my daughter was in the sixth grade in an elementary school (in an adjacent community) that had the best reputation of any school in our metropolitan area, she was required to write only *one* paper.

alternatives. I have used social studies for the purpose of illustrating how one regularity (i.e., interims) leads one to another regularity (i.e., social studies), the examination of which can be extremely productive towards one's understanding of aspects of the school culture.[13]

The purposes of this chapter were to state and illustrate the following:

1.   There are regularities of various kinds.

2.   Existing programmatic and behavioral regularities should be described independent of one's own values or opinions.

3.   Regularities exist because they are supposed to have intended outcomes.

4.   There are at least two characteristics to intended outcomes: (1) aspects of them are discernible in overt behavior or interactions, and (2) they are justified by statements of value (i.e., what is good and what is bad).

5.   There are frequent discrepancies between regularities and intended outcomes. Usually, no regularity is built into the school culture to facilitate the recognition of such discrepancies.

6.   The significance of any regularity, particularly of the programmatic type, cannot be adequately comprehended apart from the universe of "regularity alternatives" of which the existing regularity is but one item. The failure to consider or recognize a universe of alternatives is one obstacle to change occurring from within the culture, and makes it likely that recognition of this universe of alternatives will await events and forces outside the culture.

7.   Any attempt to introduce an important change in the school culture requires changing existing regularities to produce new intended outcomes. In practice, the regularities tend not to be changed and the intended outcomes, therefore, cannot occur; that is, the more things change the more they remain the same.

8.   It is probably true that the most important attempts to introduce change into the school culture *require* changing exist-

[13]The reader will recall that we and school personnel were surprised that mathematics did not produce the largest number of interims. One reason for this may be that mathematics teachers *expect* children to have difficulty and, therefore, either they proceed more slowly or they are more lenient in their grading and evaluations. I present this possible explanation in order to make the point that our understanding of the school culture requires that we try to understand why an expected regularity (or pattern of regularity) does not occur.

ing teacher-child regularities. When one examines the natural history of the change process it is precisely these regularities that remain untouched.

The more our discussion has proceeded the more evident it has become that a central problem to the understanding of the school culture is how to describe it so that the regularities that characterize it can become apparent. I have already suggested that our usual theories and ways of thinking about individuals are far from adequate for our purposes. We shall pursue this problem further in the next chapter, in which we shall refer to a particular approach that is quite promising, if only because it deals with the problem directly.

ᴄ7ᴐ

The Ecological Approach

In our accustomed way of thinking and acting it is extremely difficult, if not impossible, to look at and describe settings independent of the personalities of people. When we spend an evening in someone's home, sit in a classroom, or attend a case conference, we find that our thoughts largely refer either to ourselves or to what we think is going on "inside" someone else's head. That this is so is both reflected in and determined by personality theories, past and present.

Ego, self-actualization, expectancies, defense, anxiety — these and other terms in personality theories are basically conceived as *individual* characteristics or variables, and their variations are understood by looking at other characteristics of the individual as well as his interactions with other *individuals*. These theories of individuals have illuminated much and have given rise to techniques and procedures (e.g., therapeutic, educational) of practical value. To suggest that this focus on the individual may prevent us from seeing regularity and structure of the school culture that are as significant as regularity and psychological structure of the individual does not downgrade or invalidate such a focus. It would be illogical, foolish, and stupidly parochial to deny that there is much to be learned about the school culture by studying individuals. In fact, most of what we know about the school culture derives from what is explicitly or implicitly an individual psychology. But what I suggest is that there are ways of thinking, and questions to be asked, that require, at least temporarily, that we not think in terms of individuals, or in terms of what is good or bad for individuals.

To change one's way of thinking, if only, as a colleague once said, "for the hell of it," is not easy. To do so deliberately for the serious purpose of discovering new questions and problems is even more difficult, because one tends not to want to believe that one's investigative territory can be mapped rather differently and that new "lands" can be discovered by others whose perspective is different. It can be both strange and upsetting to go through most of one's life believing that two parallel lines will not meet in space, and then discover that on the basis of certain assumptions, in the context of certain facts and questions, two parallel lines will meet in space. It is strange because one set of assumptions is not right and the other wrong. It is upsetting because one is forced to recognize that there are productive ways other than one's own of looking at a particular setting or set of problems. Furthermore, if one deliberately tries to adopt another stance, one finds that it is not easy and one is plagued by such questions as: What questions do I now ask? What do I look at and how? I have no ready answers, but in this chapter I shall describe some of my own attempts at understanding, and those of others who have long concerned themselves with these issues (but who, unfortunately, have not had the influence they should have).

THE KINDERGARTEN

Among the most studied individuals in this country are children in kindergarten. In fact, if a law were passed making it illegal to study kindergarten children, the structure and direction of American child psychology would probably change in a somewhat drastic way. Kindergarten children have been studied for a variety of purposes: separation anxiety, socialization, speech development, cognitive style and development, discrimination of forms, sex play, and motor behavior, to name only a few. We have learned a great deal from studying individual characteristics of kindergarten children.

How, I asked myself, can I look at kindergartens without thinking of teachers or individual children, for initially, at least, I must not be interested in children as children or teachers as teachers. In fact, it will not make any difference if I look at a kindergarten class this year or next year or if I look at scores of kindergarten classrooms in scores of schools. Are there things I could learn about kindergarten and schools that not only would be revealing of the school culture but would also help us to understand individuals better?

I found myself thinking (without being clear why) about the following question: If on each of a number of days I was randomly to place myself in different parts of the school, how frequently would I see any occupant of the kindergarten? I do not pretend to have done this systematically but I placed myself in enough places in enough schools to be able to say at least three things. First, there are some places in which I never saw a kindergartner. Second, the frequency of seeing one seemed highly related to the distance from his room. Third, in each of the places, I saw children from other grades but I was unable to determine how many I could see from each grade. My impression was that the higher the grade the more likely its occupants could be seen in the different places.

One of the places in which I never saw an occupant from the kindergarten was the toilet, because, as in many other schools, each kindergarten classroom had its own toilet facilities. Overall, the dominant impression I received was that only infrequently does one see an occupant of the kindergarten outside the classroom. Once one gains this impression it is difficult to fail to recognize a corollary statement: *the occupants of the kindergarten relatively infrequently, and sometimes never, see parts of their physical surrounding.*[1] Having come this far, and feeling secure that our conclusion has some merit, we have a basis for asking some psychological questions about children, teachers, and the content of traditions. For instance, Why are kindergarten children, in contrast to children in other grades, infrequently found in certain places in the school?

[1] We all have the tendency to assume that inhabitants of a particular locale (e.g., a building, a neighborhood, a city) know that locale in that they have been to its parts or that they frequently can be found in those parts, an assumption that tends to be challenged only in fortuitous ways. For example, I have relatives who live in Brooklyn, which is part of New York City. I used to envy these relatives not because they lived in Brooklyn but because Manhattan was part of their city and readily available to them. I assumed they went to Manhattan. I was floored one day to learn that they very rarely went to Manhattan and for some of my relatives a year or more would go by without a visit there. We make the same assumption when we look at schools; at least, I did.

When one starts questioning school personnel, one receives a variety of answers, although the most frequent and immediate response is a mixture of silence and puzzlement, signifying that one is touching upon a tradition that no longer requires reflection and scrutiny. Although the answers are varied, there are certain common assumptions. The most common is that kindergarten children *are* different and these differences require that they be under constant, or near constant, surveillance. Related to this is the view that kindergarten is really not "school" but a preparation for school. A second assumption underlying some of the answers is that if kindergarten children interacted with older children they might be adversely affected; in undefinable ways they might pick up "bad habits" because they are so impressionable, immature, and socially unformed. When I asked one kindergarten teacher if it was really necessary for her classroom to have its own toilet facilities, in light of the fact that all of her children were fully toilet trained when they started the year, she was quite bothered by the prospect of what might happen or what they might see if they had to use common toilet facilities, leaving aside the prospect of their wandering and getting lost.

What emerges from all this is that school personnel view kindergarten children as different and that the nature of the differences requires a restriction in their sphere of mobility within the school. Equally as important, kindergarten teachers are viewed by others, and they view themselves, as a special kind of teacher *and* person. The nature of the specialness of kindergarten children and their teachers is not unrelated to the social insulation of kindergartens and their occupants from the rest of the school.

In pursuing the matter I should say at the outset that there is *some* merit to this state of affairs. But the degree of merit is, in my opinion, not so overwhelming as to prevent us from challenging assumptions and examining the always present but rarely recognized universe of alternatives. I should also remind the reader that in this discussion I am sincerely less interested in the merits of what is or could be than I am in illustrating how one can begin to look at the school culture not with individuals, or with the learning process, or even with goals and values, but rather with what may be termed ecological concerns.

Let us start the challenging process by suggesting that kindergarten children are viewed and managed in ways that are in the nature of a self-fulfilling prophecy. That is to say, their school experience is organized in ways that end up confirming the assumption that their sphere of mobility within the school should be restricted. If one makes the assumption that kindergarten children (at least most of them) can quickly learn to navigate the building by themselves, and that they should learn to do so, the task then becomes one of setting up the appropriate learning experiences with the intended outcome that a child on his own can go to and return from any place in the building. A related intended outcome might be that he learn to do so without any overt manifestation of fear.

I mention this particular outcome because my own memories of kindergarten (and I assume they are subject to the usual sources of distortion) suggest that venturing on my own from my kindergarten room was a fantasy very much associated with fear of those large, cavernous halls and those very big children, and even bigger adults, one would encounter. Then, too, there was the principal, to whom, obviously, God had delegated some of his most important powers. What if I met *him?* I am sure my kindergarten teacher knew all this and, therefore, protected me in ways that guaranteed that I would continue to feel that way!

Some readers may say, "Why make such a big deal about the fact that kindergartners live in a restricted physical locale, in light of all the things they have to learn in their own room (e.g., materials, cooperative play)? They will be spending several years in the building and that is ample time to learn all about the building." The primary answer to such a position is that I assume that the children are *very* curious about that building and all that goes on in it and that such curiosity should be taken account of and utilized for purposes of learning and motivation. They are as curious about the building as they are about their classroom. They are curious not only about its physical dimensions and attributes but also about all those other rooms and their occupants. Why should the satisfaction of such curiosity be delayed? Can one not satisfy such curiosity in ways that bring to the fore other curiosities and questions? If one takes seriously the goal of broadening the horizons (literally and figuratively in this case) of children, must not one recognize the questions about this "world of the school" that one can safely assume children have?

I wish to emphasize two points. The first is that one can think about kindergartens in a way that would result in activities that do not characterize them now — the intended outcomes of these activities are simply not possible now in most kindergartens. The second point can be put in the form of a rhetorical question: Is a *major* consideration in determining what goes on in the regular classrooms (first grade, second grade, etc.) organized on assumptions about the curiosity of children? Our discussion of question-asking in the previous chapter does not permit a strongly affirmative answer!

A somewhat atypical incident illustrates this point well. I was meeting each Wednesday with a group of ten new teachers, most of whom were in inner city schools. One of these meetings occurred after the funeral of President Kennedy. There was no school on the Monday of the funeral. We were meeting, therefore, on the second day after schools reopened. When the meeting began, the teachers continued talking about what they had just been discussing: that it had been difficult, if not impossible, to get the children to attend to their academic tasks, and the children "learned" very little of what they were supposed to learn. The interests and curiosities of the children were seen as *interferences* in learning.

Let us now examine some findings in light of our discussion of kindergartens. The specific findings are that in a large, suburban school system approximately 20 percent of all children repeated either Grade 1 or Grade 2 and in the great bulk of these grade repeaters intellectual level clearly was not an etiological factor (Sarason, et. al., 1966). There was variation in frequency of grade repetition from school to school, the lowest rate being 5 percent and the highest 29 percent. The most frequently stated reason for grade repetition was "immaturity." I do not maintain that grade repetition is caused by the nature of kindergarten experience. But I do wish to suggest that immaturity (whatever that is) is not a characteristic of a child independent of the environment in which the immaturity manifests itself (e.g., family, classroom). Within the school culture (as well as in a lot of other places) problem behavior is wrongfully viewed as a characteristic of an individual rather than as an interaction of individual and particular setting. Is it foolish to suggest that the highly protected and insulated kindergarten environment helps maintain (not cause) immature behavior? Is the children's inability to adapt to first grade *in part* a function of the sharpness of the discontinuities between kindergarten and first grade? Are the anxieties of these children maintained in part because they remain private, as do their questions about the nature and purposes of the school and schooling?[2]

I am sure that grade repetition is more complicated than those questions suggest, and the validity of these questions can only be determined by future study. What should be kept in mind is that these and other questions we have asked about kindergartens stemmed from the observation that the occupants of kindergartens are rarely, and sometimes never, seen in certain parts of the school in which they live. This observation permitted us to ask the "how come" question, which then directed us to assumptions, programs, and outcomes. At the very least, the observation allowed us to suggest that the school life of the kindergarten child could be somewhat different than it ordinarily is. There is a universe of alternatives, even for kindergartners and their teachers.

BIG SCHOOL, SMALL SCHOOL

The heading of this section is the title of a book by Barker and Gump (1964). It is for our purposes an extremely important book because it represents the most serious and systematic attempt to date to view schools (high schools) from an ecological standpoint. That is, its primary focus is not on individuals or groups of individuals — it is not primarily concerned with the psychology of individuals or those sociological variables (e.g., social class, status) by which groups of individuals may be ordered and understood, but rather with stable extra-individual units called *behavior settings*.

> If a novice, an Englishman, for example, wished to understand the environment of a first baseman in a ball game, he might set about to observe the interactions of the player with his surroundings. To do this with utmost precision he might view the first baseman through field glasses, so focused that the player would be centered in the field of the glasses, with just enough of the environment included to encompass all his contacts with the environment, all inputs and outputs: all balls caught, balls thrown, players tagged, etc. De-

[2] From our longitudinal studies of anxiety in elementary school children (Sarason, Hill, and Zimbardo, 1964; Hill and Sarason, 1966) we found that early grade repeaters were more anxious about school than non-repeaters.

spite the commendable observational care, however, this method would never provide a novice with an understanding of "the game" which gives meaning to a first baseman's transactions with his surroundings, and which in fact, constitutes the environment of his baseball-playing behavior. By observing a player in this way, the novice would, in fact, fragment the game and destroy what he was seeking. So, he might by observations and interviews construct the player's life space during the game: his achievements, aspirations, successes, failures, and conflicts; his judgments of the speed of the ball, of the fairness of the umpire, of the errors of his teammates. But this would only substitute for the former fragmented picture of "the game" the psychological consequences of the fragment, and thus remove the novice even further from the ecological environment he sought. Finally, the novice might perform innumerable correlations between the first baseman's achievements (balls caught, players tagged, strikes and hits made, bases stolen, errors, etc.) and particular attributes of the ecological environment involved (speed of balls thrown to him, distance of throw, weight of bat, curve of balls, etc.). But he could never arrive at the phenomenon known as a baseball game by this means.

It would seem clear that a novice would learn more about the ecological environment of a first baseman by blotting out the player and observing the game around him. This is what the student of light and sound does with elaborate instrumentation, and it is the approach we have taken in the present studies.

It is not easy, at first, to leave the person out of observations of the environment of molar behavior. Our perceptual apparatus is adjusted by our long training with the idiocentric viewing glasses of individual observations, interviews, and questionnaires to see persons whenever we see behavior. But with some effort and experience the extra-individual assemblies of behavior episodes, behavior objects and space that surround persons can be observed and described. Their nonrandom distribution and bounded character are a crucial aid. If the reader will recall a school class period, some of the characteristics of an environmental unit will be clearly apparent:

1.   It is a natural phenomenon; it is not created by an experimenter for scientific purposes.

2.   It has a space-time focus.

3.   A boundary surrounds a school class.

4.   The boundary is self-generated; it changes as the class changes in size and in the nature of its activity.

5.   The class is objective in the sense that it exists independent of anyone's perception of it, *qua* class; it is a perceptual ecological entity.

6. It has two sets of components: (a) behavior (reciting, discussing, sitting) and (b) nonpsychological objects with which behavior is transacted, e.g., chairs, walls, a blackboard, and paper.

7. The unit, the class meeting, is circumjacent to its components; the pupils and equipment are *in* the class.

8. The behavior and physical objects that constitute the unit school class are internally organized and arranged to form a pattern that is by no means random.

9. The pattern within the boundary of a class is easily discriminated from that outside the boundary.

10. There is a synomorphic relation between the pattern of the behavior occurring within the class and the pattern of its nonbehavioral components, the behavior objects. The seats face the teacher's desk, and the children face the teacher, for example.

11. The unity of the class is not due to the similarity of its parts at any moment; for example, speaking occurs in one part and listening in another. The unity is based, rather, upon the interdependence of the parts; events in different parts of a class period have a greater effect upon each other than equivalent events beyond its boundary.

12. The people who inhabit a class are to a considerable degree interchangeable and replaceable. Pupils come and go; even the teacher may be replaced. But the same entity continues as serenely as an old car with new rings and the right front wheel now carried as the spare.

13. The behavior of this entity cannot, however, be greatly changed without destroying it: there must be teaching, there must be study, there must be recitation.

14. A pupil has two positions in a class; first, he is a component of the supra-individual unit, and second, he is an individual whose life space is partly formed within the constraints imposed by the very entity of which he is a part.

This entity stands out with great clarity, . . . it is a common phenomenon of everyday life. We have called it a . . . *behavior setting.* We have made extensive studies of . . . behavior settings and found much evidence that they are stable extra-individual units with great explanatory power with respect to the behavior occurring within them. It is the central hypothesis of our studies that . . . behavior settings constitute the ecological environment of molar behavior, and the theory of them, based upon the earlier work, provides the guides for the investigations.

According to the theory of behavior settings, a person who inhabits and contributes behavior to one of them is a component part, a fixture of a behavior setting. As such, he is anonymous and replaceable, and his behavior is subject to the nonpsychological laws of the superordinate unit. At the same time, however, every inhabitant of a behavior setting is a unique person subject to the laws of individual psychology, where his own private motives, capacities, and perceptions are the causal variables. This is the classical inside-outside paradox, involving in this case persons who are governed by incommensurate laws on different levels of inclusiveness.

One of the sticking points of social and educational psychology is how to account for the consensus, the norms, and the uniformities associated with school classes, business offices, and church services, for example, at the same time account for the individuality of the members. This problem cannot be solved by either individual or group psychology. It requires a different conceptual treatment, the unnamed science mentioned earlier.[3]

The ecological theory and methodology worked out by Barker and his associates (Barker, 1968) represent the work of decades. What we need to know about *Big School, Small School* is that it is concerned with the effects of high school size upon the behavior and experience of high school students. The first task was to locate and describe the numerous (and they *are* numerous) behavior settings that make up a school. Having done this it then became possible to determine the extent to which students participated in each of the behavior settings — not unlike the question I asked about the frequency of appearance of kindergarten children in different places in the school. Still another question asked was the relation of school size to the number of different behavior settings in which the average student participated. Once the behavior settings were identified and their population density determined, then the more psychological kinds of questions could be studied: What satisfactions did students derive from the behavior settings? What were the forces influencing participation in behavior settings?

Barker and Gump (1964) have well summarized the results and their significances:

> Results from this study and the partial replication yielded general support for the theory of the effects of behavior setting size, indi-

[3]Reprinted from *Big School, Small School: High School Size and Student Behavior* by Roger G. Barker and Paul V. Gump with the permission of the publishers, Stanford University Press. ©1964 by the Board of Trustees of the Leland Stanford Junior University, pp. 15-17.

cating that the theory is a powerful predictor from ecology to the experience and behavior of individual persons. Students from the small schools, where settings were relatively underpopulated, reported more own forces (attractions) and foreign forces (pressures) toward participation in behavior settings than did students from the large school. Furthermore, a sizable group of students emerged in the large school who experienced few, if any, forces toward participation. The small schools in the present study did not contain any such outsiders; all of the small school students reported experiencing many forces toward participation. Preselected marginal students in the small schools experienced as many forces as did regular students, while in the large school, the preselected marginals experienced very few forces, far fewer than the regular students.

Another important finding is that the responses of the small school students reflected more felt responsibility and obligation. Many persons feel that the development of a sense of responsibility is essential to good citizenship, and that it is one task of schools to encourage this sense of responsibility in students. The frequency of responsibility responses in this study followed the same pattern as the data on forces, with extreme differences between schools and the emergence of outsiders, persons in the large school who reported no felt responsibility.

Second, motivation is often seen as purely a function of the person. Attraction and sense of responsibility, especially, are often seen as such "inside-the-skin" variables. Yet, when similar persons were compared in different environments in the present study, attraction and felt responsibility were found to vary with the outside environment also. The data . . . offer some evidence on the question of the comparative influence of ecology and kind of person in determining the experience of forces. Within the limits of the methods used to identify and select regular and marginal students, one would expect, if the kind of person were more important than the ecology of the school, that similar groups of students would report similar experiences in different ecologies . . . Marginal students from the small schools reported more forces than regular students from the large schools. Marginal students from the large school were a group apart, a group of outsiders. These findings indicate that the academically marginal students had very different experiences in the two ecologies. In the small school, marginal characteristics made no difference; marginal students experienced almost as many forces toward participation as the nonmarginal students. In the large school, however, the marginal students experienced relatively very few attractions and pressures toward participation.

The correlations between forces and participation provide further evidence that ecology is a powerful factor in determining participation. The consistently high correlations between foreign forces and participation suggest that ecology was a powerful determinant of participation among the subjects of the present study. The studies reviewed . . . almost entirely disregarded this variable so strongly associated with size.

Third, there are implications for developmental theory. If it is assumed that "the best way to learn is to do," or "the best way to learn responsibility is to have it," then the implications of the present study are clear. Individual students in small schools, with their relatively underpopulated settings, live under greater day-to-day attraction, pressure, and responsibility felt toward taking active part in the voluntary activities of their school environments. They are more motivated to take part.[4]

Barker and his associates did more than study the interrelationships between size of school, behavior settings, and psychological variables. They went on to study the consolidated or regional high school, which requires commuting on the part of students and "attendance at a larger school than the one that had previously existed, or could exist, in the local community." They present the intended outcomes of consolidation put forward by its proponents and opponents.

Consolidation of high schools, like most educational issues, has given rise to considerable controversy. On the one hand, its supporters claim that *students benefit* through better and more varied curriculums, better classifications, better facilities, especially in such subjects as science and music, contact with better teachers, opportunities to participate in better and more varied extracurricular activities, wider social opportunities and experiences, and more regular attendance as a result of being, in some cases, transported from door to school; *parents benefit* through reduced expenditure on education: the *community benefits* through the creation of closer ties with neighboring communities.

On the other hand, the opponents of consolidation claim that *students lose* through increased breaks in their education, loss of contact with local teachers who know the community and the families well, spending time on commuting which might be spent with greater profit on other activities, and fewer opportunities to par-

[4]Ibid, pp. 133-135.

ticipate in extracurricular activities; *parents lose* through being denied opportunities to participate in the control of their school; the *community loses* through being denied the facilities of an active school, which could serve as a cultural and educational center, and through the breakdown of community cohesion and participation, especially in youth activities.

These and other similar arguments have customarily been advanced by those who enter the controversy on consolidation. However, few systematic attempts have been made to examine the assertions empirically. Apart from studies on school size . . . almost all of the literature on consolidation deals with alleged economies and administrative procedures. The few reports involving student reactions that we found dealt with changes in intelligence quotients and the like. These are important reports, but our interest lies rather in the experiences and processes that underlie changes such as these, and the published work has been of little direct benefit to us.[5]

The findings they come up with on consolidation effects "suggest that the current assumption of consolidated school superiority is, in at least some respects, like the first report of Mark Twain's death — exaggerated." The intended psychological outcomes hoped for by proponents of the consolidated high school are far from realized.

In following our discussion of Barker's ecological approach, the reader may have discerned a kind of kinship with the approach of our man from outer space, who was parked on his space platform above a school, could observe everything that was going on, was unable to comprehend the meaning of oral and written language, had no way of comprehending "motivation," but, like the fantastic organism he was, had fantastic computers that permitted him to discern and interrelate every conceivable form of overt activity in any part of the school. In short, the man from outer space could not come up with psychological data or questions. He was, by virtue of our fantasied restrictions, forced to adopt something akin to the ecological approach. To requote Barker and Gump: "It is not easy, at first, to leave the person out of observations of the environment of molar behavior. Our perceptual apparatus is adjusted by our long training with the idiocentric viewing glasses of individual observations, interviews,

[5] Ibid. From the chapter "Some Effects of High School Consolidation," by W. J. Campbell, pp. 139-40.

and questionnaires to see *persons* whenever we see behavior. But with some effort and experience the extra-individual assemblies of behavior episodes, behavior objects, and space that surround persons can be observed and described. Their non-random distribution and bounded character are a crucial aid."

POPULATION EXCHANGE AS AN ECOLOGICAL VARIABLE AND BASIS FOR CHANGE

One of the most thorny, fascinating, and productive consequences of an ecological approach is how we utilize it for understanding differences among individuals and how the setting can be changed to obtain certain intended behavioral outcomes. In looking over the large body of work by Barker and his colleagues it seems clear that their major goals have been to develop theory and methodology. Although this work has clear implications both for understanding individual differences and the problem of changing settings, it does not address itself, except secondarily, to these implications. In recent years Kelly (1968) has pursued these issues, and his starting point has been the ecological concept of population exchange.

The current research is planned as a longitudinal study of four cohorts of male high school students, who vary in their preferences for exploratory behavior, and who are attending high school environments that contrast in the number of students who enter and leave during a school year. Two high schools of equal size have been slected from a suburban area of Detroit. One of these high schools has an exchange rate of students that is 22 per cent, while the other school has an exchange rate that is only 6 per cent. Two other high schools of equal size and of equal demographic characteristics have been selected in the inner city of Detroit. One of these inner city schools has an exchange rate of 50 per cent of its students, while the second school has an exchange rate of 15 per cent.

Population exchange has been selected as the main independent variable for defining the social environments of these two schools, because of the premise that rate of population turnover has predictable effects not only upon the social functions in these two environments but also upon the coping preference of the students. For example, one hypothesis states that students who have high preferences for exploration will have a high probability of emerging as adaptive members in a fluid environment but will develop maladaptive roles in a constant environment. Male high school students who are low explorers will have a contrasting adaptive history and are predicted to emerge as effective members in a constant society, but are more likely to assume maladaptive behaviors in a fluid environment. The research will involve studies of the peer society, and faculty-student relations as well as naturalistic observations of relevant social settings in order to present a comprehensive view of the context of exploratory behavior.

My interest in developing principles of intervention from an ecological conception of adaptation is derived from the conviction that most programs of individual or organizational change focus on either organizational behavior or the activities of specific individuals, with only slight consideration of the interdependence of individuals and the organization or the benefits and costs of any intervention for individuals or organizations. What this research is aimed toward is the creation of empirical knowledge of the interdependence of societies and their members. It is my belief that without knowledge of the process of adaptation to varied environments, it will not be possible to evolve a science of interventions.[6]

It is interesting to note that Kelly's interest in population exchange is not only in terms of human behavior but in other forms of life as well.

This particular ecological variable was selected for study not only for its intrinsic value but because of the number of parallel predictions that can be generated for the effects of this type of environment upon a range of plant and animal populations. The other primary reason for the selection of this particular variable is that it should be possible to document the simultaneous effects of how individuals (explorers) respond (take adaptive roles) in varied environments and how organizations respond (generate social settings and adaptive roles) to varied rates of immigration and emigration.[7]

As Kelly clearly points out, ecological theory and concepts cannot be accused of parochialism.

Kelly's discussion about his ongoing research program goes beyond illustrating how one might study the relationships between

[6] J. G. Kelly, "Towards an Ecological Conception of Preventive Interventions." In "Research Contributions from Psychology to Conceptions of Community Mental Health," J. W. Carter, ed, *Community Mental Journal Monograph*, 1968.

[7] Ibid.

a particular ecological variable, on the one hand, and the ways it impinges on particular kinds of individuals and organizational structure and adaptiveness, on the other hand. Equally as important is his emphasis on a point that is simple and obvious (once we are confronted with it!) but rarely taken seriously: strategies of intervention and change should vary depending on whether one is dealing with schools high or low in population exchange.[8]

THE NEED FOR THE ECOLOGICAL APPROACH

There are two major reasons I have in this book emphasized what broadly and loosely may be called an ecological approach to the school culture. The first reason is one that is as neglected as it is obvious: there *are* different "positions" from which one can view the school culture and each has much to commend it. However unassailable and obvious this statement is, one is still left with the puzzling fact that the ecological approach is hardly represented in the literature on schools. This is a result of a number of factors, historical and otherwise, and chief among them is that the major professional influences on American education have come from people and fields — psychology in general, educational psychology in particular, child development, certain aspects of psychiatry, and educational philosophy — that have been dominated by a focus on the individual and individual differences. For example, at the present time the most dominant influence on the field of child development unquestionably is Jean Piaget. It is not surprising, therefore, that many psychologists and educators have begun to apply his ideas to the educational scene — and there is much to apply. It is in no way to deny this man's giant contribution to child development to point out that his theory and studies focus on the individual organism and the ways in which its internal psychological structures develop in response

[8]I am indebted to Drs. Trickett, Kelly, and Todd for allowing me to read a draft of a forthcoming monograph that attempts to review existing literature on high schools in terms of ecological theory, and to develop strategies for programs of intervention and prevention. One can only hope that this monograph will bring the ecological approach closer to the focus of those involved in educational research.

to experience.[9] As in the case of Freud, and somewhat less so of Dewey, the *person* is in center stage, and this has facilitated overlooking the fact that a stage, be it a theatrical or educational one, has what Barker has termed "extra-individual" structured characteristics that affect the actors, even though they are unaware of these characteristics and their effects.

A second reason for the neglect of the ecological approach is that it appears to be dreary stuff. One would not want to be stranded on a desert island with the collected works of Barker and his colleagues (although, come to think of it, they would probably be more useful for survival than the collected works of Freud). The task of defining and describing the "natural" (non-investigator produced) aspects that comprise a complicated setting, as well the tasks of determining their population density and the fluidity of boundaries among these aspects, are laborious and extremely time-consuming in their execution. In addition, it is not an approach or methodology that lends itself to the quick recognition of patterns and structure. In short, it lacks the glamor that is ordinarily attributed to scientific investigation.

The third reason for the neglect of the ecological approach is that it requires us to do something that, particularly in relation to schools, is extraordinarily difficult to do, and that is to suspend one's values, one's conception of right and wrong, good and bad, and instead to describe what is "out there." It is probably impossible to do this fully. I am impressed with how difficult it is to do this even to a small extent. As a previous quote from Barker indicated, we have overlearned to such an extent to see persons and not behavior that when we are forced to describe behavior independent of what we think about why it occurs and how we personally feel about it, we find it both difficult and upsetting.[10]

[9] It is not to contradict this statement to point out that Piaget's thinking and concepts (e.g., assimilation, accommodation) have been very much influenced by biological-ecological considerations and that among his most illuminating contributions have been those concerned with the child's understanding of the attributes of external reality such as time, space, and number.

[10] The experience of difficulty and upset are expected reactions when one is forced, or has to learn, a new way of listening and looking. For example, if one is accustomed to listening to the sentences of people in terms of literal meaning it is not easy to adopt a set that gets at other possible meanings and significances, e.g., to follow Freud's dictum that one has "to listen and not listen," a kind of double-bind, which, as he demonstrated, could give one new perspectives and data about human behavior.

A final reason for emphasizing an ecological way of thinking is that one of its fascinating aspects is that one cannot predict the regularities that will be discerned and the significances of these regularities for the problem of change and for the understanding of the motivational and cognitive aspects of behavior. To illustrate this point I would like to return to our man from outer space who is parked in his vehicle above an elementary school, unseen by everyone but seeing everything. Let us assume that he has become interested in a particular room in the school in which a child never, or extremely rarely, appears. It is a room always populated by big people, although it is unusual that more than a small fraction of the big people in the school are ever in that room at one time. For a good part of the school day there is no one in the room. Aside from the one time when they eat it is usually the case that no more than one or two of them are there. In fact, he observes, even during eating time a number of the big people eat in a much larger room with the small people. At the end of the year what does his data say about the amount of face-to-face contact the big people have with each other in and out of the teacher's room?

1. During the course of the average day the teachers spend almost all of the time with small children.

2. Leaving lunchtime aside, during the course of the average day, the amount of time teachers spend in face-to-face contact with each other is extremely small. In fact, it is likely that our space man's computers would show that it is unusual for these face-to-face contacts to exceed one minute.

3. During eating time in the teachers' room there is considerable variation in how much the different teachers talk, and in the degree to which any one teacher will talk to any other teacher.

4. It is extremely rare for a teacher to be physically *alone.*

5. Approximately ten times in the year, and each time after the children have left school, all the teachers meet with someone who ordinarily spends practically all of his time in a room with no children. On these occasions this person — the principal, of course — does most of the talking. In fact, there are some teachers who in the ten meetings never say anything. Most teachers do say something but the extent of their talk is far less than that of the principal.

The earthling who attempts to replicate the space man's findings will, I predict, not come up with markedly discrepant data. And now let us go from these kinds of regularities to their possible psychological significances.

What are the possible consequences of the two facts that during the course of the work day (a) teachers are primarily with small children and (b) there is very little contact with other teachers or any other adult? (The average mother who is at home with pre-schoolers probably has more contact with adults, e.g., via neighbors, telephone, visiting.) What does it mean to go through a work day with no sustained personal contact with another adult? Being and talking with children is not psychologically the same as being and talking with peers — and I am not suggesting that one is necessarily more satisfying than the other, only that they are different. I am suggesting that when one is almost *exclusively* with children — responsible for them, being vigilant in regard to them, "giving" to them — it must have important consequences. *One of these consequences is that teachers are psychologically alone even though they are in a densely populated setting.* It is not only that they are alone but they adapt to being alone (and this adaptation, as we shall see in later chapters, does not have desired intended outcomes).

The loneliness of teachers is not something that I became aware of initially by identifying with a space man. My awareness stemmed from two considerations. First, anyone who like myself was clinically trained spent a good deal of his time in case conferences with colleagues: presenting one's own cases, reacting to those of others, and in concert with others pooling data and thoughts with the aim of arriving at a diagnostic formulation and plan of action. As Murray Levine so well put it, clinics need two staffs: one to go to the conferences and one to do the work. The other consideration was that the tradition of the case conference did not exist in schools, except in certain rare instances.

In our book (Sarason et al., 1966) describing the activities of the Yale Pyscho-Educational Clinic in relation to schools there is a chapter titled "Teaching Is a Lonely Profession." Interestingly enough, it is this chapter that teachers have mentioned most frequently and spontaneously as the one that "hit home." This reaction is one felt most keenly by the new teacher who up until her first teaching position has always worked in the company of peers or other adults. The loneliness of teachers, and again particularly so in the case of the new teacher, is further reinforced by a characteristic of the school culture we have discussed elsewhere (Sarason, Davidson, and Blatt, 1962). I am referring to the expectation, sometimes verbalized by school administrators but in practice shared by most, that a teacher should be equally adequate to the management of *all* children and problems in the classroom. This presumptuous expectation tends also to be shared by teachers, with the result that they have no difficulty finding occasions that prove their inadequacy. Over the years I have made it a practice to ask two questions of teachers: how many children do you have about whom you feel that you are not for them and vice versa?; how many times have you gone to the principal with the request that a child be removed from your class because the two of you are not a good mix? Of the scores of teachers with whom I have worked there may have been a handful who never made the request of a principal, although in the case of all the teachers there was always at least one child in the class about whom the teacher felt the match was a bad one. This expectation of which I speak increases the likelihood that the psychological loneliness of teachers will contain a good deal of felt inadequacy as well as simmering hostility to administrators who seem insensitive to the teacher's plight. In this connection it is interesting and important to note that one of the demands being made with increasing frequency of boards of education by teacher unions, particularly in our large urban centers, is that teachers should not be required to have to deal with a variety of difficult children. We shall have more to say about this in a later chapter, but I have mentioned it here in order to make two points: (a) *one* of the many reasons contributing to the rise in strength and militancy of teacher unions is that they have helped dilute somewhat the felt loneliness of teachers as teachers, and (b) over time one can expect that teachers will demand a greater role in determining the criteria to be used in composing a class of children and in transferring or excluding them.

It was not until I began to think and observe in a more ecological way that I began to see the dimensions of the problem, for example, that not talking with each other was but one instance of the general tendency for teachers in a school to have very little sustained interpersonal adult contact. But even this general tendency is but one aspect of still another tendency: teachers have very little contact with their principal and others in superior administrative positions. The opportunity — the sheer possibility by virtue of face-to-face meetings — for a teacher to receive a personal sort of "professional message" is amazingly small. Teachers are alone with their children and problems in a classroom, and the frequency and pattern of contact with others like themselves are of a kind and quality that make new learning and change unlikely. When in the course of one's day-to-day professional existence the gaining of rewards is dependent almost exclusively on one's relationship with children, and these rewards are frequently indirect and nonverbal, and when the frequency of such rewards is not greater that the frustrations one experiences, it should not be surprising if the well of motivation should run low or dry, or if behavior becomes routinized. To expect otherwise is to assume that one is not dependent to some degree, at least, on contact with and stimulation from one's colleagues. If one further assumes that teachers have a need for novelty, this unmet need may be extinguished, and the process becomes an obstacle to change.

At this point I am less interested in how one interprets the spaceman's findings than in the fact that his findings can serve as a basis for asking and pursuing psychological questions the answers to which can be very illuminating of the school culture. To some readers his findings may have seemed obvious. To others the non-psychological (in the sense of being non-motivational, non-cognitive, and unconcerned with individuals and individual differences) nature of the findings may have seemed to lack relevance or interest. The ecological way of thinking and investigating may seem to lack glamor, but there is no question that it is a productive one.

THE DEFECTS OF THE VIRTUES
OF STRONGLY HELD VALUES

In this and the previous chapters I have been in different ways emphasizing two themes. One of these has been that we know far less than we should about many aspects of the school culture and that a major cause of this has two facets: we look at and describe the school culture in terms of values and personal experiences, which, however productive of insights, put blinders on what we look at, choose to change, and evaluate; and it is inordinately difficult to adopt approaches that require us to recognize and suspend our values in the quest of achieving distance from our habitual ways of thinking and working. It is most understandable — it is, in fact, inevitable — that we should feel strongly about *our* schools and *our* school experiences. What would not be understandable would be affective and intellectual indifference. *We* have spent years in schools, *our* children's school experiences are of vital concern to us, and in contemporary America concern with schools is in the forefront of our national consciousness. But our strong interests have the defects of their virtues in that they narrow our focus, blind us to the obvious, and rob us of the capacity to recognize that the emperor may be quite naked. Because our values and assumptions are usually implicit and "second nature," we proceed as if the way things are is the way things should or could be. We do not act but we react, and then not with the aim of changing our conceptions — or, heaven forbid, our theories from which our conceptions presumably derive — but to change what is most easy to change: the engineering aspects.[11] Books get changed, new and more specialists are brought in, specialized programs and curricula are added, and new and more meetings (between students and teachers, teachers and parents) are institutionalized. It is meaningless to ask if one is for or against these and other kinds of procedural changes unless one assumes that change in itself is a good thing. What passionate devotion to our values does is to prevent us from asking: *are these changes intended to change existing regularities or are they new regularities that will exist side-by-side with the existing ones?* Which of these one intends makes the difference between change and innovation.

One of the most illuminating descriptions of American culture was written in the nineteenth century, not by an American but the Frenchman, DeTocqueville (1956). He saw and described regularities and characteristics that have stood the time test. Like our man from outer space, he did not have our passions and blinders and he did not confuse what we said with what we did, what we intended with what we accomplished. Fortunately, we do not have to await the space man to begin to look at the school culture with the freshness of a foreigner, earthling or otherwise.

[11] This point is well documented and delightfully discussed by Stephens (1967) in the context of his attempt to show the role of spontaneous psychological forces in learning, forces that long antedate the formal beginning of school. Although his book is not directly concerned with the culture of the school or life in the classroom, it goes a long way in explaining why schools accomplish as much and as little as they do. Stephens is obviously a person who, by taking the obvious seriously, comes up with some important but disquieting conclusions.

⌒8⌒

The Principal

In this and subsequent chapters we shall depart from the emphasis of previous ones by looking at certain types of school personnel and attempting to understand them in social psychological or sociological terms, that is, as individuals in roles central to the activities of a school. It might be correct to say that our purpose will be to try to comprehend how these different types of personnel view the school culture. We shall not hesitate, as we did in previous chapters, to state what we think goes on inside the heads of people.

WHY START WITH THE PRINCIPAL?

There are many reasons for starting with the principal, but for our purposes the most important is his relationship to the problem of change. The change may be of two kinds: that which the principal initiates in his own school, and that intended for all schools in a system. In either case the principal plays a fateful role. Particularly in our urban centers where schools have become a battleground involving community groups, city, state, and federal government, teacher unions, and student groups — and where the role of proposals of change has to be reckoned in terms of weeks rather than months and years — the "leader" of the school would seem to be a good starting point. But, one could argue, while it may be true that the principal is the most influential individual in *a* school, is it also not true that a school is part of a larger system that has characteristics, traditions, and a history that determine not only the role of the principal but the activities of everyone in all of its schools? The extreme of this position is that unless one deals with "the system" — unless one's efforts involve changing system characteristics — it is unlikely that one's efforts will be more than shadow boxing with the real problems. This position has been most clearly represented in the New York City school controversies where various groups have concerned themselves with how to change the educational system by realigning the forces and sources of power.

By adopting the principal as our initial focus I do not mean to suggest that system characteristics are less revealing of the school culture or less important in terms of efforts at change. In fact, as I hope to make clear, the role of the principal may well be unique in the light it sheds both on the characteristics of the system *and* life in the classroom. The danger of focusing narrowly on the system and the ways it should or could be changed is that it tends (it need not tend but in practice that is what happens) to bypass the question of how changes are to be reflected in what goes on in classrooms, *and if this question remains unanswered or remains in the realm of boring platitudes or unanalyzable abstractions we stand a good chance of demonstrating that for the child the more things change the more they remain the same.* One could put up a number of arguments for decentralizing large school systems and changing the forces of power and decision-making between its parts and the community, that is, changing the characteristics of the system *qua* system. But if one of these arguments is to effect change in what children experience in classrooms, the changing of power relationships within the system, and between the system and the community, are only the beginning of a process the intended outcome of which is to change life in a classroom. The beginning of the process (like the Supreme Court desegregation decision) may take courage, but let us not confuse initial acts of courage with the achievement of intended outcomes. We begin with the principal because any kind of system change puts him in the role of implementing the change in his school. I have yet to see any proposal for system change that did not assume the presence of a principal in a school. I have yet to see in any of these proposals the slightest recognition of the possibility that the principal, by virtue of role, preparation, and tradition, may not be a good implementer of change. If this turns out to be the case, it clearly forces one to reconsider one's goals of change. It would also suggest that most of those individuals and groups, both within and without the school system, who clamor for system change are far from knowledgeable about the culture of the school.

THE CLASSROOM AS PREPARATION FOR THE PRINCIPAL'S OFFICE

We begin with a glimpse of the obvious: a person cannot become a principal without first being a teacher for a number of years. The major justification for this seemingly reasonable requirement is that unless a principal has had long experience in teaching and managing children in a classroom he cannot appreciate or understand the goals and problems of a teacher and, therefore, cannot be of much help; in fact, he would create more problems than he would solve. A variant of this justification is that without sustained teaching experience one simply cannot know what a school is all about. Although the different justifications are not without merit, there are other considerations that should cause one to pause before accepting what seems obvious and reasonable.

1.   The fact that a teacher has spent a number of years in a classroom *with children* is no compelling basis for assuming that it prepares one for a position in which one's major task is working *with adults*. Put in another way: being a "leader" of children, and exclusively of children, does not necessarily prepare one for being a leader of adults.

2.   As we indicated in an earlier chapter, teachers are relatively autonomous in their classrooms, and within a school they have surprisingly little to do with each other. More often than not the teachers within a school do not feel themselves to be part of a working or planning group. They may identify with each other in terms of role and place of work, and they may have a feeling of loyalty to each other and the school, but it is rare that they feel part of a working group that discusses, plans, and helps

make educational decisions.[1] Teachers are "loners" — initially certainly not by their design — and this undoubtedly affects what they think about, and how they view, a school. Over a period of years they absorb and *accept* a tradition, which, if they become a principal, they are not likely to change. In fact, one of the major criteria for choosing a principal is that they were "good" teachers and good refers not only to their quality of teaching but to their implicit acceptance of the way things are.

3. What selective factors operate as to who wants to become a principal? There are at least three such factors. The first of these is that the classroom is no longer a challenge to the teacher: it has lost its novelty, next year will be like this year, and the sense of intellectual growth has perceptibly decreased. A second factor, operative more in men than in women, is that more money can be made as a principal. Another factor is that one wants to be in a greater position of influence, power, and prestige. These are not unrelated factors. What needs to be said in the clearest terms is that there is nothing wrong or bad about these types of motivation. That one wants to enlarge one's intellectual horizons, or to earn more money to provide better for one's family, or to test oneself in a position of greater responsibility — in our society, at least, these are understandable and desirable motivations. But one has to say in equally clear terms that possessing these motivations is far from an adequate basis for deciding whether one could or should be a principal. The decision to become a principal is almost always a personal one; only rarely does a school system "call" a teacher. Having made the personal decision the teacher then is required to enroll in a graduate program consisting almost exclusively, and in most instances it is exclusively, of academic courses.

4. Although a teacher and principal are in the same building and they do interact, albeit far less frequently than one would think, it is easy to overestimate how realistic a picture the teacher obtains of the complexity of the role of the principal. The one thing we can be sure of is that the teacher's picture of the role of the principal is primarily determined by *their* relationship. The

[1]The situation I am describing can best be contrasted to what happens when teachers in a school organize themselves into a union and conduct their meetings. There is a sense of common purpose and responsibility, a sense of belonging, and a give-and-take kind of discussion that they only minimally feel in their usual contacts with each other in their educational roles.

teacher may *hear* of the principal's interactions with others (other teachers, special personnel, parents, and children) but it is literally impossible for a teacher to *observe* the principal in the wide variety of relationships in which he engages. This point deserves emphasis because it forces us to recognize that the teacher's perception of the role of the principal is based on a narrow sample of experience that may have undue weight in the teacher's decision to become a principal. The narrowness of the experience is certainly not compensated for in those instances where the teacher's experience is limited to one principal and one school. The picture of the principal that teachers have may be gleaned in the following (Sarason, 1969):

> Is it necessary for each school to have a principal? I have put this question to friends who are not connected with schools. There are three types of responses to this question. The first is one of mild surprise that the question should be asked. The second response is that the individual simply has no basis for considering alternatives, although he would not in principle be opposed to alternatives. The third response, and the least frequent one, is one in which alternatives are stated and the pros and cons evaluated. If I have sensed anything common to these responses it is that the question is an open and interesting one. Now how do teachers respond to the question? As you might expect, their response is far more strong than it is to my question about physical education programs. Once emotions were relatively out of the way, a variety of answers were given and they tended to have one thing in common: there are "practical" matters of an everyday sort (that do or could occur) which could bring the operations of a school to a halt if the principal was not present. Who would keep the attendance data? Order supplies? Handle behavior problems and sick children? Supervise fire drills? Talk to parents when they phoned or visited? One could go on listing housekeeping matters which were considered to require the presence of a principal. What is most interesting to me is that teachers rarely, if ever, responded in terms of the factors I presented earlier, i.e., the principal's educational or leadership role, his evaluation functions, his role as representative of the teachers to other administrative bodies, and the importance of personal as contrasted to professional relationships with him.[2]

[2]S. B. Sarason, "The Culture of the School and Processes of Change." In *The Yale Psycho-Educational Clinic: Collected Papers and Studies*, S. B. Sarason and F. Kaplan, eds. Monograph Series (Boston: Massachusetts State Department of Mental Health, 1969).

As we shall soon see, this picture of the principal's role is true but disturbingly incomplete.

In making these points I am not only questioning the relevance of teaching experience as a preparation for becoming a principal. *What I am suggesting is that being a teacher for a number of years may be in most instances antithetical to being an educational leader or vehicle of change.* There is little in the nature of classroom teacher, there is little in the motivation of the teacher to become a principal, there is little in the actual experience of the teacher with principals, and there is even less in the criteria by which a principal is chosen, to expect that the role of the principal will be viewed as a vehicle, and in practice used, for educational change and innovation.

THE TEACHER BECOMES A PRINCIPAL

Our understanding of the role of the principal can be approached in a number of ways, but the one we shall begin with requires that we focus on the period between the appointment and the first few months in the job. The major reason for this focus is that in this period the individual is confronted with and experiences a major personal and professional discontinuity, and how he views and manages this difficult transition is illuminating of many things. But here we must sharply differentiate between two situations: one in which the principal will be in charge of a new school, and one in which he takes over an ongoing school.

Practically everyone, within and without the schools, automatically assumes that becoming principal of a new school is much to be preferred over assuming leadership of an older school. The reasons seem obvious enough: a new school is expected to have better physical facilities; school personnel, children, and parents will take greater pride in the new school; the principal will have greater freedom to organize things his way, that is, it will be easier for him to innovate and to depart from past practices; the principal has more of an opportunity to choose teachers who fit in with his plans; he will not have to deal with an entrenched faculty who, because of their loyalty to a previous principal (or other reasons), are not likely to change their accustomed way of doing things. The fantasy that one is starting "fresh" is shared both by principal and teachers, a fantasy that engenders a great deal of motivation, enthusiasm, and much hope that *life in this school will be different than life in their previous schools.* But why call this a fantasy? It is a fantasy because it denies certain aspects of reality and because its wish-fulfillment aspects overwhelm and obscure what would be required to achieve change. I shall illustrate this by using a number of opportunities I and others at the Yale Psycho-Educational Clinic have had to observe or participate in the development of new schools.

    1. From the time of appointment until the formal opening of the school the new principal spends almost all of his time in what can only be called housekeeping matters: ordering books, supplies, and furniture, assigning rooms, arranging schedules, negotiating the transfer of students from other schools, interviewing and selecting prospective personnel, making up bus schedules, etc., etc., etc. Particularly in the case of the principal new to his role the complexity of housekeeping is more than he imagined and was prepared for. In very quick order the principal sees as his major goal — a goal determined by others but which he fully accepts and in relationship to which he has increasing anxiety — *opening the school on time and in good order.*

    2. Up until the opening of school the bulk of the meetings in which the principal participates are with administrative personnel not only for the purpose of setting up house but in order for the principal to learn the rules and regulations relevant to whatever decisions he must make and plans that he has. The principal views these meetings — which are frequently with those responsible for his appointment or with those who can be helpful with the plethora of housekeeping matters — in terms of accommodating to the roles and power of others ("the system") and not in terms of seeking how to use the system to achieve his purposes.

Let us pause for a moment to emphasize a major consequence of what I have just described: up until the opening of the school the principal is not concerned with such issues as what life in a classroom should be, how teachers will be related to decisions and planning about educational values and goals, the role of parents and neighborhood-community resources, the handling of problem children, the purposes of evaluation, and other issues that bear directly on the educational experience of all those who have or should have a vested interest in a school. In fact, up until the opening of school there is precious little discussion of children or education. From the standpoint of the principal, however, the issues I have listed tend not to be issues about which he is set to do anything, or very much. It might be more fair, in some instances at least, to say that the principal is concerned with these issues but he is acutely aware that he does not know what to do about them, a problem we shall have more to say about later. If in the situation we are describing the principal was not so totally absorbed with matters of housekeeping and organization, he would be faced that much earlier with questions that will later plague him: *in what relationship should he be to what children experience in classrooms? How does he get certain teachers to change their practices and attitudes? What does one do when one feels that a problem child is a reflection of a problem teacher? How should he handle the situation in which a complaint by a parent about a teacher may be legitimate? On whose side is the principal: child? teacher? system? neighborhood?* It is extremely important to note how the principal asks these questions (and other questions) of himself because the form of the question assumes that *he and he alone* must answer the question. It is not in his head — and nothing in his previous experience would put it there — that these are the kinds of basic issues that he *and* his faculty must face, discuss, and resolve because these are the kinds of issues that affect all and, if they remain private, will contribute to the personal and intellectual loneliness of all, including the principal who escaped from one kind of role loneliness to another. To think and act in these ways would be an example of changing certain aspects of life in a school. But we are here also touching on the issue of the power of the principal, and as we shall see later, his view of it operates in ways antithetical to changing life in a school. But let us now return to the opening of the new school by the new principal.

3. There is nothing the new principal in the new school desires more than an "orderly" opening, a desire particularly strong in the neophyte who feels, and who regards others as feeling, that his worth will be judged by how smoothly things go — identical to what the neophyte teacher experiences when he begins to teach his first class. Smoothness of operation tends to become an end in itself and anything and anyone interfering with smoothness are not favorably looked upon.

4. A variety of problems inevitably arises concerning parents, children, teachers, and various assortments of visitors, formal and informal. But of greatest concern to the principal are those with teachers who

have changes to suggest, difficult or problem children they wish to discuss and about whom they want the principal to take action, or emerging conflicts with other teachers about procedures and practices. In addition, it is at this time that the new principal begins to be aware that
his teachers, whom he may have had an important hand in choosing,
are far from a homogeneous group in terms of the way they relate to
the principal, the way they handle problems, and the way they relate
to each other. It is not one big, happy family, but the principal has no
basis in thinking and training for realizing that this is inevitable in any
organized group. More important, however, the principal has no way
to handle these problems except by avoiding them, or handling them,
usually indirectly, on a one-to-one basis as they come up.

I can summarize our observations and experiences by saying that
by the end of the first year, life in the new school is remarkably
similar to that in old ones: what children experience in classrooms, the quality of relationships among teachers and between
them and the principal, the relationship among parents, community, and the school, the criteria by which everyone judges
themselves and others — in none of these can one discuss a difference that makes a difference.[3]

It is really not necessary for us to go into any detail in the
case of the new principal who takes over an ongoing school. We
shall do so in Chapter 9. Although the problems, on the surface at least, are somewhat different, the "phenomenology" of the
principal, his practices and the results are much the same. If
there is any difference, it is the speed with which the problem of
power and influence comes up.

POWER AND INFLUENCE

When most people think about a school principal they almost
always think in terms of what a principal can do, and attribute
to him a good deal of power and freedom to act in his school.
They rarely will think in terms of what he cannot do or the

---

[3]The reader who may think this an unkind or unfair conclusion — or who
felt similarly about what we have described in this and previous chapters —
should read Goodlad's (1969) conclusions based on the visits he and several colleagues made to 260 kindergartens through third grade classrooms in 100 schools
clustered in or around the major cities of thirteen states. "Neither principals nor

numerous restrictions, formal and informal, that limit his freedom of action. This tendency to think in terms of, and to over-evaluate, the power of the principal is no less mistaken in the case of the principal than it is when we think of the power of the President of our country. It may well be that we are more realistic about the presidency than we are of the principal, if only because we all were children in a school and viewed the principal as a very powerful person. We have had more opportunity to correct our over-evaluation of the power of the President than in the case of the principal.

The tendency not to think of restrictions is a reflection of a rather pervasive tendency to confuse "ownership" of something with complete freedom to use it. For example, we tend to be more aware of what we can do with our car than we are of the scores of restrictions governing its use, for example, speed limits, license and registration fees, stop lights and signs, parking areas and time limits, use of head lights, when and where to pass, and so on. A similar kind of list can be drawn up in regard to what one cannot do with one's house.

The point is that when a person is "in charge," as in the case of the principal, we tend not to think of the restrictions, formal or informal, that are inevitably present. When I say "we" I mean, of course, the outsider. School personnel know otherwise, and no one knows this more than the principal.

Let us begin by asking a deceptively simple question: what responsibility does the principal have for what goes on in a classroom? I have yet to know a principal who could not name several of his teachers about whom he had serious question as to their classroom behavior, for example, this teacher is too repressive, that teacher is too permissive, this one is unorganized, that one cannot teach reading, this one wants to get rid of all of her problems, that one cannot interest her children, this one is always stir-

---

teachers were able to articulate clearly just what they thought to be the most important for their schools to accomplish. And neither group was very clear on changes that should be effected in the future . . . . Studies have shown that administrators favor teachers who maintain orderly classrooms, keep accurate records, and maintain stable relations with parents and community. Other studies reveal that middle managers in the educational system, such as principals and supervisors, tend to be recruited from among teachers who demonstrate these orderly qualities. Because they are rewarded for maintaining the system, administrators are not likely either to challenge it or reward subordinates who do."

ring them up, and that one should not be a teacher. Regardless of the "philosophy" of the principal, he has no difficulty pointing to teachers whom he regards as problems.

There is no doubt that the principal feels a responsibility in these matters, as there is no doubt that we, as outsiders, expect the principal to feel such a responsibility. The problem of the principal is how to discharge the responsibility, and it is here that the principal's experience as a teacher asserts its strong influence. The principal views going into the classroom for purposes of evaluation and change as an act that will be viewed by the teacher as a hostile intrusion. The presence of the principal in a classroom, particularly if it is in the context of a problem in that classroom, is experienced by the teacher with anxiety and/or hostility.

The dynamics of this situation are well illustrated in the joke about the man who starts over to his neighbor's house to borrow a rake. On the way over he starts to fantasize about the possibility that his neighbor will not want to lend him the tool. By the time his neighbor has answered the doorbell, the man has decided that his neighbor will refuse the request and so his first and only words to the neighbor are, "You can keep your damned rake." What the joke assumes we know, and what makes it applicable to our discussion, is that the man projects onto his neighbor feelings and attitudes he himself has experienced toward his neighbor or others.

Although he has the power to do so, and feels a responsibility to do so, the principal prefers not to visit classrooms, a preference very much shared by teachers. But there is more at work here than the principal's past experience as a teacher, and that is that he quickly learns that telling a teacher what is wrong or insisting upon a change is a far from effective means for changing attitudes and practices. The power to legislate change is no guarantee that the change will occur — a principle the principal learned when as a teacher he was confronted with changing the behavior of children. From the standpoint of the principal there is little that he feels he can do about what goes on in a classroom, particularly if the teacher has tenure or has been a teacher for a number of years. As a result, the principal tolerates situations that by his values or standards are "wrong." Because this toleration is frequently accompanied by feelings of guilt and inadequacy it frequently has an additional consequence: the tendency to deny that these situations exist in the school.

THE PRINCIPAL VS. THE YALE PSYCHO-EDUCATIONAL CLINIC

To concretize some of the general points we have been making, it is appropriate to describe here some of the experiences members of the Yale Psycho-Educational Clinic have had with principals. One of the several reasons for starting the Psycho-Educational Clinic (Sarason et al., 1966) was to have a vehicle for studying the school culture in the role of intervener or changer. In choosing such a role we clearly and deliberately were being guided by our clinical experience, and that of hundreds of others, which demonstrated that the understanding one gains of human behavior when one is in the helping role is extraordinarily difficult to obtain in any other way. One *sees* behavior ordinarily not made public and is forced to the realization (if one had not gained it in other ways) that man's desire to change is more than matched by his ingenuity in avoiding change, even when the desire to change is powered by strong pain, anxiety, and grief. We were aware that there were different ways we could study the school, but our clinical background was decisive in determining that we would go the clinical route. This is not at all to suggest that we viewed children or school personnel as patients or that we had any intention of applying any of our theories or techniques to whatever problems we encountered. We were far from naive about schools, but we were aware that our views of schools and what we thought they needed were not the results of tranquil reflection and scientific objectivity. We knew we had much to learn and unlearn and that *whatever we had learned about resistance to change would be as applicable to us as to those we hoped to be in a position to help.* (The reader may be assured that these are words much easier to state than to implement!) In order to give the reader more of an idea of the role we wished to be in, I give below the contents of the presentation we always made to the entire faculty of a school with which a helping relationship was being considered:

For a number of years some of us in the Department of Psychology at Yale have been engaged in different research projects involving elementary schools. In addition to our experiences in the elementary schools, some of us have long been interested in various aspects of special education and in the preparation of teachers. As a consequence, we became increasingly interested in the day-to-day problems facing schools in general and teachers in particular. Let me say right off that there are two conclusions to which we have come. The first is that anyone who teaches in the public schools for less than $15,000 per year ought to have his head examined. The second conclusion is that a law ought to be passed making it mandatory for each parent to teach a class by himself for a day each year. Although these recommendations may not solve all problems, they would certainly help bring about changes that all of us would agree are necessary. All of this by way of saying that our experiences have given us an understanding of what is involved in teaching and managing a large group of children, each of whom is a distinct character, for several hours each day over a period of 10 months. It is not flattery but rather strong conviction underlying the statement that the classroom teacher performs one of the most difficult tasks asked of any professional person. It would indeed be nice if all a teacher had to do was to teach. You know, and I know, that a teacher is a parent, a social worker, a psychologist, and a record-keeping clerk. Hopefully there is time to teach once the duties associated with these other roles are discharged. We are living at a time when everyone seems to be an expert on the schools and ignorance seems to be no barrier to articulating strong opinions. There is no doubt, as I am sure you will agree, that there is much one can criticize about schools, but there is also no doubt that unless one understands what a school is like and what it is faced with in its day-to-day operation the benefits we would like to see from these changes will not be so great as they should be.

One of the most staggering problems facing our society concerns the degree of serious maladjustment in many people. One has only to look at the size and number of our mental hospitals, psychiatric clinics, reformatories, and the like to begin to grasp how enormous a problem this is. We are talking about millions of people and billions of dollars. What needs to be stressed is that in the foreseeable future we will have neither the personnel nor the facilities to give these troubled people the quality of treatment they need. In all honesty I must also say that for many of these people our knowledge and treatment procedures leave much to be desired.

As a result of our experiences, we at the Psycho-Educational Clinic in the Yale Department of Psychology have come to two conclusions: first, far too little is being done either to try to prevent the occurrence of problems or to spot them at those points in the individual's life where with a little effort a lot may be accomplished. Second, if we believe what we say, we ought in a very limited kind of way to attempt to see what we can do. I do not have to emphasize to a group of elementary-school teachers the significance of a preventive approach to problems in the early grades. As I am sure all of you know as well as, if not better than I, you are faced daily with children whose behavior, learning difficulties, and interpersonal relations (with you or other children) arouse in you concern, bewilderment, anger, and a lot of other reactions. On the basis of all the talks and meetings we have had over the years with teachers there would seem to be in any one classroom of 25 children anywhere from three to six children about whom the teacher is concerned in the sense that she has a question about their academic learning and personal adjustment in the school setting.

What do we propose to do? It is easier for me to tell you what we do *not* intend to do. For one thing, we do not intend to come into a school in order to see how many problem children we can refer out to various agencies. There is no doubt that you know a lot of children who could utilize the services of a child-guidance clinic or family service society. To come in with the intent of referring them out is both unfair and unrealistic because these agencies, particularly the child-guidance clinics, are overwhelmed with cases and generally have long waiting lists. *Even if the child-guidance clinic could take the child on, it would take them quite a while to get to first base with the child and in the meantime you still have that child in your class.* Treatment procedures are neither that quick nor that effective to allow you to expect that *your* difficulties with the child are over once you know he is being seen in a clinic. The question we have asked of ourselves is how can we be of help to the teacher in the here and now with whatever questions and problems she raises with us. In short, we want to see how we can be of help within the confines of the school.

It is not our purpose to come into a school to sit and talk to teachers, however helpful and interesting that might be. When we say we want to be helpful in the here and now within the confines of the school, we mean that in addition to talking with the teacher about a child *we have to be able to observe that child in the context of the classroom in which the problem manifests itself.* For help to be meaningful and practical it must be based on what actually goes in the classroom setting. For example, it is in our experience of no particular help to a teacher to be told that a child needs individual attention, a need which differentiates him not at all from the rest of us. What a teacher wants to know is when, how, and for what goals this "individual attention" will occur, and this requires a first-hand knowledge of what is going on.

We do not view ourselves in the schools as people to whom questions are directed and from whom answers will be forthcoming. Life and the helping process are not that simple. We have no easy answers, but we have a way of functioning that involves us in a relationship to the teacher and the classroom and that together we can come up with concrete ideas and plans that we feel will be helpful to a particular child.

We are not the experts who can come up with solutions even though we have no first-hand knowledge of the context in which the problem has been identified.

I hope I have made clear that when we say we want to help it means that we want to talk to the teacher, observe in the classroom, talk again to the teacher, and together come up with a plan of action that with persistence, patience, and consistency gives promise of bringing about change. It is not a quick process and it is certainly not an easy one.

I cannot state too strongly that we are not coming into the schools with the intent of criticizing or passing judgment on anyone. *We are nobody's private FBI or counter-intelligence service. We are not the agent of the principal or some other administrative officer.* In fact, we are in no way part of the administrative hierarchy or power structure of the school system. We have no special strength or power except that which flows from our being able to establish a situation of mutual trust between teachers and ourselves. To the extent that we can demonstrate to you by our manner, gesture, and verbalization that we want to help, to that extent we make the development of this mutual trust more likely and quickly to occur.

There is one aspect of the way we function that I think needs some elaboration. I have already told you why it is essential for us, if our efforts are to be maximally useful, that we spend time in the classroom. Another reason this is essential resides in the one advantage we have over the teacher, i.e., we do not have the awesome responsibility of having to handle a large group of young characters five days a week for several hours each day, a responsibility that makes dispassionate observation and clear thinking extraordinarily difficult. We can enjoy the luxury of being in the classroom without the responsibility of the teacher for managing and thinking about 25 or more unique personalities. We do not envy you although I am quite sure that you will envy us for not having your responsibilities. It is precisely because we are "free" that we can observe what is going on in a way not usually possible for a teacher.

In order for us to help in a school it is crucial that we know that school as a physical entity and as a kind of social organization. Consequently, we usually make the request that for the first six weeks or so we visit classrooms and get to know you and what you do in the different grades without any obligation to get involved with any problem. A school and a classroom are not simple settings and it takes several weeks until we get the feeling of familiarity. We will be here on certain days of the week so that you can count on when we will be here. We try to spend a day and a half a week in each school.

We do not know to what extent we can be of help to you. We do not present ourselves as experts who have answers. We have much to learn about this helping process. If our previous work with teachers is any guide, the type of service we want to develop is one that they feel they need. The only thing we can guarantee you is that we want to learn and to help. We have much to learn from you, and together we may be able to be of help to children in school.

For our present purposes the most important aspect of this presentation was that *we were going to be in classrooms*. Although we expected that our role would cause discomfort for the principal, we did not expect the degree of difficulty we in fact encountered in most but not all instances. The following summarizes our experience:

1. In diverse ways the principal would attempt to structure our role so that we would work with children rather than teachers. With us, at least, the principal tended to describe problems as existing inside the child's head independent of the classroom he was in or the teacher he had. It was children who were problems and needed help.

2. Principals were bothered and puzzled by the amount of time we spent "observing" in classrooms. Were we observing children? the teacher? the whole classroom? But amount of time was less puzzling than what we did with our observations. Since we had and wanted no power to tell anybody what to do, and we were not evaluators, how did we use our observations? What did we talk about with teachers?

3. In a number of instances the principal became visibly upset when he found out that in order to cope with certain classroom problems the teacher and clinic member had worked out and implemented a new procedure or approach. If the teacher had made these or other changes on her own, as is frequently the case, she would have felt no need to check with the principal who would then have nothing to be upset about. What seemed to be the chief basis for upset was that in some way the relationship between the teacher and clinic member had resulted in the teacher changing something about *her* procedures, practices, and thinking, i.e., in each instance the teacher had willingly changed in some respect.

4. In some instances the principal suggested, and in some cases demanded, that we not go into the classrooms of the new teachers, claiming that the new teacher is very anxious, that she usually has difficulty in matters of discipline, and that she would become more anxious and ineffective if an "observer" was in the room. Interestingly enough, it was always our experience that in contrast to older teachers

the new ones were more likely to seek us out, invite us to their class-rooms, and more quickly and openly present their problems. As we have pointed out elsewhere (Sarason et al., 1966), where for a period of months we had to stay away from new teachers we spent the last half of the year trying to help the teacher undo what had been done in the first half.

5. Much of what has been said above was put spontaneously, and in the context of heated discussion, by two different principals: *"You are doing what I am supposed to be doing."*

From the standpoint of many principals the conflict with the clinic member did not stem from a perception of differences in roles but rather from a perceived similarity in which we seemed to be able to relate and work with teachers in ways in which the principal would like to function but cannot or does not know how. It was very difficult for the principal to recognize that our relationships with teachers did not develop in the context of power and evaluation. Although the principal and the teacher are acutely aware that their relationship takes place in the context of power and evaluation, neither of them knows how to minimize the negative consequences of such a context except by minimizing contact. In an informal study I conducted in several schools the average frequency of appearance of the principal in a class-room during a two week period was between 1 and 2 times (for some classrooms it was zero) and the duration of such appearances varied from 2 - 10 minutes.[4] In a fair proportion of the times there was no subsequent communication about the visit, and this was to be interpreted that all was well. Where there was communication, it was the rare teacher who would state that the communication was helpful.

THE PRINCIPAL AND SPECIAL SERVICES

There used to be a time, we are told, when a school was a rela-tively simple affair consisting of children, teachers, principal, jani-

[4] These figures are based on observations in elementary schools. In the junior and senior high schools, which have many more pupils and classrooms, the princi-pal and his assistants rarely visit classrooms in other than the most perfunctory ways. Since these schools tend to be organized along departmental lines one would expect that the departmental chairman would play the role of educational leader, but since he himself is a teacher he literally has little or no time to visit classrooms.

tor, secretary, and, on certain days, a nurse. Not only was there consistency in type of personnel but one could also count on the particular individuals in these roles being in the school over long periods of time. In our large urban settings, at least, this situation no longer obtains. As we indicated in an earlier chapter, the percentage of children who are in a school in September but are no longer there in June is high. However bothersome this may be to a principal it presents far fewer problems than the increasing presence of a wide variety of special people or services who have duties to perform in the school. School psychologists, psychiatrists, and social workers, remedial reading teachers, speech and hearing specialists, special class supervisors, curriculum supervisors, representatives from different social agencies, a wide assortment of volunteers, class mothers, teachers' aides — these are only some of the special services that are represented in a school. During one week 93 different people (not counting personnel full time in the school) performed a service in one of the inner city schools in New Haven, and we had no reason to believe that it was an atypical week. Undoubtedly, there are few such people coming into suburban schools, but this does not controvert the fact that more people, representing services, come into our schools than ever before.

This situation — and there is every reason to believe that the numbers will increase rather than decrease — exacerbates almost every problem of the principal we have thus far discussed. The fact that so many different people come into the schools bears witness to at least two things: there are problems in the school, and the usual personnel cannot, or have not been able to, resolve them. In addition, the titles of many of these people convey that they have knowledge or competencies that regular school personnel do not have. In short, these specialists are a constant reminder that regular school personnel, including the principal, cannot do the job themselves. Up to a point the principal agrees with and accepts this formulation, and indeed there are principals who are constantly pressuring for more special services. But the conditions for conflict are present and we detail some of them here:

1. The relationship between the principal and the specialist is unlike that between principal and teacher in that the specialist is expected to have knowledge and skills not possessed by the principal. Consequently, the principal cannot determine or tell the specialist what to do. The principal, however, being acutely aware that it is *his* school and he bears responsibility for what takes place in it, feels a strong need to

know what the specialist will do, and he feels even a stronger need to decide whether or not the recommendations of the specialist should be implemented and in what ways. A person with the greatest amount of power is dependent on a person with greater knowledge and skill. Although this type of relationship does not necessarily have to result in conflict, it frequently does. Personality differences may contribute to the degree of conflict, and too frequently such differences are used as if they explain everything, but one cannot overlook the existence of conditions of role conflict.

2. The specialist is acutely aware of a problem that is compounded of administrative and professional aspects. On the one hand, in almost all instances he is *not* administratively responsible to the principal — he is usually part of a pupil personnel services department — and, on the other hand, he knows that in a real way he is also responsible to the principal. At the very least, he is accountable to the principal. The specialist frequently finds himself in the situation where he cannot act in accord with his professional knowledge and standards (i.e., he cannot do what he thinks is best to do) because the principal is determining what he can or cannot do. As any specialist will attest, there are some schools to which he goes with the greatest reluctance because he feels he cannot perform his duties according to his professional standards. The specialist would like to feel that what he has to say and do is respected and followed; the principal would like to feel that he is not merely a servant of the specialist but an important participant in and determinant of what goes on.

3. From the standpoint of the principal the specialist is a transient whose expertise does not include an intimate knowledge of what is distinctive about *that* school and its occupants, and if for no other reason the principal must be vigilant about what the specialist does and recommends. This is difficult for the specialist to comprehend and when it happens that his work and recommendations are not acccepted or followed, his tendency is to explain such behavior in terms of narrowness, obtuseness, and rigidity. Such attributions may be true but when it is not seen in the context of the principal's perception of his role, the response of the specialist tends to increase conflict and psychological distance.

4. The nature of most problems referred to the specialist involves him with teachers. To the principal for whom relations with teachers is a source of conflict and personal dissatisfaction, the relationship between specialist and teacher can be one more source of trouble. Messy triangular relationships are by no means infrequent, and it is not unusual for the teacher to feel caught in the cross-fire.

The relationship between the principal and any one type of specialist has to be viewed as but one instance of an increasing series of relationships in which the principal has less expertise than someone else in his school. From the standpoint of the principal these increasingly frequent relationships confront him with a recurring question: what should a principal know and be?

A MAJOR DILEMMA

To understand the dilemma of the principal one must begin by recognizing that he views his role, as do many others, as implying leadership. Whatever his motivations for seeking the position, they did not include being a housekeeper, or highly paid clerk, or embattled figurehead. Initially, at least, the principal expects and wants the school ("his" school) to bear the stamp of his conception of what good education and a school are. This conception may be vague, and depending on one's point of view, it may be regarded as liberal, conservative, progressive, punitive, permissive, and so on. The principal wants to be and to feel influential. His dilemma begins when he realizes that words and power, far from guaranteeing intended outcomes, may be ineffectual and even produce the opposite of what he desires. When he encounters hostility and resistance to his recommendations or ideas for change, (e.g., with a teacher) he feels he has one of two alternative means of response: assert his authority or withdraw from the fray. The usual consequence of either response is to widen the psychological gap and to increase the feelings of isolation of those involved.

When I look back at all the new principals I have known or observed, their "administrative styles" vary but two of the most frequent types are relevant here. One of them includes those principals who, as one teacher said about her new principal, "acts as if everything before him was lousy and we should be thankful that the truth is here." The other type is far more favorably viewed because he does not impose his ideas on anyone, i.e., he leaves the teachers alone. There is a third type which, in my experience, I have only observed in our urban centers and this is the principal whom everyone considers favorably because he is "strong" with the children. A number of these principals were, in fact, strongly for "law and order" at the same time they were highly effective with difficult children in the sense of being able to listen to them, talk with and not at them, and conveyed to them a desire to help. But as one of these principals said to me: "*I* know how to handle these poor kids in *my* office. But there are about 300 of them in this school (which had an enrollment of 1200) and I can't do it myself. How do I get some of my teachers to be able to change what and how they are teaching them?" This principal, who spent most of his time handling pupils sent "to the office," literally had no time to spend in classrooms or with those teachers he regarded to be as much of a problem as he did the children.

The dilemma of the principal is further complicated when he has to deal with people who have a different type of expertise and with whom the principal is not in the role of leader. What is important is that the principal's problems of leadership with "his" people interact with the same kinds of problems encountered with special services. The consequence of this interaction is that the principal is constantly wrestling with the problem of leadership with the feeling, which increases in strength over time, that he is losing the battle, that he is not the leader he expected to be, or would like to be, or that others expect him to be.

In large measure we have been discussing the principal in the context of his experience in matters that he would like to affect, or changes he might want to make, that is, matters in which he would like to be influential because they reflect *his* conception of what life in a school should be. His dilemma in leadership is further aggravated by the fact that often proposed changes for his school (e.g., the introduction of a new curriculum) do not come from him but from sources in the system ("downtown"). The point that we must not overlook is that regardless of whether or not the principal likes the proposed changes he is in large part responsible for implementing these changes *in fact and in spirit*. When he is in favor of the proposed changes, he is faced with the task of leading the process of change so that its intended outcomes are realized, which is another way of saying that he has to help and insure that other people change. As we have seen, this is precisely the problem about which the principal feels most inadequate or, in practice, does inadequately. When he is not in favor of the proposed change, his dilemma may be simultaneously increased and decreased: increased because he must do something he does not favor, and decreased because he does not personally feel responsible for the change and can so represent himself to others in the school who are also affected by the change.

THE INCOMPLETE PICTURE

In this chapter we tried to make a number of points. First, as an initiator or implementer of change the principal is in a crucial role. Second, neither by previous experience nor formal training nor the processes of selection is the principal prepared for the requirements of leadership and the inevitable conflicts and problems that beset a leader. Third, these background factors may not only be inadequate as preparation, they may be antithetical to appropriate performance in the role. Fourth, with increasing frequency the principal is involved with a variety of special services that are beyond his own areas of knowledge and expertise and, because they are administratively not under his jurisdiction, complicate his problems with leadership, responsibility, and power.

This is not a happy picture. Although what I have described is based on the extensive experience of myself and others at the Yale Psycho-Educational Clinic, I would like to emphasize that our experience includes candid discussions with principals, discussions that could only take place after we had demonstrated that we were not in the schools to judge or criticize, that is, *really* we were not in a school to compete with or supplant or undermine the authority and functions of the principal. There was conflict, there were differences of opinion, there were battles — some of them quite stormy — but in a number of instances these confrontations brought issues out into the open, which were then worked through and resulted in productive and enduring relationships. (As we shall see in the next chapter, the "psychology of confrontation," which we consider to be a most important aspect of the problem of change, is where the principal feels most at sea.) What I consider to be the most important points made in this chapter could have been written using little else than what some principals actually said in the context of confidential discussion. But for obvious and understandable reasons principals do not and will not make their dilemmas public.

What I have just said is a consequence of the anticipation that some people would view the contents of this chapter as critical and derogatory. Verbal disclaimers are usually held suspect and are rarely effective. Nevertheless, I have to say that the intention of this chapter was to describe a particular educational role and the dilemmas and problems encountered in performing the role, independent of the personalities one finds in this role. When

I have used judgmental terms (e.g., inadequate) I was referring not only to my perception of the relationship between theory and practice of the role but to that of principals as well.

But the picture we have attempted to describe is incomplete in at least two respects. For one thing we have only alluded to the principal's perception of "the system" and how this perception affects what he does and, more important, what he does not do because he feels he cannot do it. A related aspect, and one we stated and bypassed in the beginning of this chapter, is the legitimacy of using the concept of "the system" as the sole etiological scapegoat for whatever one may think is bad in the school culture, and no role allows this question to be raised with greater cogency than that of the principal. These aspects are the focus of the next chapter.

↶9↷

The Principal and the Use
of "The System"

In this chapter I shall again be discussing the principal. The
thinking described and the points made are applicable in varying
degress to all school personnel.

Particularly in our larger urban centers one quickly finds in
conversation with all school personnel, from janitors to the school
superintendent, that they are acutely aware that they are part of
a very complex arrangement of roles and functions, purposes and
traditions, that are not entirely comprehensible either as a whole
or in part. Where it is comprehensible, it is often not viewed as
"rational." The dominant impression one gains is that school personnel believe that there is *a* system, that it is run by somebody or
bodies in some central place, that it tends to operate as a never-
ending source of obstacles to those within the system, that a major
goal of the individual is to protect himself against the baleful influences of the system, and that any one individual has and can
have no effect on the system *qua* system. There is no doubt in
anyone's mind that the system "works" in the sense that children
are in school, teachers teach, administrators administrate — everyone is doing something for or with someone else — but rarely
does one meet someone who believes it is working well and that
his own job could not be done better if the system operated
differently.

The important point is not that everyone has a conception of
the system, but that *this conception governs role performance even*

though it may be a correct or faulty conception. Although in this chapter I shall be emphasizing the ways in which faulty conceptions affect role performance (i.e., by constricting the range of activities and the capacity to act), I am not unmindful of the fact that the consequences of a correct conception may be very similar to those of a faulty one. While I do not in any way question that characteristics of the system can and do have interfering effects on an individual's performance, it is the major theme of this chapter that "the system" is frequently conceived by the individual in a way that obscures, many times unwittingly, the range of possibilities available to him. Too frequently the individual's conception of the system serves as a basis for inaction and rigidity, or as a convenient target onto which one can direct blame for most anything. The principal illustrates this point as well or better than anyone else in the school system.

VARIABILITY AMONG PRINCIPALS

Let us start with a simple but actual instance:

An outside agency offers a service to several schools. The service involves a weekly, one hour meeting with groups of teachers around problem cases in their classrooms. It is necessary that these meetings take place during school hours. Each of these elementary schools has two teacher aides who can take over the classrooms of the teachers who will attend these weekly conferences. Since the outside agency feels that it would be better if more teachers could attend, each principal is asked if there is not some way by which more could be accommodated. Most of the principals respond by saying that there is really no way to free more teachers. One principal says that she could take a classroom for the hour and her secretary could take another. One other principal says that two more teachers can be freed and that their classrooms would be unattended for the hour, i.e., the children would be on their own doing assigned work.

For a principal to take over a class is, of course, not an unusual matter, particularly under certain emergency conditions. It is unusual for a principal to do this once a week over a period of months; it is more unusual to assign a secretary to a classroom on a regular basis; and it is extremely rare, again on a regular basis, to leave a classroom unattended for one hour each week. The reasons for the rarity of these instances are several, among them being the feeling of most principals that these represent bad practices and that they are unfair to the educational progress of children. But more important and pervasive than these reasons is the feeling that these are not "legal" or permissible or responsible practices. When the principal is occupied in a classroom, or a secretary takes over a class, or children are unattended by a "responsible" educator, many untoward things can happen for which the principal will be held responsible, and it is a major concern of most principals that they not permit a practice that may produce criticism by administrative superiors or others. The major basis for this attitude is that "the system" does not view these practices either as permissible or desirable, and most principals do not question this position. But one also finds principals who have seriously considered such practices but who refrain because of their conception that the traditions of the system are wise and not to be countered. The facts that some principals within the same system do permit these practices and spontaneously develop and support them, and that these practices become known to and tolerated by "the system," indicate that as important as the system itself is the conception of it held by the principal.

To further illustrate this point I shall present below part of an extended discussion of how "the unmanageable child" can be handled by classroom teachers. The excerpt concerns a way of thinking and a procedure that one member of the Yale Psycho-Educational Clinic was able to implement in one inner-city school. The question the reader should bear in mind is why most principals have been opposed to trying the procedure.

> The enormous effort and inventiveness required of a teacher in fostering good relationships both between herself and her children and among her children is sometimes defined as a distraction from her educational role by even the most kindly teachers. After all, she has a curriculum guide to cover and her children are evaluated against local or national achievement test norms. The psychologist can be of some help by pointing out how neglected emotional undercurrents festering in the class considerably reduce the teacher's educational effectiveness as much as they work against a child's developing his most human character traits. To neglect emotional factors in the classroom with an unmanageable child is to invite upheaval.

Relationship-building techniques for influencing the unmanageable child are indispensable to involving him constructively in the classroom, but they are usually insufficient to produce the dramatic suppression of hostile defiance that is necessary if he is to be allowed by the principal to remain in school. For the child's own welfare, therefore, it is necessary to work out with the teacher influence techniques that effectively suppress the child's defiant outbursts almost at once, unless teacher and psychologist feel that he would profit from a brief exclusion from school. The use of exclusion from school as an initial influence technique, however, is usually not nearly so effective with the defiant child as other measures. One of three techniques for suppressing defiant outbursts is implemented along with the relationship-building techniques in the case of each unmanageable child.

The most commonly recommended technique for suppressing defiant behavior is that of excluding the disobedient child from his classroom and placing him for half an hour in a classroom nearby. The success of exclusion depends on the preparation given by the psychologist to the teachers and school personnel involved, the support or toleration of the principal, and the precise manner in which the teacher prepares her class and implements the technique. Any such dramatic recommendation, of course, requires the approval and comprehension of the principal, whose begrudging acceptance of the plan could undermine teachers' use of it. The principal must also participate in selecting the relatively experienced teacher with whom the unmanageable child's teacher pairs. Teachers have an antipathy to imposing on each other: the excluding teacher usually feels embarrassed about depending on another teacher, and the receiving teacher is concerned about her class being unsettled by the visitor. These understandable concerns must be recognized and assurance given that the play may be stopped if it creates more problems than it solves. The participating pair of teachers must be fully briefed on the rationale and dangers in the plan so that they experience as few surprises as possible in implementing it. From our experience with the exclusion plan we now routinely brief participating teachers on several points. When a child is received in another room, he is to be given a seat at the back and excluded from any form of participation or interaction in the class. Before making this clear to teachers we occasionally found the excluded child excitedly participating in the receiving teacher's classroom activities. We also now prepare the excluding teacher for the problem of a child refusing to leave the room. He is to be carried out by the pair of teachers if he is in kindergarten through second grade.

Older children refusing to leave their rooms are to be informed that unless they do so their parents will be phoned immediately. Never has a child refused to respond to either pressure. Never has an excluded child posed the slightest problem in the receiving classroom. Never has a child greeted the exclusion with anything but distasteful embarrassment.

So far the exclusion plan has the ingredients of an effective technique for suppressing defiant outbursts: it immediately terminates the disobedient behavior without introducing complications in either the receiving or excluding classrooms. Its unpleasant quality for the child renders it an effective influence technique in shaping more compliant subsequent behavior. The most significant source of power adhering to the plan, however, is probably not its unpleasantness per se but its decisive ability to force on the consciousness of the child the limits beyond which he may no longer go; in short, to underline by dramatic action those rules that other children remember and obey through verbal injunctions alone. It also gives the teacher a measure of authority she had been lacking in verbal injunctions. If the plan is to maximize the child's chances of remembering and following classroom rules, it must be introduced to the whole class not as an angry punitive retaliation by a distraught teacher but as a way of helping children to remember to follow rules that allow them to enjoy learning. It should be explained to the children repeatedly that a child will be excluded not because he is unwanted or disliked but because he needs the brief opportunity in another classroom to reflect on the rules he has been disobeying. By introducing the procedure to the entire class in a group discussion it does not appear as though the defiant child is being singled out; the shock of implementing the technique is reduced to more manageable proportions; and its rationale is communicated during a period of relative calm in the classroom. In their actual implementation of the plan teachers are cautioned against excluding children when they are furious with them, waiting instead until they have regained their composure. At that point the child is to be given one private, unembarrassing warning that clearly states that if a specific behavior does not cease he will be excluded. If several children are acting up defiantly they are to be warned publicly, but in no case is a child excluded unless he has had one and only one private warning from the teacher to remind him clearly of the rule he is breaking and of impending exclusion if he does not stop disrupting the class. Contained in such private warnings must be the teacher's attempt to explain to the child how he is disrupting the class, together with whatever relationship-building techniques she feels appropriate and feasible. Should the child subsequently defy the warning intentionally, he is to be led out of the classroom by the teacher who explains to the entire class in the presence of the child why he is being excluded.

On returning to the classroom after delivering the child to the receiving teacher, the excluding teacher reviews the situation with her class, emphasizing the reasons behind the relevant rules and alternative ways in which the excluded child might have acted. Whenever possible her remarks are channeled into a group discussion that can be used to marshal the support of the class in helping the excluded child. Once children have expressed their expected bitterness toward the defiant child in such discussions, the teacher can elicit more sympathetic interest from them in helping him, especially when she points out that she needs help from the class in teaching the excluded child to follow class rules. Such discussion that can be used to marshall the support of the class in a meaningful basis for the teacher to develop with her children a casual and change-oriented view of surface misbehavior. If the excluded child is to derive from his exclusion the maximum incentive and minimum discouragement to changing his ways, the teacher must schedule a short after-school interview with the child on the day of his exclusion. Like the class discussion, the follow-up interview is an essential ingredient in effecting a rapid suppression of his defiant outbursts. During the interview the teacher can explain how she excluded the child to help him remember class rules rather than to embarrass him, how she hopes that in the future a warning will be sufficient to induce the child to control his behavior, how it is the child himself and not the teacher who decides whether he is to be excluded from the room. Finally, the teacher can use the interview to explore with the child whatever difficulties he is experiencing in the classroom, promising the child confidentiality if he wishes to reveal something personal. Throughout the interview the teacher makes clear her affection and respect for the child, indicating how his misbehavior is at least as discrepant with his own hopes for himself as it is with hers for him. The psychologist can be helpful in reducing the aversion some teachers express about "psychoanalyzing" their students. As long as they do not probe deeply and listen warmly and acceptingly to any problems the child discusses, their common sense and professional ethics, he tells them, are adequate guides. Most of the inner-city children who require psychotherapy will never receive it; thus the teacher's may be the only interest ever expressed in their emotional lives. Of course, the psychologist is always available to review with a teacher any material that baffles or disturbs her. We have never regretted encouraging teachers to conduct such therapy-like interviews, though we have played down the suggestion with some teachers more than others. One outcome of such interviews is that they establish an open line of communication between child and teacher by dramatizing the teacher's wish to help him by talking with him rather than by forcing him to change.

The exclusion plan has proved an effective defiance-suppression technique for influencing children through the fourth grade. Especially when applied as calmly and consistently as possible, in a program of relationship-building, the exclusion plan can greatly reduce mounting classroom tension in a relatively antiseptic way. We have not yet experimented with its use for unmanageable children above the fourth grade.[1]

This description allows us to raise two questions: what objections to this procedure have principals raised? Why did one principal accept and warmly support the procedure? The most frequent objection raised by principals was a variant of the "legal" question and goes like this: "I personally do not see anything wrong in the procedure except that we are not supposed to lay our hands on children, and if we have to carry a screaming child from one classroom to another we are breaking the rules. I would be accused of poor judgment, to say the least, and I stand a good chance of having the parents on my neck with all that that implies. This is not something the school system would tolerate." In short, the principal's view of the system — what it will or will not tolerate — was a decisive factor. I should emphasize that a number of principals were sincere in saying that they *personally* had no objections but that they could not agree to the procedure because it was counter to rules and regulations, i.e., the system and its traditions.

How can we understand why one principal went along with the procedure? Another principal answered that question in this way: "He is a fool and he is asking for trouble." The tendency to anticipate trouble *in relation to the system* is characteristic of many principals and one of the most frequent and strong obstacles to trying what they conceive to be an atypical procedure. But the principal who went along with the procedure saw things somewhat differently: "Right now the only thing I can do with those

---

[1] S. B. Sarason et al, *Psychology in Community Settings* (New York: John Wiley and Sons, Inc., 1966), p. 143.

kids, and I have a lot of them, is to send them home. The system says I can do that, except that it doesn't do any good. You can't teach a child who is not there. We are not going to hit the child or manhandle him. We are not going to descend on him like a bolt out of the blue. There may be trouble but that's what we have now. This is not being done to make life easier for us — in fact, it means more work — but to help a child in school. What are we here for? Certainly it is not to send kids home." It is not important that the procedure worked beautifully in this school, for which this principal's unequivocal support was no small factor. What is important is that he did not conceive "the system" as preventing him from discharging what he saw as his responsibility to extremely difficult children. In fact, it was his strong sense of responsibility that frequently put him in opposition to the "system," and he won far more battles than he ever lost. Rather than saying that he won battles, which is the way he saw it, it would be more accurate to say that what he demonstrated was that the system could "tolerate" diversity. But to test tolerance requires that one assume that "the system" can be or should be or will be malleable. Without this assumption one begins with a conception of the system that, in the tradition of the self-fulfilling prophecy, one ends up confirming.

Let us take one more example:

In a particular inner-city school there was a major problem in controlling a rather large group of first and second graders during the recess period following lunch. In the fall and spring the recess was held in the school playground, and in bad weather it was held in the gym. Two teacher aides had been assigned to organize and oversee the activities of the seventy or so children during the recess. Chaos was the norm, in part due to the absence of any meaningful or interesting play materials. As part of his work in a clinic seminar a Yale senior had been assigned to work with one of the first grade teachers, and shortly after he began he became aware, like everyone else, of the chaos during this particular recess. After several months, during which he tried to be helpful with the recess problem, the student suggested to the principal that a couple of seventh or eighth graders from an adjoining school be gotten to help out during recess by organizing smaller groups around certain games. The first response of the principal was that insurance policies might not cover the seventh and eighth graders if they were somehow injured. The second response, upon which the principal dwelled for some time, was that the superintendent would not accept students functioning as teachers. Close questioning by the undergraduate produced nothing to indicate that the principal was not sincere in her belief that using students in the proposed way was frowned upon, if not directly against the rules. *The fact of the matter was that other principals in the same system had been using older students in the proposed way for some time.*

In choosing examples I have deliberately selected those that had either or both of two characteristics: an element of risk and, in the mind of the principal, a possible legal question. In each of these instances (many more could have been presented) at least one principal did something that most principals could not do because of their conception of what the system would allow or tolerate. The fact that at least one principal conceived of his responsibility and the system in a way that permitted him to take an action accepted or tolerated by the system indicates that for the other principals the decisive factor was their conception of what the system would permit.

The role of the principal cannot be understood by a listing or description of what he can or cannot do, if for no other reason than that conditions change and new problems arise. Any job description of a principal consists essentially of a set of generalizations, which, if anything, states or implies the *minimum* limits or scope of the position. It does not describe the maximum limits or scope of the position. For example, the job description may state that the principal is responsible for the quality of instruction in the school; it will not state the myriads of ways by which the principal should or could discharge this responsibility. The job description may state that the principal is responsible for insuring that parents are informed about the progress of their children; it will not state the numerous ways by which this may be accomplished. The description may state or imply that the principal is responsible for keeping "law and order" in the school; it will not state the many different ways in which this may be viewed or done. The scope a principal permits himself, so to speak, is a function of several things (e.g., personality, imagination, etc.) and the one I am emphasizing here is his conception of the system and its relation to what the system permits and tolerates. I have, of course, stated the opinion that too frequently the principal's conception of the system simply does not square with what the system in fact permits or would tolerate. Why this should be so is less important at this point than the fact that it is so. I have discussed some of the causative factors in the previous chapter, and we shall return to the problem at the end of this one.

It is perhaps necessary that I make clear what I have *not* been saying or describing. I have not said or implied that the modal urban school system (its traditions, structure, practices, role relationships, and "atmosphere") encourages or facilitates innovative or bold thinking and action on the part of the principal. I have not said or implied that the system does not present numerous obstacles in the path of a principal who may want to venture in new directions. In short, the modal urban school system does not have the soil in which the seeds of new ideas can grow and thrive easily or well. To argue otherwise requires a capacity to deny reality that goes well beyond ordinary psychopathology.

But having said this one runs the danger of overlooking three important considerations. First, the knowledge on the part of the principal that what he wants to do may and will encounter frustrating obstacles frequently serves as justification for staying near the lower limits of the scope of his role. Second, the principal's actual knowledge of the characteristics of the system is frequently incomplete and faulty to the degree that his conception or picture of what the system will permit or tolerate leads him to a passive rather than an active role. Third, and perhaps most important, the range in practices among principals within the same system is sufficiently great so as to suggest that the system permits and tolerates passivity and activity, conformity and boldness, dullness and excitement, incompetency and competency. One of the most distinguishing characteristics of the modal urban school system is the diversity in quality and practice it contains. If "the system" is to be blamed for whatever one considers its defects, it would seem that it also should be blamed for its virtues, however occasional and infrequent they may be. But diversity within the system is not explainable by the system *qua* system. One has also to take account of the variations in the way in which individuals conceive of the system.

LOCUS OF CONTROL

To understand diversity in role conception and performance requires that we look at factors ordinarily relegated to a secondary status when we think in terms of the school system or the culture of the school. One such factor, which has emerged rather clearly from our work with and observations of principals, concerns the degree to which the principal feels that he is what he is *as a person* because of forces external to him in contrast to those he perceives as internal. That is to say, there are principals who act as if *they* are primarily in control of their destiny, and there are those who act as if what they have been, are, and will be are largely a function of external conditions and forces over which they have had or will have little control. I know that I am drawing too sharp a distinction and perhaps conveying the idea that there are "types" according to which people can be conveniently labeled and pigeonholed. I do not intend such a typology but overdraw the distinction in order to emphasize a factor that has clarified for me the diversity in role performance among principals. I should hasten to add that I do not attach goodness or badness to this factor. Because a principal acts on the basis that he must be governed not by outside forces, changes, and demands but rather by considerations that internally govern him in no way means that the consequences of his actions are good or bad. One's actions are mediated not only by how one views "locus of control" but by a set of values as well.

A principal was discussing with me a child who had been and still was presenting behavior problems in his classroom. She related to me that a month earlier the child did something the principal did not like and she slapped him. The child's father complained to the superintendent. In discussing this with the superintendent the principal said that if he, the superintendent, would send the father to her he would also get his face slapped.

I could write a fair-sized monograph on this principal demonstrating in diverse ways how her actions were determined not by external conditions or requirements or demands but by her view that *she* would determine what she did, when she did it, and how she did it. The reader may conclude that I am merely describing an authoritarian personality but this conclusion can obscure the fact that the same view of locus of control can be found in non-authoritarian individuals. I do not question that this principal was authoritarian but I also do not question that she viewed herself as the primary determiner of her destiny as a principal and person. That the relationships I am discussing are far from simple are illustrated in the following, which concerns not a principal but a teacher who unknowingly taught me a great deal.

This was a woman who had been teaching in this school for forty years. She was four years away from retirement. The school had changed drastically in the previous decade. In earlier years its student body was primarily Jewish and Italian but now it was almost exclusively black and Puerto Rican. When I began to work in this school this Jewish woman was one of the first teachers with whom I had a discussion and it was not one to generate happy thoughts about the future. She struck me as somewhat aloof and cold, very reserved and proper, and not someone who would easily change her mind about anything. These personality characteristics bothered me less than her organized presentation about how the neighborhood and its people had changed (all for the worst), and how the nature of schooling could no longer be considered as serving educational goals. Whereas it had once been a joy to teach the children who came to this school, it was no longer so. I concluded from this discussion that for this teacher the world had changed and that there was nothing she would or could do about it, i.e., she was now in a situation where a changed and still changing world were the primary determinants of what she did.

I did not look forward to visiting her classroom, expecting, as I did, that it would be the modal, unmitigated, boring disaster characteristic of most other classrooms in that school. What I found over a period of months was quite the reverse. To see how this woman put out for her pupils, the ways in which she managed to work individually with children, the interesting home-made instructional materials she used and the interesting and sometimes exciting ways she used them, the complete fairness with which she set and enforced rules, the games they played (there was no gymnasium) and her own physical involvement (despite her age and poor health) — my amazement was only matched by my puzzlement. Two other facts: at the end of each year the academic achievement of her second-graders was, on the average, above national norms, and in the four years we were in that school no child in her class was ever referred by her as a behavior problem. My puzzlement was simply that I did not understand what kept her going in this remarkable fashion. The more I thought about it the more I began to understand that, despite her perception of how the school, the school system, and the neighborhood changed, she could not or would not change her way of conducting herself as a teacher. It is almost as if she had said to herself: "I do not care how much things have changed, or what other people do about these changes, I can (must?) only continue to function in a certain way and if I do I'll achieve my goals. I can make these children learn." She had to feel that she was the primary determiner of her behavior in her role and that she was not going to be unduly influenced by external factors, forces, or changes.

Thus far in this chapter I have attempted to bring several factors into relationship with each other. First, there is a very marked tendency for school personnel to view the school system in negative terms. Second, in the case of the principal there is an equally marked tendency to view the system as the primary determinant of his role performance. Third, the principal's view of what the system will permit or tolerate tends to be faulty and incomplete and obscures the diversity in role performance. Fourth, an important factor shaping the principal's view of his role and the system is, in part at least, determined by the degree to which he feels *he* rather than external factors will govern his course of action.

In trying to understand diversity in role performance among principals we should not overlook the obvious and momentous significance of the diversity, and that is that the potential scope of the role is far more broad and important than modal performance would suggest. What the principal could do should not be confused with what he does do. What the modal principal does should not be confused with what the school system would permit or tolerate.

A principal and his faculty in a suburban school found themselves in agreement that they would prefer not to have report cards except at the end of the year. They felt that the anxiety and competitiveness that surrounded report cards were unwholesome, and they also felt that what was communicated to parents by report cards was as frequently misleading as it was helpful. What they preferred was to take the responsibility of talking to parents whenever they felt that a discussion was necessary and also to encourage parents to take more initiative in coming to school whenever they wanted to know how their child was doing. The group was ready to terminate the discussion because it was the feeling of all that the school system required report cards and that there was no point in taking on a losing battle. The principal wondered aloud whether they should not take the issue up with the PTA, if only to find out how they viewed report cards. The meeting was held and a majority of the parents not only agreed with the principal and teachers but urged them to try to implement the plan. The principal then took the matter up with the superintendent, stressing the feelings and support of the parents, and he was told to go ahead and try it.

The school system sets the lower limits of the scope and responsibility of the principal. The upper limits of the role are far less determined by the system than one might think by looking at modal performance.

IDEAS: THE NECESSARY INGREDIENT

It is very likely that some readers will have concluded that I am advocating that the principal should be one who views himself as the primary determiner of his courses of action rather than someone who views himself as a kind of victim of external forces and changes. I intended no such conclusion, and if I had, it would not have been justified for one very obvious reason: there are principals (just as there are many other kinds of people) who do view themselves as the primary determiner of their courses of action but whose ideas and values — the ingredients that empower and give substance to their actions — can be questioned on numerous grounds. Actions, regardless of whether they reflect an internal or external orientation, are always mediated by a blend of ideas and values.

The principal of a junior high school was indisputably a person who viewed it as necessary that he feel that his actions and decisions were primarily controlled by factors internal to him rather than by the way things happened or changed "out there in the world." When he became aware that boys' hair styles were changing, he was quite bothered although he did nothing when these styles started to be evident in the school. He stewed over the matter for some time. The school did have explicit rules about what was proper attire and he did not consider the new hair styles as falling within these rules. He was also aware that some of the parents were permitting or tolerating the new fashion. One day he decided that he had to take a stand and so he instructed each teacher to send to his office any boy whose hair style was clearly long. Approximately twenty boys appeared at his office where he informed them that they were to go home and not return until their hair was cut. This they all did.

There are those who would applaud this principal for viewing himself as he did *and* for the specific ideas and values reflected in his actions. There are others who would applaud this principal for viewing himself as he did *but* who would disagree with the ideas and values giving rise to the course of action, in terms both of means and ends. And so we come to the heart of the matter: the fact that a person has a particular orientation toward himself and the world is important, but equally important are the ideas and values to which the orientation is related. When I say ideas and values I refer to a number of things: one's knowledge and conception of what children are and the kinds of problems they inevitably have in the course of growing up; to what extent and how the interests, problems, and characteristics of children should be reflected in and determine the school experiences; to what extent and how decisions and planning in the classroom are discussed and made; how a faculty should think about how it confronts and resolves problems concerning their relationships with each other, administration, pupils, and parents; how should a faculty avoid the usual situation in which they feel intellectually and personally isolated and lonely; what makes a classroom interesting for the teacher? Is the intellectual growth of teachers less important than that of pupils? Can pupils learn and change if teachers are not continuing to learn and change? Many more statements and questions could be formulated and asked concerning what the nature of life in a school should be but they would only underscore two facts: life for everyone in a school is determined by ideas and values, and if these are not under constant discussion and surveillance, the comforts of ritual replace the conflict and excitement involved in growing and changing. The principal may be this or that type of personality, he may be experienced or inexperienced, he may be likeable or otherwise, he may be intellectually bright or average — if he is not constantly confronting himself and others, and if others cannot confront him with the world of competing ideas and values shaping life in a school, he is an educational administrator and not an educational leader.

Most principals are administrators.[2] That this is so is not entirely explained by the characteristics, traditions, and practices of "the system." The fact that one cannot say that all principals are administrators should make one pause about using the con-

---

[2] The problem of the school administrator has been briefly but well discussed by Usdan (1968). For a more detailed discussion the reader should consult Grass and Herriott (1965) as well as Goldhammer, Suttle, Becker, and Aldridge (1967).

cept of the system as the sole etiological factor. That there is
some (not much) diversity among principals is a characteristic
of the school system that requires recognition and explanation.
What I have been suggesting in this chapter is that the modal
school system permits and tolerates diversity, and that limits of
this tolerance are *in part* determined by the principal's conception of himself in relation to the system and how this conception
is powered by ideas and values. That one may not agree with a
particular blend of ideas and values should not blind one to the
more general point that the ultimate fate of ideas and values depends on the principal's conception of himself in relation to the
system.

The position I have taken has an important consequence for
the current scene in which our urban school systems are under-
going, or are the object of, change. The type of change that has
aroused the greatest controversy is that concerning decentralization and community control, although I confess that it is by no
means clear to me what these terms mean or what their specific
intended outcomes are supposed to be. To those who like to
play around with organizational charts illustrating the new administrative structures and redefinition and realignment of forces
of power, I suppose these terms have clear meaning. There is no
doubt that those who want to change the school system hope that
by changing structures and forces of power they will better the
system. "The system is faulty and must be changed" — this is the
most frequent comment one hears, and I, for one, cannot disagree. However, what is missing in these proposals for change
(and missing in those instances I have observed where some of
these proposals have been put into effect) is any recognition that
the principal is the crucial implementor of change. That is to
say, any proposal for change that intends to alter the quality of
life in the school depends primarily on the principal. One can
realign forces of power, change administrative structures, and increase budgets for materials and new personnel, but the intended
effects of all these changes will be drastically diluted by principals whose past experiences and training, interacting with certain
personality factors, ill prepares them for the role of educational
and intellectual leader. In fact, and this point has tended to be
overlooked, *many of the intended outcomes of the proposed
changes could have been achieved by the principal before these*

proposals ever were made or became matters of official policy.
That they were not made in no way means that they could not
have been made. That they were not made reflects, in part, the
factors we have been discussing in this and the previous chapter,
and it is these same factors that contribute mightily to what I
have too often witnessed when the new policies are stated and
then implemented: the more things change the more they remain
the same.

THE PRINCIPAL AS SCAPEGOAT

It may be all too easy for some readers to conclude that I have
presented a diatribe against principals, blaming them for the ills
of our school system. This reaction is justified only in the case of
those readers whose need to avoid complex problems is so strong
as to require them to oversimplify reality. This reaction will also
be characteristic of those who see complicated social systems (like
the school system) and the different roles within them as a collection of individuals with differing personalities that creates conflict that can only be resolved or prevented by selecting "better"
personalities. Whatever the sources or functions of these reactions
I part company with those who share them.

It is as unjustified as it is easy to try to understand the complexity of the role of the principal solely in terms of individual
personality dynamics, with the usual result that one ends up with
"good guys and bad guys." Personality factors are certainly important, as is the necessity at some point to make judgments on
this score. However, as I have tried to make clear, the complexities, ambiguities, and responsibilities of the role are not only the
result of individual factors or dynamics but rather of traditions
colliding with changing conditions. It would perhaps, be more
correct to say that changing social conditions have brought to the
fore with dramatic force what have always been the dilemmas
within the role and between that role and other roles within the
educational system.

At the time this book was written, 1969, there were two jobs
in which turnover had dramatically increased and for which it
was far from easy to recruit. One of these jobs, of course, is that
of the college president. The other is that of the public school

principal. When it is half facetiously said that these are impossible jobs, the attribute of impossibility does not refer to the characteristics of individuals but to the inordinate complexity and demands of these roles. If there was any single purpose to the contents of this and the previous chapter, it was to counter the tendency to describe the role of the principal in oversimplified terms that when used as a basis for action and change at best produce the illusion of change and at worst strengthen the feeling that it is all a hopeless affair. I cannot refrain from adding that the tendency to oversimplify, and in fact not to understand, the role of the principal is characteristic not only of those within the school culture but of those from without who seek to effect change.

ᴄ10ᴑ

The Teacher: the Role
and Its Dilemmas

In all the previous chapters we have, in varying degrees, discussed the classroom teacher. Although in this chapter we shall concentrate on communalities among teachers, the reader should not forget how diverse a group classroom teachers are. Teachers vary in a number of dimensions, for example, the grade level they teach (kindergarten, elementary, junior, and senior high), the kind of child they teach (retarded, disturbed, physically handicapped), area of subject matter specialization (physical education, math, etc.), length of teacher experience, type of teacher training background, and sex. Each of these dimensions could serve as a basis for understanding the role of the teacher in the culture of the school. In fact, the diversity is of such a degree as to rule out the possibility that any one individual can know the culture of the school in terms of all or even most of these dimensions. We will have to content ourselves with the modest goal of trying to see some of the communalities underlying obvious diversity. In this attempt I shall inevitably be influenced by my own immersion in schools as well as my interest in the problem of change.

151

THE PERENNIAL PROBLEM: NUMBER AND
DIVERSITY OF CHILDREN

From the standpoint of teachers the complexity of their task reflects in large measure the fact that a classroom of twenty-five children or so *is a lot of children for any one person to handle.* In addition, the children vary enormously in terms of academic achievement, intelligence level, behavior, interest, likeability, and maturity. The modal teacher divides the adult world into two groups: those who understand this complexity and those who do not, and in the latter group they place many school administrators and most parents. However, the complexity of the teacher's task is not easily understood by pointing to numbers and diversity of children. Perhaps the major reason that causes the teacher to point to these factors is something that intrinsically or logically has nothing to do with the process of education. I am referring here to the fact that the teacher feels, and is made to feel, that her worth as a teacher will be judged by how much her class learns in a given period of time. The strong feeling that teachers have about the complexity of their task stems from the awareness that they are expected to bring their children (if not all, most) to a certain academic level by a time criterion in regard to which they have no say. Faced with numbers and diversity of children *and* the pressure to adhere to a time schedule presents the teacher not with a difficult task but an impossible one. *I say impossible because I have never met a teacher who was not aware of and disturbed by the fact that she had not the time to give to some children in the class the kind of help they needed — and the need for help, it should be emphasized, is frequently not due to any basic intellectual defect.* There are, of course, other reasons why a teacher cannot help certain children, but none of them is more important than the felt necessity to have the class reach a particular level of skill and knowledge in a fixed period of time.

What is deserving of note here is that, by and large, teachers accept this state of affairs. They may criticize the amount of material they are expected to cover, they may feel badly that in the process certain children fall by the wayside, and they may bitterly resent that their worth as teachers is judged primarily by the average achievement level of their class, but they do not question that a time criterion is necessary. An alternative to this situation is the concept of the ungraded classroom in which children move along at their own pace and not all are expected to reach a certain level at a certain time. But in the instances where I have observed ungraded classrooms I have been impressed by several things. First, principals and other administrators still judged the worth of teachers by how much material was covered in a fixed period of time. Second, teachers, no less than before, felt under pressure to show the usual rate of progress. Third, I could discern no difference, favorable, or unfavorable, between graded and ungraded classrooms. Fourth, as one teacher put it, "you can ungrade a classroom of 25-30 distinctly different children but you still have one teacher to handle it all." I am not calling the concept of the ungraded classroom into question. All that I wish to indicate is that teachers and other school personnel have inordinate difficulty in thinking other than in terms of covering X amount of material in X amount of time. It would indeed be strange if they thought otherwise. After all, the school is organized according to grade levels, children are expected to be promoted at a certain time on the basis of achievement, and teachers at one grade level expect that the teachers of the previous level have adequately prepared their pupils, just as they know that the teacher to whom their children are passed on will expect that a particular amount and kind of material will have been covered. One of the major sources of psychological distance or interpersonal conflict among teachers in a school is when a teacher feels that the previous teacher of her pupils did not adequately prepare her children or did not cover an adequate range of material.

The effects of time pressure, as well as one of its potent sources, are seen in its most clear form in the new teacher who comes to school armed with the concept of lesson plans and the knowledge that these plans will be scrutinized and evaluated by the principal and other supervisory personnel. There seems to be wide agreement that keeping control of the class is one of the new teacher's major problems and about which she has much anxiety. Superficially, this appears to be the case on the basis of my own experience. Although difficulty in keeping control has several sources, one of the most important of these is the preoccupation with lesson plans and the need to cover them by a certain time. Time and again I have seen new teachers successfully complete a forty-minute lesson — in the sense that the points to be covered were covered — only to have lost the children some-where around the ten-minute mark — and "lost" could mean lost in behavioral chaos or a fog of confusion. On those occasions when I have asked the new teacher why she persisted with the lesson plan when it was clear to her (as it often is) that she was losing the class, I have met with several reactions the two most frequent of which were: she could think of no alternative to con-tinuing, and relief that someone else verbalized what she herself would have liked to have verbalized and acted on.

I have been stressing the point that a major problem of the teacher inheres in the interaction between number and diversity of children, on the one hand, and the felt need to adhere to a time schedule, on the other hand. There are two types of time pressure, short and long, and I have only been referring to the one that may involve weeks, months, or the span of the school year. If one focuses only on the single day and attempts to under-stand why the classroom day is organized the way it is, one quickly sees that time considerations are fairly decisive in determining how the class day is to be apportioned. A certain amount of time is apportioned to social studies, math, and so forth. The amount of time any one activity receives is a function of some scale of value and the number of activities that have to be represented. In short, the absolute amount of time any one activity receives is generally predetermined and is not a function of what teachers feel their class of pupils requires. As we shall see later, few teachers feel free to depart from the predetermined time allocations.

We should not lightly pass over the fact that the teacher has little, and more often than not, nothing to say either about num-bers and diversity of children in the classroom or the time per-spective by which her teaching is governed. What we are saying in effect, and what most teachers are aware of, is that teachers are far from having a role in some important decisions that affect life in the classroom.[1]

[1]With the rise of militancy in teacher unions and associations it was to be expected that numbers and diversity of children would become a controversial issue. The demand for smaller classes and reduction in the intellectual and emo-tional diversity among children in the classroom is put forward on the basis that meeting the demand will enable teachers to cover adequately the material they and the school system want covered. I do not think that I need elaborate on the further point that the rise in strength of teacher associations is related to the in-creasing awareness on the part of teachers that much of their professional work is shaped by forces and groups other than themselves.

SEGREGATION: THE PREPOTENT RESPONSE

From the beginning of his career the teacher copes with two kinds of dilemmas: professional and personal. The professional one, which we have discussed, stems from the knowledge that the teacher is unable to do justice to each child in the classroom. Within the limits of time and capability the teacher may try to reach and help each child, but these attempts are rarely sufficient to enable the teacher to maintain the myth that she is indeed helping each child. Some teachers feel guilty that they cannot help those with one or another kind of learning problem; some teachers feel badly that they are not doing all that they would like for the bright student; other teachers are frustrated that they do not have the time to reach and understand children with obvious personality problems. The personal dilemma, which stems in part from the professional one, consists of the need to adjust in some non-disabling or disorganizing way to the personal consequences of the professional dilemma and, in addition, *to cope with the equally upsetting realization that part of the problem resides in the teacher's inadequacies in knowledge, understanding, and technique.* As has been pointed out elsewhere (Sarason, Blatt, and Davidson, 1962) no group more than teachers is as aware that the preparation of teachers ill prepares them for the realities of classroom life. That teachers do not proclaim this is understandable in the same way that principals, as we saw in the previous two chapters, do not go about proclaiming the disconnectedness between their world of training and their world of work.

These are not easy dilemmas to live with. In one way or another the dissonance is resolved, at least to the point where its return is only occasional. One of the most frequent ways the dissonance is resolved is through the idea that certain children cannot be accommodated in the ordinary classroom. That is to say, for the sake of the academic and personal development of the child it would be best if he were put in a special class or program. Sometimes, of course, it is also maintained that it is unfair to the majority of the children in a classroom to have their progress impeded or slowed by a small number of children who are not "with it." However the position is articulated, the consequence has been that in recent years there has been a dramatic increase in the number of special classes for the "emotionally disturbed," the mentally retarded, the perceptually impaired, and the slow learner. If money were not a factor, and if appropriately trained teachers were in greater supply, the rate of increase would be even sharper. Segregation of problem children is the prepotent response to the professional and personal dilemmas teachers face. If in addition to the children segregated in special classes one were to include those excluded or suspended from school, one begins to understand what is meant by those who characterize the urban school system as comprised of two systems: the regular and the special.[2]

The prepotent response or attitude shows up in ways less obvious than placement into special classes. One of these ways is manifested in the relation between the classroom teacher and the increasing number of "specialists" whose job it is to help the regular classroom teacher with problem children. Psychologists, psychiatrists, social workers, reading specialists, and resource or roving teachers are only some of the personnel available to the classroom teacher. One of the major complaints teachers articulate about these specialists is that they define help in terms of what

[2]The dramatic increase in special classes of all kinds is a relatively recent phenomenon, but it has a long and stormy history as Wallin (1955) has made all too clear. That it is of recent origin is not due to any fundamental change in viewpoint of school personnel to handicapped children, a viewpoint that at worst is strongly negative and at best is tolerant, but rather to mandatory legislation and the availability of federal funds. As a consequence, these classes tend to be viewed as alien bodies in the school culture, with the result that children in these classes, as well as their teachers, feel different and apart from the school. The relationships between the regular and special class teacher are not made any easier by the fact that special classes contain fewer children than the regular ones, i.e., too many regular class teachers think that the special class teacher has an easy time of it. In addition, the special class in a school presents many problems to the principal who has no competence (he feels) with special education and does not know how to relate to the special class teacher or *his* supervisor. Underlying all this are two important characteristics of the school culture: the higher a child's intelligence level the more valued he is as a person (it's better to be rich than poor!), and that one needs a special psychological theory for different kinds of special children, which is like saying that one needs a special theory for the hydrogen atom and a special one for helium. The second characteristic is reinforced by the fact that those books on teaching or schools that have been generally influential in this country are concerned only with the regular classroom. In the school culture special education over the years has been treated in much the same way that the race problem was treated by the larger society. Just as the larger society is painfully changing, the school culture is changing somewhat in its view of special education (Sarason, S. B., and Doris, J., 1968).

the teacher can do with the child. As one teacher put it, "I do not need someone to tell me what more I should or could do with the child. When I ask for help I am asking someone else *to do something.*" Another teacher put it this way: "The next time someone tells *me* to give Johnny more individual attention, I'll either scream or invite him out." What the teacher has difficulty understanding or accepting is that the number of specialists is pitifully small (both on an absolute and relative basis) to provide the kind of help she desires. In fact, another frequent complaint of the teacher is that special services are available "too infrequently, too late, with too little." If the relationship between the classroom teacher and special services personnel is not exactly one characteristic of a mutual admiration society, it is in large part due to two factors: both the classroom teacher and the specialist are keenly aware that they cannot give the necessary degree and quality of help, and, perhaps more fateful for their relationship, *each tends to be unaware that they are both in the same boat.* It is not unusual, therefore, for the specialist to view many teachers as uncooperative or resistant, and for the teacher to view the specialist as unhelpful and unsympathetic. The loneliness of teachers (and others) has many sources, but heading the list are the feelings that their plight is neither understood nor appreciated and that they have only themselves to fall back on.

THE FANTASY OF REDUCED CLASS SIZE

Fantasy is a double-edged sword in that it solves problems and gives expression to wishes at the same time that it denies external reality. One of the most frequent fantasies in which teachers indulge — and it is by no means restricted to teachers — is how enjoyable life in a classroom could be if class size were discernibly decreased. Like the heavens of religions, reduced class size is a teacher's ultimate reward in comparison to which inadequate salaries pale in significance. The reason I label this a fantasy is not only because it is incapable of fulfillment but because those who hold it tend to be unaware that it is unrealistic. Let us put it this way: if Congress in its infinite wisdom were to pass legislation making it financially possible to reduce class size in half, *the legislation could not be implemented.* It is conceivable that over a period of a decade the necessary physical plant could be built — our society has rarely failed in crash programs of a technological nature. What would be impossible would be to train teachers and other educational specialists in the numbers necessary to implement the legislation. Our centers of training simply cannot train discernibly more people than they are now doing. In fact, our centers of training are quite aware that they are not now doing the quality job that is required in terms of selection of students and quality level of faculty. These centers cannot, nor will they, discernibly increase the numbers being trained. In short, the goal of dramatically reducing class size is far from a financial problem.

What I call the 'fantasy of numbers of professionals" is not peculiar to the culture of the school. Following and in large part because of World War II, the mental health professions convinced themselves and the public that the solution to the problem of mental disturbance was to engage in a crash program in the training of psychotherapists. That there was a good deal of governmental support for these programs had the effect of maintaining the illusion that university training centers could in fact meet the demand, an illusion recognized as such by only a few people. It took two decades for this illusion to be shattered on the rocks of reality and social change. As a consequence, and one that has direct relevance for the culture of the school, there is beginning to be an accommodation to the idea that the solution cannot be based on the assumption that the traditionally trained professional will ever exist in adequate numbers. Other human resources will have to be tapped and developed. But in the case of the school, as we shall now see, this accommodation has not been without its major problems and is inevitably a reflection of the modal way in which change occurs in the culture of the school.

In the past decade, and particularly in our urban school systems, the use of teacher aides has increased perceptibly. More often than not these aides have a high-school education or less, are indigenous to the area served by the school, and are given a modicum (at best) of preparation for being in a classroom. When these programs have been initiated it has usually been with a good deal of fanfare proclaiming that teachers are finally going to receive some of the help they long asked for and needed. I have been in the position of observing these programs and talking to many teachers who received aides. Why do so many teachers view teacher aides as being quite far from an unmixed blessing? Some teachers, by no means all, rather bitterly resent the implication that someone without college education and training can play a significant role in the education of children — a position identical in principle to that held by the field of psychiatry two decades ago that someone who did not have a medical background could not be an effective psychotherapist.[3] Some teachers complained that while the aides were appropriately motivated and eager to work with children, the teacher simply did not have the time to instruct and supervise the aide and, therefore, used them primarily for clerical purposes. Some teachers frankly said they could not work with another adult in the room — they anticipated that it would be distracting both to them and the children — and, therefore, did not request an aide. There were, of course, some teachers who were enthusiastic about having an aide, although the number of such teachers was definitely small.

The negative or lukewarm reactions of the teachers can be understood from several standpoints but the one that can be easily overlooked — and it certainly is by administrative personnel — is the one that focuses on the role of the teacher in formulating, developing, and carrying out the aide program. *In every such program I observed, the teachers were presented with a ready-made program, and in some instances they learned about it in the local newspaper.* The advice of teachers was never sought, the problems that could occur were never discussed, teachers were given no role in formulating a training or selection program, and, needless to say, teachers had no opportunity to express the professional and personal problems and questions they might have about the use of aides.[4] The change process in regard to

[3] This controversy, by now interred, must be viewed as but one instance of the real crisis in the delivery of health services and the woefully inadequate number of medical personnel being trained. There are at the present time several projects being conducted in leading medical centers involving the use of nurses in matters of diagnosis and treatment that two decades ago would not have been seriously considered or could have received governmental support.

[4] As we shall see in the next chapter, the relationship of teachers to program planners is similar to, if not identical with, that of the teacher to the children in the classroom.

aides was as "modal" as the change process in regard to the new math. What I think deserves special emphasis is the difficulty many teachers had in verbalizing their resentment about having little or nothing to say about decisions that could or would affect their work. It may well be that this difficulty in recognizing and verbalizing resentment reflects the degree to which teachers are accustomed to being treated as lowly proletariats. It may also be that it reflects a kind of preconscious awareness that they should do something about the conditions that produce such resentments, but doing something that would change their perception of themselves and their role is not easy for teachers or anyone else. As a teacher once said to me: "teachers are not militant by nature, only from sheer desperation."

Zax and Cowen (1967), who have done and are still doing some of the most systematic research on the training and introduction of teacher aides, have well demonstrated that when teachers are an integral part of the development of the program, have an important role in the training of aides, and come to know them before they are introduced into the program, the teachers and the aides not only find it a mutually productive experience but the gain to children is great. What is particularly instructive about this report is that in the pilot studies they proceeded with the training program for the aides with little or no involvement of teachers. After the aides were introduced they quickly sensed the sources of teacher dissatisfaction, they realized that as people from outside the school system they had excluded teachers in planning in much the same way as insiders do, they changed strategies, and the level of cooperation and enthusiasm of everyone markedly increased.

One can expect that in coming decades more and more efforts will be made to create and introduce new roles in the schools for people with little or no formal training in education. This process has already begun and will probably accelerate. These efforts are both laudable, necessary, and overdue. However, to the extent that these efforts are implemented in the usual way in which changes are introduced into the school culture, one cannot set one's expectations very high.[5]

---

[5]It should be emphasized that recent efforts to utilize so-called non-professional personnel in the schools (particularly in urban schools) are far from being the first of such concerted efforts. Levine and Levine (1970) have documented the

In the case of the classroom teacher what is at issue is not involvement for the sake of involvement or to satisfy the elementary requirements of courtesy. What is at issue, but rarely clearly stated, is how the change process can enable the teacher to perceive her role differently, that is, to perceive the role not as threatened or derogated but as expanded in scope and importance. Any conception of change that does not explicitly recognize that changing perception of role is never an easy task and that it cannot be accomplished by legislation or regulation — or by virtue of laudable goals or the pressures of external reality — is likely to result in strengthening the rigidity of role boundaries. Involving teachers in those decisions or plans that will affect them can be justified on several grounds. First, involvement makes it more likely that responsibility will be assumed and not be attributed to others. Second, it makes it more likely that problems of attitude and goals will surface and be dealt with. Third, and of crucial importance, it increases the chances that the alternative ways in which problems can be formulated and resolved will be scrutinized and act as a control against premature closure and the tendency to think that there is only one way by which problems may be viewed and handled. There is another factor, and precisely because it is so rarely recognized and discussed, and because of its importance in understanding the classroom teacher in the context of the culture of the school, I shall deal with it separately in the next section.

THE EFFECTS OF BOREDOM AND ROUTINE

With the reader's indulgence we shall, as we did in earlier chapters, imagine that we are someone from outer space parked in a space platform, incapable of comprehending language or writing, capable of seeing everything that goes on in the school, and possessed of a mind and advanced computers that allow one to re-

---

visiting teacher movement at the turn of the century, a movement that largely involved non-professional workers from settlement houses. The school social worker of today is a direct descendant of the visiting teacher except that, as the Levines point out, in the process of "professionalizing" the work of the visiting teacher most of what was distinctive in their role went by the boards. The reader is urged to familiarize himself with the Levines' account.

cord anything in the nature of a regularity. Let us further imagine that we have been parked above the school for a long time, perhaps two years. The reader may recall from earlier chapters that one of the things that the man from outer space discerned as a regularity was that the frequency with which "big people" engaged in face-to-face contact for more than a couple of minutes was amazingly low. His computers also told him that on those infrequent occasions when all or most of these big people would be together in one room (e.g., faculty or PTA meetings) the frequency with which sounds emanated from their mouths was fantastically less than when each big person was alone in a room with the small people. We discussed these findings in terms of "teaching is a lonely profession" by which we meant that the teacher is alone with her problems and dilemmas, constantly thrown back on her own resources, having little or no interpersonal vehicles available for purposes of stimulation, change, or control against man's capacity to act and think foolishly.

But what are some of the regularities that our man from outer space would observe about the teacher in the classroom? One of the more obvious regularities he would observe is that the teacher does much the same thing on each of the 180-plus days of the school year with much the same children and in exactly the same classroom. From the rituals associated with the beginning of the school day to those associated with the end, each day is very much like every other day. Occasionally there are variations that the man from outer space might have difficulty comprehending because they are so infrequent, for example, fire-drills, assemblies, shortened days due to snow storms, visiting policemen and firemen, business-in-education week, Christmas parties, and so on. These occasional events causing some kind of change in the daily routine only emphasize that there is a routine.

We have to leave the man from outer space because he can only (*only?*) discern overt behavioral regularities and he cannot help us in understanding the covert significances of what we have learned from him. In leaving him let us note that as a result of making observations for more than one year he saw something else: there was a marked tendency for the same teacher to be with the same *kinds* of children; in successive years the same teacher tends to teach the same kind of child. We now have to ask the crucial question: to what extent and in what ways does this routine — this identity among days, the degree of age specialization — affect the thinking and feelings of teachers? What enables a teacher to resist the effects of a routinized existence? Before attempting to answer these questions I should hasten to point out that the regularity we are describing is about the elementary school teacher whose degree of routine contains far more diversity than that of the junior or senior high-school teacher who teaches *a* particular subject, for example, math, English, French, and so on. Whereas the elementary school teacher tends to teach all the major subjects, the junior and senior high school teacher within the course of the day tends to teach the same subject matter to five or more different groups of students.

The questions I raised earlier are not easy to ask of teachers and they are far less easy for teachers to think about and answer. After all, if one's job is not very interesting, if it is the only type of job one is likely to have in life, and if in the public's mind it is a job that is thought to be interesting, it should not be easy to talk freely about how one thinks and feels about that job. On the basis of my discussions with teachers it seems clear that how teachers respond to these questions in part is related to the length of their teaching career. Without exception those who have been teaching for five or more years admitted that they no longer experienced their work with the enthusiasm, excitement, sense of mission, and challenge that they once did.[6] (I should make it perfectly clear that these teachers were *not* saying that they disliked being a teacher, although in a minority of instances I felt that to be the case.) For the most part they felt as competent as they ever were going to feel, and they verbalized no expectation that they would be teaching or thinking differently sometime in

---

[6]Green (1968) has written an extremely stimulating general discussion of the concepts of work, labor, and play, and the different consequences of each on the individual. In the last chapter of his book he relates this discussion to the schools, with particular attention to the teacher as a producer. "Our understanding of teaching as an activity has tended to become focused primarily on the results; what counts is not the process, but its outcome. The tendency is therefore to view teaching, to assess its excellence, in terms of its product." What I am describing about teachers, what they have told me, are consequences of viewing what one does as work, i.e., as a kind of activity that makes sense only when it has a connection with a result or a product. This is radically different from play and, as a result, it is difficult, if not impossible, for someone who views his role as work to maintain enthusiasm, excitement, sense of mission, and challenge.

the future. Almost without exception each teacher had at one time considered, or was still considering, moving out of the classroom and even moving out of education. Some teachers were clear that this consideration was motivated by the knowledge that there was much to learn and do in education and the rest of the world and they were not going to learn this by remaining in the classroom. In one way or another these teachers indicated that they rarely experienced anymore the sense of personal or intellectual growth. The shape of the future was quite clear and there were aspects of it that bothered them. The future contained a routine with which they were already quite familiar.

All these older teachers had taken or were taking advanced courses in education in local colleges and universities, and their motivation for taking these courses was not simply to meet a requirement in order to gain a salary increase. There was a passive desire or need to be intellectually stimulated and to have horizons expanded; they knew well that there was much to learn. There seemed to be the unverbalized hope that by virtue of these courses something new would be injected into their working lives. What I learned from these discussions, which I did not fully realize before, was that in a fair number of instances these courses did serve as a source of intellectual stimulation — it did confirm to the teachers that there was a world of interesting and conflicting ideas — but they did not, or could not, see the relevance of these courses to their daily work in the classroom. On the basis of nearly three decades of teaching and working with teachers I cannot refrain from pointing out, in these days when "relevance" is uppermost in the minds of those in the college community, that as a group teachers have long been living with the knowledge that their college experiences were for the most part irrelevant to their work. If one thinks one understands and sympathizes with what so many in the university community, students and faculty, call irrelevance and alienation, he then understands a good deal of the phenomenology of the classroom teacher.

The picture that emerges from discussion with the younger teachers is more complex and somewhat less clear, and primarily for two reasons. First, to oversimplify the matter, they grew up and went to school in a society rather different than that experienced by older teachers. Second, the discussions took place at a time in their careers when problems of identity, professional and personal, were ever present and poignantly so. A surprising number of these younger teachers were already convinced that they did not want to remain in the classroom.[7] There were many reasons for this but for the purposes of our present discussion the one requiring our attention is that they did not see the school as an intellectual community in which they could look forward to growth and change. *In fact, some explicitly pointed to some older teachers in the schools as examples of what they feared they might become.* Here, too, I must emphasize (and shall discuss later) that these teachers were not complaining about being teachers of children or that there were no rewards in what they were doing, but rather about the painful awareness that their present and future seemed all too similar. By and large they had all the commendable features of youth: the need to give to others, to eradicate injustice, to question tradition, and to experience the sense of learning, changing, growing. Some of these needs could and were being met, but neither in relationship to their colleagues or to children was the need for new ideas and intellectual growth met.

After working for some time with a young, unmarried woman who taught French in a junior high school, I finally got the courage to say to her: "You teach French each day to six different groups of children. You have been doing it now for three years. It occurred to me the other day that if I had to do what you do, even if it were psychology, I would go crazy. What keeps you going? And you are a good teacher. Where are the kicks?" I was surprised by the speed with which she responded — obviously, my statement and question touched on something about which she had been thinking. "Two weeks from this Saturday I have appointments at the UN and the French Consulate to find out about job possibilities, and it well may be that if it is necessary for me to learn shorthand and really be able to type for these kinds of jobs, I will do it. As to kicks, there are some. For instance, when you get a student in beginning French who for some mysterious reason has just the right intonation and pronunciation, it is a real pleasure to see him or her blossom. Or the student who went on his own to the library and got out some French books he wants to discuss with you. I enjoy their interest *in me,* and I get a good feeling when they want to talk with me alone and tell me something personal. But most of the time it's push push,

[7] The reader will recall that in the study by A. Levine (Chapter 5) of a MAT program, a rather large number of students said that they were not going to pursue a teaching career.

stimulate stimulate, and sometimes *I* get the feeling that I think many of the kids have: is it all that necessary and important? I have learned a lot and probably could and will learn more but I am not honestly convinced of that. It has turned out to be much more of a grind than I ever imagined. What do other teachers tell you?"

Not all the younger teachers were as frank with me as this young woman, and they certainly did not talk over these matters very much (if at all) with each other. Overall I gained the distinct impression that the younger teachers were acutely aware of a discrepancy between what they were personally and intellectually experiencing as teachers in classrooms and their earlier fantasies or expectations about what life in school would be like. If they experienced the sense of intellectual growth and excitement except on occasion, I did not pick it up.

Toward the end of a year-long series of weekly meetings with a group of young high-school teachers, organized around whatever problems they were having as teachers, one of the teachers said that he was seriously thinking of leaving teaching. There were several reasons why this and the other teachers would not have wanted to remain at this school (and indeed two were making arrangements to go to another system), but the discussion centered on the lack of intellectual stimulation, which all experienced. They complained that their days were not varied, school was a well-insulated fortress, and that they felt locked into a system that had some characteristics of a factory.

There are, of course, teachers who give no indication that they are bothered by an awareness that their working lives are fairly routinized or that they have settled into a mold about which they should be disturbed. They do not view the classroom, now or in the future, as something closing in on them. I cannot estimate the size of this group, although it is probably not as large as some critics would have us believe. As I said earlier, if teachers are intellectually dissatisfied with their lot, if they come to view teaching as a job lacking the attributes of excitement and personal growth, one should not expect them to parade such feeling in a very public manner.

If my observations have merit, they force one to raise a most serious question: *if teaching becomes neither terribly interesting nor exciting to many teachers, can one expect them to make learning interesting or exciting to children?* If teaching becomes a routine, predictable experience, does this not have inevitable consequences for life in the classroom? The modal classroom does not allow me other than to conclude that children and teachers show most of the effects of routinized thinking and living.[8] It would be strange if it were otherwise.

There is still another factor, again infrequently recognized, which often has the effect of facilitating the development of a protective routinized existence. This factor is the obvious one that inherent in teaching is *giving,* that is, the teacher is required to give of himself, intellectually and emotionally. At the beginning of his career this presents no particular problem because most new teachers come to their task with that sense of mission and enthusiasm that makes giving a natural, unreflective act. But even where this feeling is weak, or even absent, children, in different ways, need, want, require, and demand giving by the teacher. Constant giving in the context of constant vigilance required by the presence of many children is a demanding, draining, taxing affair that cannot easily be sustained. Even where it is sustained on a high level it still does not always prevent guilt feelings because the teacher cannot give all that she feels children need. To sustain the giving at a high level requires that the teacher experience *getting.* The sources for getting are surprisingly infrequent and indirect. One can get from children but this is rarely direct; one can get from colleagues and administrators, but this is even more infrequent. One can get from oneself in the sense that one feels one is learning and changing and that this will continue, but this crucial source of getting is often not strong enough to make for a better balance between giving and getting.

[8]This is not a conclusion that should be restricted to the modal public school. Among the many different things our college students are telling to, and (literally) demonstrating for, us is that their life in the classroom is often all too dull and predictable. Although the extent of my direct observations of college teachers is far less than those of public school teachers, I have no basis for contradicting the assertion that the modal college teacher is no more stimulating than the modal classroom teacher. If someone ever determines that the college teacher is more stimulating, it will not be unrelated to two facts: the college teacher (particularly in our major universities) is in a classroom far less than the public school teacher, ordinarily he is not expected to teach the same course year after year after year, and he does have the time *during the working day* to talk and be with colleagues and others. The point is that in talking about the public school we should not allow ourselves to forget that the "teacher problem" is by no means peculiar to the public school.

One of the consequences of a marked disparity between giving and getting is development of a routine that can reduce the demand for giving.[9]

Dr. Murray Levine had a student keep a diary during his first year of teaching in an elementary school. In the diary the student makes quite clear the guilt and conflict a teacher can experience around the problem and necessity of giving. To illustrate the point the student describes a five-minute interval during which one child broke a class rule, one child joyfully completed an assignment he showed to the teacher, and one child needed the teacher's help with something he did not understand. Each of these required of the teacher a different cognitive orientation, each engendered different emotions, and in sequence they necessitated the teacher, chameleon-like, quickly to change thought, feeling, and action. Not all five-minute intervals are like this one but it is not as infrequent as the lay public imagines. It is frequent enough within the course of a day to emphasize not only the extent of giving required of the teacher but also the difficulty the teacher has in sustaining a high level of giving and not resorting to strategems of routine that reduce giving at the expense of meeting the needs of children. I have often said, only somewhat facetiously, that we ought to pass a law requiring each parent alone to teach or to manage a class of children for one day. At the very least, it would educate the public to what a teacher is confronted with day in day out, year in year out. It might also raise the level of discussion about where and what kinds of changes we should be thinking about in our efforts to "improve" our schools.

What I am describing here is no more than what many teachers have told us in the context of our working relationship with them (Sarason et al., 1966). At the beginning of the relationship, usually initiated by the teacher around a problem child, we would frequently sense an ambivalence: wanting discussion and help and yet fearful that *we* would be putting more demands on the teacher to do and give more. This ambivalence would not dissipate until the teacher recognized that we were asking

[9]One sees the same process among physicians despite the obvious fact that they enjoy more getting, psychologically (probably) and materially (certainly), than teachers do; they generally feel under strong pressure to give more than they think they can, or should, or are able to. Like teachers, they frequently do not know what to do for a patient, or they feel they do not have enough time to handle all problems in the way they would like. Frequently this results in a style or routine or rationalization that reduces the guilt associated with not meeting the external or internal demands to give.

for more giving but we were prepared to give as well — by being in the classroom, giving time, being available, and obviously being interested and concerned. It was only after the dissipation of the ambivalence that some teachers could tell us what it was like constantly to feel that one has to give with little expectation either that one will get or that what one will get will be direct or predictable. One member of the Yale Psycho-Educational Clinic has maintained that a good part of whatever success we have had in working with teachers was due to the fact that we were giving to them and this was atypical in the working lives of the teachers.

There is nothing evil about a routinized day. But as each succeeding routinized day passes and it adds up to years — sometimes in the same classroom with the same kind of child with the same subject matter — one is justified in asking what are the internal and external factors that prevent what is overtly a routine from resulting in routinization of thought and action? I have suggested that in the culture of the school where the teacher is alone with many and diverse children, subject to all kinds of internal and external demands to give and do, and where the level of giving tends to far exceed getting, the modal teacher is hard put to escape the psychological effects of routine.

THE OUTSTANDING TEACHER

In a recent book entitled *Life In Classrooms,* highly recommended to the reader, Jackson (1968) presents conclusions based on interviews with a group of outstanding teachers, so labelled and chosen by administrators and supervisors who presumably knew their work well. Four themes emerged from these interviews and Jackson, skillfully, using the teacher's own words, illustrates how these themes are verbalized in the interviews. The first of these themes is immediacy, which can be described as an acute sensitivity to the "here-and-now" — what I have earlier described as the need for a state of constant vigilance. The second theme is informality, which is not easy to summarize or characterize but can be described as the opposite of an emphasis on undue routinization, that is, an emphasis, relatively speaking, on the importance of freedom of movement and thought for children. A third theme is individuality, which "deals with the teacher's interest in the well-being of individual students in his class and becomes particularly evident when the teacher is asked to describe the satisfactions he derives from his work. Although he confronts an entire class, it is what happens to individuals that really counts." A fourth theme is autonomy, which was most clearly verbalized in response to at least two hypothetical conditions: the possibility of an inflexible curriculum and the "possible invasion of the classroom by administrative superiors bent on evaluation" — to both hypothetical conditions they were quite emphatic about how strong their resistance would be.

We shall have occasion in this and the next chapter to comment on Jackson's observations and conclusions. At this point I would like to make a comment that is a glimpse of the obvious: Jackson's teachers do not *talk* in ways that suggest that they have suffered the consequences I have described earlier in this chapter. They certainly talk as one would imagine outstanding teachers would talk. Let us leave aside the unanswerable question of the relation between what these teachers say and what they actually do. The fact is that I have met and worked with these kinds of teachers in their classrooms. In my experience they exist in very small numbers. Jackson makes no claim that his sample of teachers is a representative one. He points out that at best his sample comprises the top 5 or 10 percent of the instructional staff as perceived by administrators.

How do we account for the fact that so few teachers are considered outstanding? Is it that outstanding teachers were outstanding in the relevant characteristics *before* they became teachers, that is, are they a special breed of person who is always in short supply? How many young teachers left the classroom and teaching precisely *because* they had the relevant characteristics and could not tolerate the interferences or constraints they experienced? How many "average teachers" had the potential to be much better teachers but either because of the lack in training or the schools in which they worked this potential could not be developed? Is the quality level of a teacher completely or largely independent of the school in which he works? Would Jackson's outstanding teachers, who were from suburban schools and one private school, be outstanding in inner-city schools? By these questions I am, of course, returning to a dominant theme of this book: *characteris-*

tics of individuals are always, to some extent, a reflection of the setting in which these characteristics are manifested. "Outstandingness" may be seen by others as a characteristic of an individual, but the very fact that it is seen and responded to *by others in the setting* indicates that we are dealing with more than the characteristic of an individual.

I, for one, have no difficulty accepting the idea that the characteristics of the outstanding teacher, as Jackson so well describes, probably characterized them before they became teachers. I do have difficulty accepting the notion that their becoming a good teacher was independent of where they were teaching. My experience with very young teachers has brought me to several conclusions. First, by and large they are an eager, anxious, malleable group searching rather desperately for some kind of acceptable compromise between the realities of the classroom and their fantasies about being able to help all children. Second, they are often torn between the perception that they must adhere to a schedule and a curriculum (and in some instances daily lesson plans are required) and their frequent feeling that they should depart from the routine. Third, they are quite unprepared both for the loneliness of the classroom and the lack of relationships in which questions and problems can be asked and discussed without the fear that the teacher is being evaluated. Fourth, when an evaluation-free relationship is available — such as that we have tried to develop at the Yale Psycho-Educational Clinic — a fair number of these young teachers are able to change, and sometimes dramatically so. As we have pointed out elsewhere (Sarason et al., 1966) the direction in which the teacher changes (in matters of discipline, curriculum, and handling of administrative personnel) often involves doing what the teacher wanted to do but for which there was no "authoritative support." The first two years of teaching are a baptism of fire in which many things can be consumed, including some of the ingredients that make for a good and even outstanding teacher. The important point is that what happens in these years, *for good or for bad,* cannot be understood by narrowly focusing on the teacher, but by seeing the teacher as part of a matrix of existing relationships, practices, and ideas.

I suppose I feel strongly about these matters because a lot of my experience has been with the young teacher in the inner-city school about which a number of people have written a good deal (e.g., Kohl, 1967; Kozol, 1967). I am thinking particularly of those who were becoming outstanding teachers, and those who had the potential to become good teachers. All of them chose to teach in inner-city schools. Some left teaching after a year or so, others stayed on with the knowledge that they would someday leave, and some succumbed in the sense that they retrogressed rather than progressed as teachers and as individuals. To understand their development and fate in individual terms would be grossly incomplete. Similarly, to look only to external factors ("the school or the system") would also be a partial explanation, although these young teachers tended to explain everything in terms of such factors. What became clear to me, as a participant observer and helper, was that the problem could not be formulated in cause and effect terms or by dichotomizing factors into external and internal. Their inadequate formal training for the realities of the classroom, their sheer ignorance of and lack of preparation for what life in a school would be, the demands and willingness to give and the consequences of sustained giving in a context of constant vigilance, the absence of meaningful helping services — all of these and other factors interact in ways that should make simple explanations suspect. I have by now seen many inner-city schools demolished and new ones built with the not surprising result that the more things change the more they remain the same. Why this should be so I have only partially discussed in the chapters on the principal. We shall take this problem up again in a later chapter. I wish here only to make one observation: in all the new schools and new programs I have seen (inner- and outer-city) I rarely heard any discussion about how life in the classroom for teacher and child would be or should be changed. There was discussion of special services to teachers and children and the need for teacher aides, but this discussion hardly seemed to reflect other than the most superficial recognition of the problem of the effects of teaching on the modal teacher in the modal classroom. There was much talk about the need for teachers to be flexible, creative, stimulating — everyone was against sin and for virtue — but no one, in my memory, asked the question: to what extent may the development and maintenance of these virtues be hindered by what we know about the modal teacher in the modal classroom?

But, the reader may ask, how do we understand how Jackson's outstanding teachers, albeit in suburban and private schools, did it? The answer is a simple one: we do not know and it has barely been studied. We know some of their characteristics, but surely there is more to it than that. When we listen to a symphony we are set to pick out and respond to the melodic theme, and it is all too easy to forget that the way we hear that theme is very much determined by literally scores of instruments that are not playing that theme but nevertheless are part of the whole. If we look at teacher characteristics in this way we can learn much — just as we can enjoy the melodic themes in a symphony — but just as the melody is not a symphony, teacher characteristics are but one aspect of a more complicated orchestration of factors. That we are set to respond to and think about teacher characteristics probably tells more about our accustomed ways of thinking than it does the complexity of the culture of the school. All of this would be no more than an interesting problem in theory were it not for the fact that our actions and proposals for change are determined by the way we formulate problems.

In this chapter I have attempted to look at aspects of the phenomenology of the teacher that reflect several givens: the pressure of externally determined criteria of performance, the pressure of internally determined criterion of personal and professional worth, the demandingness of the role, and the developmental consequences of the interaction of these and other factors. In this attempt I have deliberately emphasized in the teacher's role the conflicting, the affective, and the deeply personal. This I have done for two reasons. First, although I am certainly not the first to point these things out, it is still true that these aspects of the teacher's role are little appreciated and deserving of more study. Second, any effort to change the nature of life in the classroom must deal with these problems, and precious few of these efforts have dealt with them. Put in the terms of the first half of this book, most efforts to change the *classroom* have not started with a clear statement about what behavioral regularities, overt and covert, were to be changed, and it is small wonder that when the fanfare accompanying these efforts died down the old regularities were still very much alive: teachers and children were still doing the same things and feeling the same way.

But there is much more to the role of the teacher than what we have discussed here. As important as the affective factors is what teachers know, and how they plan, that is, the cognitive aspects inherent in the role. These aspects we take up in the next chapter.

ᴄ11ᴐ

The Teacher: Constitutional
Issues in the Classroom

In the previous chapter our primary aim was to convey how in the modal school certain internal and external forces, extending over time, are experienced by and influence the modal teacher. In this chapter our focus will shift to what teachers think and do in regard to a number of specific and predictable events or issues that arise in any classroom. We can consider only a few of these events or issues, and they have been deliberately chosen to illustrate the general and obvious point that life in the classroom is a function of what and how teachers think about children, and how such thinking reflects the teacher's conception of his role. In a real sense this chapter is concerned with the teacher's "theories" of human behavior and group living. As we shall see, it is only when these theories are made explicit, and are seen in contrast to alternative conceptions, that we get a deeper understanding of certain behavioral regularities in the culture of the school. Let us not forget that the existence and pervasiveness of a behavioral regularity are two of the best indicators of a covert regularity involving the relationships between thinking and conceptualization, on the one hand, and a scale of values (what is good and what is bad), on the other hand.

CONSTITUTIONAL ISSUES

Almost all teachers meet a new group of pupils on the first day of school. The beginning phase of the school year certainly extends beyond the first day, but by the third or fourth week a routine is established, and teacher and pupils have, so to speak, sized up each other; the rules of the game by which everyone will be governed are fairly well known. How does this come about? How do teachers present and explain these rules of group living? Are these rules discussed? Are they for children only? What role do pupils play, if any, in the formation of rules? These questions and others comprise what I like to call the constitutional question because in each classroom there is a constitution, verbalized or unverbalized, consistent or inconsistent, capable or incapable of amendment, that governs behavior. Constitutions tell us a good deal about history, tradition, and conceptions of human behavior.

We did an informal observational study of six classrooms, two each in grades 3, 4, and 5 in a suburban school system. In each of these six classrooms we had an observer who sat in the classroom for the first month of school beginning on the first day. The task of the observer was to record any statement by teacher and child that was relevant to "constitutional issues." The results were quite clear:

1. The constitution was invariably determined by the teacher. No teacher ever discussed why a constitution was necessary.

2. The teacher never solicited the opinions and feelings of any pupil about a constitutional question.

3. In three of the classrooms the rules of the game were verbalized by the end of the first week of school. In two others the rules were clear by the end of the month. In one it was never clear what the constitution was.

4. Except for the one chaotic classroom neither children nor teachers evidenced any discomfort with the content of constitutions — it was as if everyone agreed that this is the way things are and should be.

5. In all instances constitutional issues involved what *children* could or could not, should or should not, do. The issue of what a *teacher* could or could not, should or should not do, never arose.

On a number of occasions I have presented these findings to groups of teachers with the question: How do we explain them? In every group the question produced silence. In one group a teacher responded in a way that I think verbalized what most teachers were thinking: *What* is there to explain? I would then follow my initial question with another question: What do we have to assume to be true about children and teachers in order to justify these findings? These discussions were by no means easy or pleasant, and understandably so, if only because the teachers had never been called upon to make explicit the conceptions and values upon which these practices were based. But what were some of the assumptions that teachers could, after prolonged discussion, recognize and state?

1. Teacher knows best.
2. Children cannot participate constructively in the development of a classroom constitution.
3. Children want and expect the teacher to determine the rules of the game.
4. Children are not interested in constitutional issues.
5. Children should be governed by what a teacher thinks is right or wrong, but a teacher should not be governed by what children think is right or wrong.
6. The ethics of adults are obviously different from and superior to the ethics of children.
7. Children should not be given responsibility for something they cannot handle or for which they are not accountable.
8. If constitutional issues were handled differently, chaos might result.

If one does not make these assumptions, which is to say that one thinks differently about what children are and can do, one is very likely to think differently about what the role of the teacher might be. In this connection it is instructive to note that as I pursued the issues with the groups of teachers, and the assumptions could be clearly verbalized, *many of the teachers found themselves disagreeing with assumptions they themselves recognized as underlying their classroom behavior.* Equally as instructive was the awareness on the part of a few that if one changed one's assumptions one would have to change the character of one's role, and this was strange and upsetting, as indeed it should be because they realized that life in the classroom for them and the children would become different.

The problem we are discussing goes beyond the classroom, and its generality hit me with full force during one of these discussions with teachers. That it hit me with such force in this particular group was in part due to the fact that several of the teachers were quite adamant in maintaining that young children had to have their lives structured for them by adults because they were too immature to participate in and take responsibility for important decisions governing classroom life. *What I became aware of during the discussion was that these teachers thought about children in precisely the same way that teachers say that school administrators think about teachers, that is, administrators do not discuss matters with teachers, they do not act as if the opinions of teachers were important, they treat teachers like a bunch of children, and so on.* The rise and militancy of teacher organizations have a complex history, but one of the important factors was the unwillingness of teachers to be governed by a tradition in which they had no part in decisions and plans that affected them. We are witnessing the same development on the part of students in our high schools, junior high schools, and, needless to say, in our colleges. The amending of constitutions has been and will be accompanied by strong conflict for two reasons: there are differences in conception of what people (teachers, students) are, and it is recognized that what is at issue is what life in a school is and could be.

It is not the purpose of this book, except in a very secondary way, to say how things should be. The primary purpose is to describe some of the important regularities in the culture of the school and to relate them to the conceptions and theories that "justify" these regularities. In order to do this I have tried, wherever possible, to contrast these existing relationships with the ever-present but neglected universe of alternatives of conceptions from which derives a universe of alternative actions. This tactic not only serves to make one aware how the weight of habit and tradition can obscure the difference between what is and what could be, but it also helps force those who want to introduce changes to be more precise about what it is they want to change. The "constitutional problem" is a case in point. I have known many teachers, principals, and school administrators who pride themselves on their adherence to democratic principles and feel strongly that the needs and rights of children have to be taken into account. In addition, these same people can point to colleagues whom they label as authoritarian or restrictive, with the implication that these characteristics are anti-educational in spirit and effect. Without denying in the slightest that these differences exist, I have also to say that, constitutionally speaking, the differences are not all that great; in terms of how and on what basis the classroom constitution is determined, the "democratic" and "authoritarian" teacher are not as far apart as one might think.[1] In both cases I have been impressed by three things: constitutions are for children and not teachers, complete power is retained by the teacher, and children passively accept the constitution developed for them. Those who wish to change life in the classroom are dealing with constitutional issues and not, as is too frequently the case, with high-sounding slogans whose conceptual underpinnings remain unexamined with the usual result that there is a discrepancy between what is said and what is done.[2]

I should remind the reader that in this chapter we are attempting to understand the relationship between what teachers do (or do not do) and how they think about children and themselves, to understand the "theories" of teachers — not their feelings or values but their conceptions of what people are. And teachers, like the rest of us, have such conceptions, which, again like for the rest of us, are usually implicit rather than explicit. In this connection we now turn to another issue that was the major reason we did our little observational study.

[1]This conclusion is similar to that made by Jules Henry (1963), based on his observations of life in the suburban classroom. Henry is one of the very few anthropologists who has directly studied the classroom. His description and discussion of life in the classroom are illuminating and provocative. Given the emphasis in anthropology on foreign and so-called primitive cultures, it is not surprising that this important discipline has not focused on the classroom in our society (e.g., Spindler, G. D. [ed.], 1963).

[2]The constitutional issues, as well as others to be raised in this chapter, could be regarded as relevant to, or subsumed under, a theory of instruction. This would be a matter of indifference to me were it not that theories of instruc-

THE STUDENT'S AND TEACHER'S CONCEPTION OF LEARNING

Prior to the observational study, I had, in connection with numerous studies on anxiety in elementary school children (Sarason, Davidson, Lighthall, Waite, and Ruebush, 1960), sat in scores of classrooms. It took quite some time for me to become aware that something was missing, and that was discussion in class of why and how people learned. It is obvious enough that however one defines such words as learning, schooling, and education they refer to things or processes that take place in a school. They can and do take place outside of a school, but they are involved in what goes on in a classroom. What do children in a classroom think about the business of learning? Do children have their own theories (as indeed they do) about how and why one learns? Are there discrepancies between the theories children think about and the theories they are asked or required to adopt? Would children like to talk about these matters? Are they able to talk about them? How do teachers explain and discuss their theories of learning and thinking with their students? In short, to what extent were the whys and hows of learning and thinking an explicit focus and subject of discussion in the classroom? My observations left no doubt that how children thought about the processes of learning and

---

tion do not deal with constitutional issues but rather focus on the cognitive characteristics of the individual child, and on how these characteristics develop and could be taken account of in curriculum building. As often as not the theory talks about *a* child, and not a child in a group of children. Any theory of instruction that does not confront the reality that the teacher does not instruct *a* child but a group of children is not worth very much, to teachers at least. Even where the teacher intends to instruct a particular child, it takes place psychologically (for the child, teacher, and the other children) in the context of being part of a larger group and set of relationships. I quite agree with Jones' critique (1968) of Bruner's (1966) theory of instruction, that is, his overemphasis on cognitive skills and curricular skills and underemphasis on the affective. Jones comes close to including the constitutional question in his theory of instruction but it is far from as explicit as I think will be found to be necessary. This may be because Jones, in reacting to Bruner's overemphasis on the cognitive side, gets riveted on the expression of the affective side, and what tends to get sidetracked are the constitutional arrangements between teacher and class that maximize such expression. Depending as Jones does on Freud's and Erikson's conceptions about individual development, he cannot develop what is needed: a truly social psychological theory of instruction. These objections aside, I consider Jones' book a distinct contribution.

thinking rarely came up for scrutiny in the classroom, but I was not as certain that the teacher's theories were as rarely presented and discussed. Therefore, we placed observers in classrooms to study this, and we chose the first month of school on the assumption that it would be during this interval that a teacher was most likely to make her own thinking explicit to the students. The most general instruction given to the observers was to note anything that a teacher said bearing on the whys and hows of learning and thinking. More specifically, they were asked to record anything relevant to the following questions:

1. When a child did not know or could not do something, did the teacher's response in any way attempt to find out how the child had been thinking or how he might think — in contrast, for example, to telling and showing *a* correct procedure.

2. How frequently did a teacher say, "I don't know," and go on to discuss how he would think about going about *knowing*.

3. How frequently and in what ways does a teacher take up and discuss the role of question asking in intellectual inquiry or problem solving?

There were other questions, but I expect from those above that the reader will understand that we were interested in the degree to which such topics as thinking and problem solving were discussed in the classroom. The results were quite clear: such discussions did not take place. Although unverbalized, the ground rules were not difficult to discern. First, the task of the student was to get the right answer and this was more important than how he arrived at the answer. By "more important" I mean simply that the right answer was what teacher and student obviously treasured. Second, for any one problem or question there was *a* correct way of thinking about and answering it. Third, *thinking was really not a complicated affair.*

There is nothing new or surprising in this. For example, Wertheimer (1945) well described, in the case of a geometry class, how the students were taught by their teacher to solve the parallelogram problem. When Wertheimer then tried to get the students to consider alternative ways of solving the problem they were hardly able to grasp the idea that there was more than one way one could think about the problem. When he demonstrated alternative proofs, the students said he was wrong because he did not do it "the right way."[3]

What happens when I take up these observations with teachers? One of the most frequent reactions is similar to what Susskind (Chapter 6) reports when he presented to his teachers the discrepancy between the number of questions they asked of students and the number students asked of them: distress signifying that perhaps something was wrong. Another reaction is again similar to what only one of Susskind's teachers said, although I obtained it more frequently: "that is the way things should be." In a real sense these teachers were responding in a manner identical to that of Wertheimer's students, who could not accept the idea that there were other ways of thinking. But most instructive of all were those occasions when I could raise these issues with teachers *after* a discussion in which they had critically examined their experiences as students in their college courses. *What I confronted them with was the startling identity between their complaints as students in college and what their own students might complain about if they could but talk.* Some teachers could immediately see the possible connection. Other teachers could not accept the idea that how they felt could bear resemblance to how their students felt, that is, children did not think about thinking or learning the way teachers did. Leaving aside these reactions, there were two reservations that teachers verbalized. First, there was little or nothing in their training that would enable them to handle the issues in the classrooms. Second, even if they wanted to or could handle them, the demands of curriculum coverage leave little time for such matters.

Life in the classroom can be viewed and understood from different vantage points, but in my opinion, one of the most important ones is that which looks at the implicit theories teachers have about thinking and learning. What I have tried to suggest

[3]One of the several justifications for the development of the new math was to counteract the kinds of things Wertheimer and others have described. That is to say, one wanted children to grasp the idea that there were different ways one could use and think about the world of numbers. As we pointed out in Chapter 4, the new math is taught in much the same ways as the old math. It could not be otherwise if for no other reason than those who pushed for the change seemed unaware that the theories of learning and thinking that guide teachers, in addition to the constitutional issues discussed earlier, do not permit the processes of thinking to be an object of inquiry in the classroom.

in this section is that many teachers have two theories: *one that applies to them and one that applies to children.* Put in another way: many teachers are quite aware from their own experiences of the differences in characteristics between dull and exciting conditions of intellectual activity. But their inability to see or assume some kind of identity between their pupils and themselves leads them unwittingly to create those conditions that they would personally find boring. Classroom learning is primarily determined by teachers' perceived differences between children and adults, a fact that makes recognition of communalities almost impossible.

CLASSROOM SEATING

In asking how teachers think about and what they do with children in relation to predictable issues or events, we started with what are obviously two important issues: the constitutional question and the teacher's conception of the role of discussion of the whys and hows of inquiry.[4] A recent study by A. Schwebel (1969) allows us to pursue the discussion in terms of a question that, on the surface at least, would not seem to be for our present purposes very important or productive. But complex questions tend on examination to remain complex at the same time that simple questions on examination tend to become complex.

[4]Following the completion of this book, Fuchs' (1969) *Teachers Talk* was published. Most of Dr. Fuchs' book consists of excerpts from journals kept by fourteen new teachers during the first semester in the classroom in city schools. These excerpts constitute compelling confirmation of many points I have made in this and the previous three chapters. My favorite excerpt (because of the importance I place on constitutional issues) is from a teacher's report of the first day of school: "Then I established class routines: how we would put away our clothing; how we would get our clothing; raising your hand when you have something to say, not calling out; not talking when I'm talking; not talking when I haven't given permission to talk; not talking when you are doing something. I told them that we would have free time for talking. Then we discussed fire drills, what we would do and how we would line up, and our behavior in the hall and in the yard. I also covered supplies, the things that I requested that they bring in, and any problems. I complimented them on how they were dressed and how I would like them to come to school from now on, dressed neatly and clean; we discussed routines at home, the time we go to bed at night, how we take our bath, what happens when you get up in the morning. We discussed why breakfast is called breakfast and why we eat breakfast. Before we knew it the whole morning had gone and it had been a very good morning." The book is a storehouse of accounts of life in the classroom and school.

Schwebel's study started with his observation, stemming from his work with teachers in their classroom, that children in the back of the room tended to behave differently than those in the front of the room. He did a small preliminary study (using independent observers who did not know the purposes of the study) and found confirmation for his own observations. He then developed a more elaborate study around the question: How are the seating arrangements in a classroom determined and what are their effects? Schwebel summarizes teacher descriptions of their procedures as follows:

> From the post-experimental interviews with the participating teachers it was learned that seat assignment procedures as a social-psychological problem is not included in teacher training programs or discussed by elementary school teachers. Nonetheless, the procedures the teachers described using were highly similar, suggesting that they were reacting to common psychological and/ or environmental demands. The one demand they spoke of in particular was that of *achieving classroom control.* . . .
>
> The procedure which teachers typically reported using to prevent disruption was to separate those children they had judged as "disruptive" and to assign them to seats in various parts of the room. Most teachers stated that they could identify the "disruptive" children in the first day or two of school. "Good" children were typically seated by the teacher next to those judged as "disruptive." While this suggests that teachers use physical proximity to certain types of children as a control mechanism, it raises the question of why the teachers do not assign several or all of those they judge as disruptive to seats in the front of the room where they as teacher could act as the control agent.[5]

Among his major findings were: "(1) although individual teachers were consistent, as a group they varied with respect to the location in which they assigned pupils whom they judged as attentive, shy or likeable; (2) those children assigned by teachers to the front row are more attentive to classroom activities than their classmates in the middle and back rows; and (3) occupancy of seats in the front, in contrast to those in the middle and back, affects in a positive manner, the way in which pupils are perceived by their teacher and peers, the way in which pupils eval-

[5] A. Schwebel, "Physical and Social Distancing in Teacher-Pupil Relationship" (Doctoral dissertation, Yale University, 1969).

uate themselves, and the way in which they behave." Schwebel also points out, on the basis of his interviews, that "seat assignment procedures as a social psychological problem are not included in teacher training programs or discussed by elementary school teachers." Furthermore, although teachers were aware that they had assigned some "good" and some "bad" pupils to the front, and others to the back, the teachers could not verbalize their reasons. "Either they were less aware of the considerations which they had taken into account in making these decisions or, for one reason or another, they were hesitant to report them." 6

Why were teachers rather unclear about how they consider seating procedures? Or was it that they were clear in that discipline and control were the primary considerations that governed their thinking and decisions? What complicates answering these questions is what may be Schwebel's most intriguing finding: teachers with a high need to please other people (according to the Marlowe-Crowne Social Desirability Scale) rated pupils who sat in the front of the room more positively than those who sat in the back; teachers with a low need to please others rated pupils in the front of the room less positively than those in the back. These findings suggest that characteristics of teachers may be as important in determining seating (and, therefore, behavior) as characteristics of children.

That a classroom is a social organization is a glimpse of the obvious. What is not so obvious and is suggested by Schwebel's other data from the children is that children seem to be more aware of, or attach more significances to, the social aspects of classroom organization than do teachers. To the extent that the teacher's thinking about seating is oversimple (i. e., oriented almost exclusively toward control of disruptive behavior) or determined by his personal needs, *it is almost impossible for him ever to recognize that his pupils view seating differently.* That seating may not be high in the hierarchy of important problems facing a teacher requires no discussion, but this should not obscure the fact that in small as well as large problems two things are decisive: how one formulates the problem and, equally important, how one structures the situation so that the problem can be reformulated on the basis of new information provided by

6 *Ibid.*

others. The relatively unimportant problem of seating contains within it all the constitutional issues raised earlier.

THE TEACHER AS A THINKING MODEL

Thus far in this chapter I have been, in one or another way, raising a descriptive type of question: What and how much do children know about what a teacher thinks? It is inevitable that children will know something about how a teacher thinks, how much depending on the teacher. I have never heard anyone argue that a teacher is not a model for children of how one should think and act. It is not a matter of *should* a teacher be a model but rather that he *is* a model. But the fact that he is a model of a particular kind and degree very definitely involves a variety of "shoulds," such as what children should learn, what a teacher should do, and so on. The point I wish to emphasize is that it appears that children know relatively little about how a teacher thinks about the classroom, that is, what he takes into account, the alternatives he thinks about, the things that puzzle him about children and about learning, what he does when he is not sure of what he should do, how he feels when he does something wrong — there is quite a bit that goes on in a teacher's head that is never made public to children. Well, someone can ask, are you advocating that teachers act like patients on an analyst's couch and give forth with all that is inside them? Obviously not, in addition to which I am not advocating *anything*. I am merely pointing out that whatever the degree to which teachers make their thinking public inevitably reflects the kind of "thinking model" to which they adhere. Put in another way, it reflects a conception of what is helpful to children. How does one decide what is helpful? For example, if it were true that how a teacher thinks about the classroom is something about which children are curious, is it helpful *not* to satisfy this curiosity? Is there any reason to believe that it is helpful to children to know how a teacher thinks? Unfortunately, we do not have a truly firm foundation for answering the question. However, there is a good deal of anecdotal evidence strongly indicating that the more a teacher can make his own thinking public and

subject for discussion — in the same way one expects of children — the more interesting and stimulating does the classroom
become for students, and I assume that is a helpful state of affairs. Phillip Booth (1969) put it beautifully in a review of a
book by the teacher and poet, Mark Van Doren: "His unique
genius as a teacher was to speculate publicly; in opening the
play of his mind to students, he gave each student a self-assigned
role in resolving these questions his teaching dramatized." I
would be quite surprised if Professor Van Doren's "unique genius" was not in some measure a reflection of a clear conception
of what would be helpful to his students.

The issue I am raising is well illustrated in the research
endeavor. If one reads professional research journals, it is easy to
gain the impression that research is conducted by rational people
in rational, planned ways. In the modal research paper one finds
hypotheses that are related to or stem from a theory, defined procedures, results, and then a discussion section in which one explains why things happened as they did. As often as not (probably
more often than not) the discussion section is an implicit tribute
to the researcher's ability to predict. It is hard for the reader, particularly if he himself is not a researcher, to avoid concluding that
research is a cold, cut-and-dried set of logically related cognitive
processes in which the personal and subjective are not allowed to
intrude. That this is a partially true but horribly misleading model
of how a researcher thinks and acts is something that researchers
themselves well know (e.g., Taylor, ed., 1959; Watson, 1968). Graduate students who are being introduced to the research endeavor
frequently suffer trauma when it dawns on them that published
research is a most inadequate and incomplete representation of
how the researcher thinks. The public and private model are far
from congruent. *What I have tried to indicate in this section is
that the modal teacher in the modal classroom presents a "model
of thinking" to students that is as unrepresentative of his thinking
as a published piece of research is of its author's thinking.* It may
be that the similarity does not end there. I would venture the
opinion that the similarity between teacher and researcher rests,
among other factors, on their implicit belief that their audience
would not be interested in or would not comprehend a more realistic presentation of their thinking. If my experience with school
children — in fact, with all levels of students, from elementary

through graduate school — is any guide, that large part of a teacher's "thinking about thinking," which is never made public, is precisely what the children are interested in and excited by on those rare occasions when it becomes public.

THE PREPOTENT RESPONSE
TO MISBEHAVIOR

No discussion of how teachers think can long avoid the problem of discipline. Particularly in the case of the new teacher, nothing rivals discipline as a problem (Sarason, Davidson, and Blatt, 1962). It is interesting to note that in our observational study of the first month of six classrooms, discipline as a problem in group living was never discussed. Most teachers made clear what was good and bad behavior — what the characteristics were of crime in the classroom — but these were not discussions.

We might begin by asking the following question: What is a teacher's prepotent response to a child's misbehavior? The answer is rather clear: the teacher reprimands the child in one way or another, that is, she tells him (many times gently and nonpunitively) that what he is doing is wrong. The more serious the infraction, or if it involves a child with a notable classroom criminal record, the stronger the teacher's response and the harsher the punishment. This is all very obvious. What is not so obvious is the content of the thinking that gives rise to this type of prepotent response. I say this because when on scores of occasions I have asked teachers to explain to me the justification for the prepotent response, they have been puzzled by the question. From their standpoint the answer is obvious and not necessary to justify: if a child does something wrong, you tell him so that he will then do the right thing. If I then ask why it does not always work, the answer is almost always in terms of characteristics of the child.[7] (The "theory" is correct but the child does not know that!)

[7] The experiences I shall be relating here are based on those contacts with teachers who asked to see me about a misbehaving child. In almost all classrooms there is at least one child who is a chronic misbehaver, although teachers vary markedly in seeking help with these children. The frequency of such children is quite high in inner-city schools where I have spent most of my time, and it was my experiences in these schools that forcibly brought to my attention the significance of the prepotent response to misbehavior.

One teacher (in a suburban school) had been discussing with me a particularly troublesome boy. I said that I would be back in three days to see how things were going. When I returned the teacher gleefully said, "I am not superstitious but I don't want to say anything. He has been absolutely no problem for the last two days." I then said to the teacher, "Have you told *him* how pleased you are at how well he is doing?" His facial expression was sufficient to tell me that it did not occur to him to reward the child. His theory was explicit about when one punishes, but not about when one rewards. One might say that the principle underlying his thinking was: you let well enough alone until well enough becomes bad enough.

Wherein was the approach to this troublesome boy different from that of the teacher's? Let me paraphrase what I said to this teacher, although this summary should not be viewed as a cookbook recipe:

What you are doing with this boy is not working. We do not know why it is not working and we really don't have the time to find out why. The longer this continues the worse for you and the boy. What about trying this: tomorrow morning before school opens get this kid alone and tell him that you are quite aware that your way of trying to help him in regard to misbehavior is not working. He knows it and you know it. What he may not know is that you are puzzled and bothered. You do not enjoy punishing him, although that may be hard for him to believe. You have two questions to put to him. The first is what ideas does he have about how you can help him. The second is what does he think about this: from this point on when he misbehaves the two of you are going to leave the room and the two of you are going to discuss what had just happened and why, and how it could have been avoided. This does not mean that you are throwing punishment out of the window. You will have to punish, much as you, the two of you, may not like it, but that is less important than figuring out ways in which you can help him avoid trouble and that is what you are most interested in.[8]

It is not easy, nor is it our present task, to explicate the thinking from which the above is or can be derived. That it is different than what underlies the prepotent response is obvious. The reader may have noted that one of the differences reflects the content

[8] I must emphasize to the reader that this is a paraphrase and has to be viewed in the context of a relationship of weeks with this teacher in his classroom. What I presented above was not for the purposes of describing a procedure but, simply, a way of thinking.

of the discussion in the previous section, that is, *the teacher makes public what and how he thinks about a problem*. A related difference, of course, is that *one assumes that children are really interested in what goes on in a teacher's head, particularly as that does or will affect children*. There is much more to it than these differences. The important point is that the prepotent response, which is so typical an aspect of life in the classroom, reflects only one way one could think about the problem.[9]

Let me now turn to two related questions I have asked teachers: is there something about children that makes them *completely* unable to participate in discussion and formulation of crime and punishment in the classroom? Please note that I italicized "completely" because I have never seen a classroom (although I am sure they exist) in which children participated in such discussion and formulation — and we are back, of course, to the constitutional issue. The second question: assuming that they are incapable, is it also true that they do not think about or are not concerned about crime and punishment in the classroom? To say they are completely unable is at least unjustified and at worst sheer ignorance of what children do outside of school in their spontaneous play groups. One does not need the support of formal research to assert that children in their relationships to each other have some concept of fairness — one needs only good eyes and ears.

[9]The work of Kounin, Gump, and their colleagues (Gump and Kounin, 1959; Kounin, Gump, and Ryan, 1961; Kounin, Friesen, and Norton, 1966; Kounin, 1967), based on their research on the classroom management of deviant behavior, represents what I consider to be a productive and relevant approach to a theory of instruction, more so than the efforts of Bruner and Jones (see page 179). Kounin (1967) has put it well: ". . . the management of behavior in classrooms is not a function of the techniques of directly controlling behavior as such — that is, discipline or desist style. Rather, it is a function of the techniques of creating an effective classroom ecology. Nor is it a simple issue of admonishing teachers that 'prevention is better than cure,' or 'create rapport,' or 'make it interesting.' Nor is it an evasive preoccupation with 'personality' or the listing of boy scout type characteristics. Nor is it a simple extrapolation from other adult-child relationships — whether these be parents or professional psychotherapists. Nor is it solely a matter of understanding and knowing how to handle an individual child to the exclusion of the group. Rather, the business of running a classroom is a complicated technology having to do with developing a nonsatiating learning program, initiating and maintaining group and individual movement, aiming teacher actions at appropriate targets, and still others yet to be determined. And may I add my belief in the potential value of receptive, naturalistic, ecological researches in arriving at a knowledge of what these dimensions are or might be."

The fact of the matter is that the great bulk of teachers assert (1) that children are not completely unable and (2) that children do think about crime and punishment in the classroom. *Whatever thinking allows teachers to make these positive assertions is not reflected in what they do, or, more specifically, in the justification of the prepotent response.*

There is another way of looking at the prepotent response, and the thinking surrounding it, and that is that it reflects an individual psychology. That is to say, when a teacher thinks about misbehavior he thinks primarily in terms of individual children. When he thinks about action he also tends to think about action in relation to individual children. Although the teacher is quite aware that there is a group of children, this plays far less of a role in his thinking and action than one might think. When we discussed Schwebel's study of seating we saw that teachers arrange seating patterns primarily for purposes of "control," patterns based explicitly on the assumption that one kind of child can influence another kind of child, that is, interrelationships within the group are presumed to be important. By and large, however, teachers do not think in terms of how a group can be organized and utilized so that as a group it plays a role in relation to the issues and problems that confront the group. Since this statement may be misinterpreted, I should be blatantly clear that I am not suggesting that children should run a classroom. All that I intend by that statement is what teachers themselves have asserted to the two questions I put to them. If these assertions were to be taken seriously, it would mean that one would have to think in terms of theories of groups, group processes, the relation of the leader (teacher) to the group, and the role of, as well as the phenomenology of, leadership. This is not to say that one scraps one type of psychology for another. They both have their places. It is the case, however, that in their training teachers have been exposed, almost exclusively, to a psychology of learning that has one past and one present characteristic: the latter is its emphasis on how an individual organism learns, and the former is that the major learning theories were based on studies of the individual Norway rat. If instead of putting one rat in the maze they had put two or more in the maze, the history of American psychology would have been quite different. Conceivably, the social nature of learning might not need to be rediscovered.

To illustrate further what I mean let us take the following problem which a number of first and second grade teachers have presented to me. The problem involves what to do about the dependent, crying, anxious, clinging child.[10] In a number of instances and on the basis of my observations in the classroom, I suggested to the teacher that when the child acts in this way she pick him up, cuddle and soothe, reassure him that she would do whatever she could to help, and try to find out about what he was afraid or thinking. A number of teachers responded by saying that they had thought of doing that but *if they did it with one child other children would want similar treatment.*

SBS: It is my impression that the rest of the class recognizes that Jimmy is different than they are. They seem fully to recognize that he is the only one who behaves in this way. What is your impression?

Teacher: I am sure that's true. In fact some of them have asked why Jimmy cries. And some of them try to soothe him.

SBS: But what if you were to do as I suggest and other children then ask for the same treatment — and I have no doubt that many of them would like the same treatment from you. How might you handle it?

Teacher: That's what I am afraid of — I don't know.

SBS: Well, one thing you could do is to tell the class that when anybody feels and acts like Jimmy, and that means they are unhappy and need help, you would do for them what you do for Jimmy. Do you think that if you took this up with the class, they would not understand what you were saying or how you expect them to cooperate? You seem to feel that they would take — they want to take — advantage of you.

Teacher: That's not true. I am sure they would understand. Maybe there's one who would put on an act!

SBS: You mean that you think the children are perceptive, that they would understand, and they would abide by the responsibility you are implicitly placing on them?

Teacher: I guess so.

SBS: But that means, doesn't it, that you have to present the problem to them, your way of thinking about it, your questions and hesitations, and solicit their thoughts both about what ought to be and what their responsibility should be?

[10] This problem rarely was presented to me in suburban schools. It was a very frequent problem in inner-city schools.

The point is that when one begins to think in this way one is involved in problems of group process; one is not only involved with a Jimmy, or untested assumptions about what a group of children are and can become, or imagined consequences, but with a process that is deliberately public, involves obligations and responsibilities, and deals with issues of interest and concern to all. It is not a simple process and requires a way of thinking to which teachers are not exposed. It requires one other thing that was well put by one teacher who, with a glint in her eyes, said: "You mean we should treat children the way *we* like to be treated?"

A final word about the prepotent responses to misbehavior. I have by now asked hundreds of teachers the following two questions. "How many times in the last month have you, aside from the report card, made it your business to communicate to parents that their child was not doing well, or he was misbehaving, or one or another kind of problem?" I never kept an accurate count but I would guess that 25 percent of the teachers indicated that they had gone out of their way to contact parents about a child's problem. The second question was, "How many times in the last month have you, aside from the report card, made it your business to communicate to parents that their child was doing well, or very well, or very much better than previously?" At most, 1 percent of the teachers indicated that they had initiated such a contact.

THE GOALS OF CHANGE IN THE CLASSROOM

One does not have to document the statement that there are many people, both from within and without schools, who feel that the quality of life and learning in the classroom needs to be changed. The goals of change vary in their scope and phraseology, for example, the classroom should be more child-centered, it should be more democratically organized and run, it should be more relevant to the world that children do and will live in, teachers should be more creative, and so on. A basic assumption in these statements of virtue is that the teacher will be the agent of change; the teacher will possess that way of thinking, as well as appropriately derived procedures and tactics, that will bring about the desired kind of classroom life. It is rare, indeed, to find in these discussions serious consideration of the consequences of this basic assumption for the change process. That is to say, there is a remarkable blindness to the fact that one is confronted with the extremely difficult problem of how one changes how people think. This is all the more strange when one recognizes that underlying the different criticisms of classroom life is the more basic criticism that one does not agree with how the modal teacher thinks.

The more I have read about and personally observed efforts to introduce change in the classroom the more clear several things have become. First, those who attempt to introduce a change rarely, if ever, begin the process by being clear as to where the teachers *are*, that is, how and why they think as they do. In short, they are guilty of the very criticism they make of teachers: *not being sensitive to what and how and why children think as they do.* As a result, teachers react in much the same way that many children do and that is with the feeling they are both wrong and stupid (Holt, 1964). Second, those who attempt to introduce a change seem unaware that they are asking teachers to unlearn and learn. Third, if there is any one principle common to efforts at change, it is that one effects change by *telling* people what is the "right" way to act and think. *Here, too, those who want change do exactly that for which they criticize teachers.*

The main purpose of this chapter has been to obtain glimpses of how the modal teacher thinks and how this determines, in large part, life in the classroom. Put in another way: the overt regularities that can be discerned in the classroom reflect covert principles and theories. If we wish to change the overt regularities, we have as our first task to become clear about the covert principles and theories: those assumptions and conceptions that are so overlearned that one no longer questions or thinks about them. They are "second nature," so to speak. If these assumptions and conceptions remain unverbalized and unquestioned, which is to say that thinking does not change, the likelihood that any of the overt regularities one wants to change will in fact change is drastically reduced. It would all be so simple if one could legislate changes in thinking.

It is likely that some readers will use the contents of this chapter as grist for their internal mill of prejudice and snobbery. It is not difficult, if one is so disposed, to feel superior to teachers — and many university critics (and others) are so disposed. This would not be worthy of comment were it not for two facts: many university critics spearhead the change process, and, as anyone familiar with the history of anthropology knows, the feeling of superiority ("bringing culture to the primitives") is lethal for the process of understanding and change.

My former colleague, Dr. Murray Levine, developed a concept on the basis of his intensive work with teachers in inner-city schools.

THE CHILD COMES BY HIS PROBLEM HONESTLY

From the point of view of the teacher who is concerned about teaching a large group of children any child who presents special difficulties is a nuisance. As long as education is defined in terms of the preparation and presentation of material to children, the teacher's first inclination, when faced with a difficult child, is to experience the child as trouble. Finding her own efforts frustrated or finding that she must divide her attention in more ways than she feels capable of doing, the teacher frequently feels angered and resentful of a child who demands something different by virtue of his behavior. She may also feel anxious because her image of herself as a competent professional person is threatened. Although we are taught that human behavior stems from sufficient causes, in the classroom situation the teacher is not always able or prepared to seek causes. Understandably, from her viewpoint, the child is at fault for acting as he does, and it is her feeling that both she and the child would be better off if the child were away from her. Sometimes the consultant can serve an important function by helping the teacher to see that the problem has a background. When the teacher sees that a child does come by his problems honestly, so to speak, her tolerance for the problem and her willingness to make the effort to work with the child are sometimes increased.[11]

Dr. Levine gives case examples of how the thinking and actions of teachers changed in relation to certain children once they understood that indeed they come by their problems honestly, which is another way of saying that the teacher understood the child in *his* terms and life experience. If we believe teachers have problems, and they do, we will not get very far in helping them if we do not understand that they come by their problems quite honestly.

[11]S. B. Sarason et al, *Psychology in Community Settings* (New York: John Wiley & Sons, Inc., 1966).

⌒12⌒

The Dewey School

Whenever I have discussed a characteristic of the school culture — be it a way of thinking or doing things — I have tried to contrast what is with what could be. I have not done this because I think that "what is" necessarily is without merit, or what could be is not without its problems. However I might feel about the alternatives to the modal way of thinking and acting in the school culture, the main purpose of my tactic was to demonstrate that in order to understand things as they are it is necessary to be aware of the universe of alternatives from which one could choose a way of thinking or a course of action. The other purpose of this tactic was to suggest how inordinately difficult it is to become and remain aware that there is a universe of alternatives to what one does and how one thinks.

Consistent with these purposes I shall in this chapter describe a school that can be because, in fact, it used to be. I am referring to the school that John Dewey started and directed at the University of Chicago. It existed during the years 1896 to 1904. Basically, this chapter is an inadequate summary and discussion of a most unusual book "The Dewey School" by Mayhew and Edwards (1965), who were intimate participants in the school. The book was originally published in 1936, although it is largely based on records and documents written during the existence of the school. The original manuscript was too large for publication and all chapters had to be reduced in size. The book is still 489 pages in length and is probably one of the most comprehensive descriptions of a school that has ever been written. That it defies easy summary is as much due to the completeness with which Dewey's ideas are presented, and their relation to actual practice demonstrated, as it is to the detailed descriptions of classroom activities. The reader is urged to consult this important document.

No one, critic or otherwise, has denied that John Dewey was a great thinker. It is impossible, of course, to deny that he was a prolific writer. Unfortunately, as the years go by it seems that fewer and fewer people read Dewey, although it is likely that more and more people read about what other people say or think about Dewey. The Mayhew and Edwards book artistically blends what Dewey said and helped to do in relation to education. There is, of course, the problem of the degree to which the description of the culture of the Dewey school is distorted by the fact that authors (who wrote in close consultation with Dewey) were obviously partisan. I raise this problem not only because it is valid and important, but in order to emphasize that nonpartisan description of what goes on in a classroom or school, which meets the requirements of reliability of observation, is amazingly scarce — and it was recognition of this that in part led me in earlier chapters to try to think like a man from outer space. [1] At the very least, the comprehensiveness of the Mayhew and Edwards book leaves one with far less of a feeling that one does not know what "really" went on than is the case with any other descriptive document in education of which I am aware. Another relevant consideration, about which the reader will have to make a judgment for himself, is how refreshingly candid the

[1] I regard, of course, the tactic of the man from outer space as no more than a personal gimmick for reminding me that in the normal course of living it is extraordinarily difficult impersonally to observe the external world and to determine overt patterns of social interaction. We are so caught with what goes on in our own as well as the minds of others that we are usually unable to become aware that the presumed overt consequences of our thinking frequently have a structure quite different from what we think or intend. Roger Barker, whose work I briefly discussed in Chapter 7, is the only one in American psychology who has seriously devoted himself to conceptualizing settings and developing an appropriate methodology for getting at the structure of environments. It is not that Barker is uninterested in what goes on in the minds of people — far from it — but rather in having a better basis for understanding how internal and external structure (the internal stream of behavior and the external structure of settings) can be related.

writers are about their doubts and uncertainties, particularly in the first three years, and their mistakes and failures.

In what follows I have focused on those aspects of the account that I consider to be most relevant to the issues and problems I raised in the previous chapters.

THE PRINCIPAL

John Dewey was the principal of the school regardless of whatever other titles he may have had. The significance of this is that he was a man who had a body of ideas about what life in a classroom and school should be. There was no question in his mind that his major role was to wed theory and practice, and it was not enough for theory and practice to exchange verbal vows and then, as he well knew was too often the case, lead what was essentially a divorced existence. His tasks were not only administrative but intellectual as well. He did not look upon a school as a place where only children learned and grew, but a place where children, teachers, parents, and the principal learned and grew. School was not a place where skills were mechanically learned and the predigested and crystallized wisdom of the ages poured into empty mental receptacles. It was not a place where what was learned was determined primarily by age or the calendar. School was about thought and action, ideas and their consequences, classroom and home, school and society, the past in the present, and the nature of group living. School was not preparation for life — it was life. Life in a school should be orderly, but that was not the same as saying it was predictable. Individuals learn but always in a social context.

These are, of course, noble thoughts and laudable goals. Let us now see what the principal did.

1. Dewey met weekly with the teacher "in which the work of the prior week was gone over in light of the general plan, and in which teachers reported the difficulties met in carrying it out. Modifications and adaptations followed. Discussion in these meetings was a large means in translating generalities about aims and subject matter into definite form." These meetings were not about "administrative matters" but about ideas, their implementation, success and failure. The meet-

ings were not a platform for Dewey to lecture but a vehicle for discussion of individual children. "Those who have attended discussions among parents and teachers will readily understand that there was a tendency for these meetings to devote too much time and attention to the peculiarities and difficulties of individual children. In theory, the reports on individual children were supposed to connect with the principles involved in adjustment of subject-matter to their needs and the cooperative adjustment of children to one another in the social give and take of daily life. In fact, the younger and less experienced teachers, who served as assistants, often failed to see this connection and were inclined to be impatient with the personal phase of the discussion when it concerned children they did not have to deal with. Experience showed that "principles" were too much taken for granted as being already understood by all teachers; in the later years an increasing number of meetings were allotted to the specific discussion of underlying principles and aims. Later results would have undoubtedly improved had there been more such meetings as were held in the earlier years. In these earlier years fellows and members of the faculty of the pedagogical department, graduate-student assistants, and the regular teaching staff of the school all met weekly with the directors to discuss the reports of the school in relation to theoretical principles and to revise future plans accordingly." It is obvious that this principal was as interested in the minds of teachers as in those of children.

2. "Cooperative social organization applied to the teaching body of the school as well as to the pupils. *Indeed it could not apply to the latter unless it had first taken effect with the former.*" (Italics mine) It was the principal's task to create those conditions which would be the antithesis of "teaching is a lonely profession." What comes through in the description, casually and almost incidentally, is the degree of hourly and daily interaction among teachers. It was, however, not casual thinking on Dewey's part when he recommended that elementary school teachers should have the same power and freedom *and salary* that high school and university teachers had. "Primary teachers should have the same power, the same freedom (and the same pecuniary recompense that now goes to university and, in less measure, to high-school teachers). Persons selected on the basis of their ability to respond to the needs of an educational situation and to cooperate socially and intellectually with others develop ability to work out and organize subject-matter and methods. Our "higher" education will not be really higher until elementary teachers have the same right and power to select and organize proper subject-matter, and invent and use their own methods as is now accorded in some degree to teachers of older students. In recollection of many things in our school practice and results that I could wish had been otherwise, there is compensation in the proof our experience af-

fords that the union of intellectual freedom and cooperation will develop the spirit that is prized in university teachers, and that is sometime mistakenly supposed to be a monopoly of theirs." Just as it would have been impossible for Dewey to accept ideas prepackaged by others, he did not view teachers as the transmitters of his or someone else's "curriculum." Teachers were colleagues who should not be told what to do. He presented and defended his own ideas and he expected teachers to do the same.

3. Dewey was an investigator and when the school was enlarged and put on a departmental basis he chose directors who were also investigators. Each director weekly furnished reports containing "data of the problems for study and discussion in the weekly informal conference of teachers, as well as in the more formal seminar groups and larger pedagogical club meetings."

4. Dewey considered informal interchange among teachers to be an essential characteristic of the culture of the school. Teachers had free periods in order to visit and advise *with* other groups and teachers. The function of the free period was not a respite from a wearying task but a stimulus to intellectual exchange.

5. A parent association was formed and it was expected that they would be concerned with educational issues. The association had an educational committee to which parents came with their criticisms and suggestions and "in quiet consultations with the teachers was often able to correct a bad habit formed in a teacher or, by revealing a teacher's plan to the parent, remove his objections and reconcile him to the particular method in question." In order better to inform the parents with the purposes of the school "a class was formed, open to all members of the association, in which the principles of the school were taught."[2]

For Dewey, parental involvement or "community participation" was a necessity dictated by theory and not political considerations, and precisely because it was so dictated, issues of professional preciousness and boundaries were, if present, certainly not thorny.

If anything can be concluded from what has been written about the school, it is that its principal needed to know what was going on in the classroom, in the minds of teachers and parents, and in the quality of human relationships. To him school was

[2] Quotes from *The Dewey School,* the Laboratory School of the University of Chicago, 1896-1903, Introduction by John Dewey. By Katherine Camp Mayhew and Anna Camp Edwards. Copyright, 1936, 1964, Meredith Corporation. Reprinted by permission of Appleton-Century-Crofts.

a place in which his own need to learn and change could be satisfied. Like the children he was a student.

At one point in their report Mayhew and Edwards (page 373) state: "Unhurried and unhampered as it was by arbitrary requirements imposed from above or by irritating delays in getting necessary equipment or material, the school in three years grew from fifteen to one hundred and twenty-five children. . . ."[3] This, I think, is a misleading statement. It is probably a true statement if by "unhurried and unhampered" Mayhew and Edwards are reflecting the views of the school staff. If this is true it was only because Dewey protected his school against the system in which he and the school were embedded. A quick reading of the latter half of Mayhew and Edwards' chapter on general history would be enough to dispel the notion that Dewey did not have to tangle with a variety of settings and people, both within and without the university. Dewey cherished his ideas and school too much to allow himself to be passive to numerous outside efforts that would have adversely affected the culture of the school.

As a principal Dewey led and inspired people, and not only "his own people." During his tenure at the University of Chicago it probably had as great (and perhaps greater) a group of eminent scientists and scholars as had ever been assembled in one place in this country. He was able actively to involve many of them in the school to a degree that has never been approximated.

THE TEACHER

In describing Dewey as a principal we said much about the teacher. The teacher was not an isolated individual alone with her children and problems.

> . . . There was daily and hourly exchange of results of classroom experience; a certain child was ailing and needed rest; another was inhibited by shyness and needed encouragement; certain subject-matter was going well or ill with certain groups; or a science teacher would suggest to the one in charge of number work that the children of a group were ready to mark the Fahrenheit and

[3] *Ibid.*

Centigrade scale divisions on their thermometers, then in the making in shop and laboratory. Accordingly, this topic would be taken up for work in number as opportunity presented.

Great flexibility of organization was necessary for the working out of so complicated a program of activities. This was made possible only by the willingness of the teachers to assume, when need arose, extra responsibilities to meet emergencies. In addition to the informal interchange between the teachers, there was, as already stated, the weekly meeting with Mr. Dewey and later with Mrs. Young and Mrs. Dewey present. As the school and staff of teachers grew larger, this meeting assumed more formality.[4]

It is impossible to summarize descriptions of the teacher in the classroom without losing a good deal of the feel of what went on. Hopefully the quotes below will convey some feeling for what went on:

. . . With all the younger classes, the first few minutes of each recitation were spent in a kind of council meeting with the teacher, picking up the threads of the previous period, planning and assigning the work of the present hour. The children developed their own impersonal methods of distributing important privileges, assigning the waiter at luncheon or the leader of the class for the day, etc., by alphabetical order.[5] The leader's responsibility entailed considerable independence of the teacher in following out the daily program. This was often complicated by unexpected changes of room and teachers. In this way any child who, as leader, was lacking in initiative and executive ability fell naturally into the position of one who must develop both through his own effort and without any insistence from the teacher. In like manner, the naturally executive child, instead of spending all his energy in running the school, as sometimes happens in schools of this freer type, could put it into better planning of his work and forwarding of his skill in techniques.

This method in classroom work, the result of the cooperative efforts of teachers and children, had the merit of enlisting the interest and effort of the child both in planning for the activity and in its execution. In this process of directing a self-initiated

---

[4] *Ibid.*

[5] About the age of twelve or thirteen the children voluntarily discarded the custom of following a leader and wished to be allowed to report to their classes as individuals. In case of unavoidable delay on the part of the teachers, the classes of all ages, even the youngest, put themselves to work under the direction of a leader.

activity great care was necessary to allow the child freedom to discriminate and select material according to his own idea of its purpose in what he was going to do. For example, in his pottery making, it was desirable that the form of the bowl he was making should be determined by him according to the use that he was to make of it and not according to a pattern set for him by another. His bowl completed and proven useful for *the purpose* which he had foreseen, he was asked to use it, and his difficulty in so doing became his new problem. This recalled to his mind the form of a pitcher so that he himself planned and made up the appropriate lip on the jar, thus carrying his activity forward. In this way the child gained the method of thinking and planning before doing. The stimulation of a successful accomplishment was the motive for his next act. He became, in this particular instance, conscious that shape was related to the function of use. He formed an image, in advance, of the shape of the jar he must have for the use he wished to make of it and perceived that its use should determine its shape.

This illustrates how general ideas reached the child through the teacher by means of her foresight, wise direction, or suggestion at the right moment. Always bearing in mind that the activity of the child must be self-initiated, the teacher's responsibility was to provide necessary materials and instruction in the technical skills sought by the child to attain his desired ends. There was also need to remember that there is a stage of growth when it is natural for children to acquire their techniques of construction, communication, and measurement easily and with a degree of pleasure, and that activities which were graded and adapted to a child's growing power stimulated his feeling of need and progressively increased his measure of ability. The resulting sense of satisfaction and clearer vision of achievement opened his eyes to the extension of his activity.

THE USE OF RECORDS

In the meantime, making records was a necessary part of the classroom process. This, however, was not used to stimulate a child's interest in learning to write. He was, instead, helped with the mechanics of making the record sufficiently to hold his interest in the process. It was found to be good practice, particularly with the younger children, in the council meeting at either the beginning or end of the period, for the teacher to write at dictation the children's story of the work of the hour. This story was arranged and used at the next period as a reading lesson for review. The children, seeing their own experience made lasting and useful to them and others by the written form, gradually awoke to an appreciation of its use. They were interested by skillful suggestion to find that other people had had the same experience and had written it. The desire to read for themselves was often born in children out of the idea that they might find better ways of doing and thus get more satisfactory results. With this interest as an urge, the child himself often freely set his attention to learning to read. A natural need thus became the stimulus to the gaining of skill in the use of a tool.

In such a process, unconscious to him and psychologically right because indirect, the child learns his techniques of reading, writing, and measurement as a means to a desired and immediate end of his own conceiving, and not as something he must learn because he will need it sometime, somewhere, for a purpose utterly unimportant to him. Furthermore, by using his skills to extend his ability to plan and execute his activity, he integrates his experience and furthers his growth.

REALIZATION OF THEORY
IN CLASSROOM METHOD

Too much emphasis cannot be laid on the constant and intelligent attempts to put into classroom use, and thereby test, the theory of the school. The success or failure of these attempts occupied to a great extent the weekly teachers' meetings and was the subject of the informal daily discussion that always went on between the teachers in hallways and on the way to and from classrooms. Judgment as to whether there was a right learning condition in the classroom was often based on the attitude (poised and happy, or nervous and irritable) of the child as he went to the next class. A quiet and contented attitude was considered an indication of satisfaction of desire arising from the successful accomplishment of a planned end. Such an attitude also indicated that the teacher was fulfilling her function. Although the immediate decision with regard to treatment of subject-matter and method was left to the individual teacher, each teacher's method was so checked and rechecked by cooperative discussion of results and effect on the children, that changes in viewpoint continually took place. Therefore, teachers and children, administrators and parents, as a result of sharing in the same social process, shared also in the educational benefits therefrom.

Mr. Dewey emphasized to all of us the importance of not looking for material results, but to observe carefully the effect of the processes upon the minds, not only of those who were to be "taught," but upon those who were the "teachers" or leaders. The emphasis upon the necessity of *participation* in the educational process and the equally strong and important fact that education is not a state but a process made us look upon this experimental school as something which had a working hypothesis worthy of careful consideration. . . .[6]

Over the years the word "permissive" has been used, and in a pejorative way, to characterize the classroom in the Dewey school. One can even collect jokes about the permissive teacher zealously refraining from suggesting anything to children who wander aimlessly and anxiously seeking direction from somebody. This is as ridiculously untrue about the relation between children and teacher in the Dewey school as it would be of the relation between Dewey and the teacher, *and in Dewey's thinking and theory there were no differences between the two types of relationships.* Dewey and his teachers did not confuse sensitivity to what a child thought and desired with indulging them. They did not view leading or stimulating them, or making suggestions, as forms of intellectual poison. In his foreword to the Mayhew and Edwards book, Archambault puts it well:

It is difficult indeed to see how that theory could continue to be so grossly misinterpreted if critics would read the careful descriptions of policy, curriculum, and method that we find here. It can easily be seen that the cliches characterizing the typical criticisms of Dewey's educational thought are grossly inaccurate. The school is seen to be far from "permissive," for the role of the teacher as a responsible agent is clearly defined. The school is not "child-centered," but rather "society-centered," constantly focusing as it does on social life and social occupations. The school is not "directionless." One of the most valuable aspects of this book is its description of the ways in which the notion of growth as an educational end is manifested in school practice. The reader is constantly struck by the postulation of flexible but definite aims and these aims are stated in terms of clearly discernible skills and attitudes. This attention to concrete detail is characteristic of the entire volume and as a result we have a thorough description of the role of the teacher, the principles of scientific method trans-

[6] Mayhew and Edwards, *op. cit.*

lated into concrete pedagogical principles, and the revolutionary Deweyan concept of discipline.[7]

Dewey explicitly recognized that his school had been far from a total success, and in the very brief description I have given I did not intend to describe an educational heaven. There were three purposes to what I presented. First, I wanted to demonstrate the obvious: there was a way of thinking about what a school can be that is in marked contrast to the thinking underlying what the modal school has been and still is.[8] Second, I wanted to bring to the reader's attention a setting in which this thinking was translated into actions and organization that, on the basis of all available evidence, were dramatically different from what went on, and still go on, in our schools. Third, and related to the second, this integration of theory and practice involved and necessitated principal, teachers, parents, and children in social and intellectual relationships that were and are atypical of schools. (How many of

[7] *Ibid.*

[8] Roush (1969) has made the same point in a paper ("What will become of the past?") concerned with the role and teaching of the humanities in our colleges and universities. Explicitly recognizing his debt to Dewey he goes on to ask some Dewey-like questions: "In short, to take such a theory seriously, one would be forced to ask radical questions about the way matters are normally handled now. I am in love with Chaucer, and love, I know, is a fine thing. I never had much trouble with the question: "Why do I read Chaucer?" Why do I cherish my family or eat oranges? But I have had difficulty answering the question: "Why do I teach Chaucer?" What, in fact, does it mean to say: "I teach Chaucer?" Does it mean simply to be a matchmaker, to bring Chaucer to students so that they, too, can fall in love with him? To be a matchmaker in that way is no small accomplishment, perhaps, *but why Chaucer?* There are any number of attachments students could form, and who am I to say that they should spend their time falling in love with Chaucer rather than Shakespeare or biophysics or dogs or one another? Such loves are sometimes mutually exclusive. The question makes sense only in the present context of the American academy, where *to teach* usually means to act like an inviolable expert whose task is to put his students through his paces. Assuming that definition of teaching, let me rephrase my question: What *right* do I have to teach Chaucer? What right do I have to tell adults past the age of consent what they should know or whom they should love? I refuse to accept the notion that I have the right because Chaucer is good, or because I know more than my students, or because they will be grateful to me subsequently. If I want to work within a dialectical tradition, there seem to be only two conditions under which I have the right to teach anyone anything: when he asks me to or when a community of which he is a member agrees that whatever I am teaching is something he should learn. On most campuses today, neither condition obtains." Roush's paper merits the adjective *seminal.*

those who currently talk of community and neighborhood participation and control of schools, of the need for a more "relevant"
curriculum, of the insidiousness of professional preciousness and
boundaries, and of the necessity for students to have an active role
in shaping their lives in school are aware that there was a John
Dewey who thought about these things, conceptualized them in
a grand theory of the individual in society, and specifically tested
his ideas in a school that he created?)

The reader will recall from earlier chapters our man from
outer space, parked in his space platform over a school, able to see
everything but unable to comprehend speech or to deduce the
thinking of earthlings, but quite capable with his advanced computers of discerning every behavioral regularity characterizing
the inhabitants of the school: principal, children, teachers, and
parents. If that same man from outer space previously had been
parked over the Dewey school, is there strong reason to doubt that
he would have been struck by some dramatic differences between
the regularities in the two schools? There are two major significances to the discernment of behavioral regularities. The first is
that any educational rationale or theory states or implies behavioral regularities that can be observed or recorded. The rationale
or theory may involve more than this, but it must lead to behavioral regularities different than those stemming from other
rationales or theories — if it does not it is a difference in theory
that does not make a difference. The second significance is that
behavioral regularities allow one to determine the consistency
between theory and practice. As we saw in the earlier chapters,
in the case of the modal school, present or past, either it is not
clear what the underlying rationale is or there are clear grounds
for suggesting that there is an inconsistency between theory and
practice. The beauty of the Mayhew and Edwards' description is
that educational theory is spelled out in ways that make clear
which behavioral regularities one should expect and, equally
important, the extent to which their regularities may have been
discernible. One has to say "may have been discernible" because,
despite the comprehensiveness of the description and the internal
evidence that the writers and Dewey did not gloss over problems
and failures, the fact remains that the writers were partisan, unlike
our man from outer space.

AGAIN THE PRINCIPAL

In previous chapters I have maintained that life in a school — the quality of its culture — was in large part a function of its principal. Furthermore, I have maintained, the fate of efforts to introduce a meaningful change into a school was again largely (by no means completely) a function of the principal. Nowhere are these assertions better illustrated than in the relationship of Dewey to his school. [9] But, the reader may ask (as have a number of teachers): "You are not talking about principals. You are talking about *John Dewey*! How many John Deweys are there?" Unfortunately, there are very, very few John Deweys. In fact, it is my opinion that no one of his stature, scope, and depth has been on our scene and I can discern no comparable person on the emerging horizon. But the thrust of the question does not stand up under examination. If by the question is meant that only a John Dewey can lead and infuse a quality into a school, the question is not deserving of comment. If by the question is meant that only a John Dewey can integrate in his mind theory and practice, and vigorously and vigilantly oversee and pursue the

[9] Dewey probably would have been bothered by the term "his school" because of the implication that the people within it thought and did what Dewey wanted them to think and do, just as he was bothered by the practice of having teachers and children accommodate to prepackaged ideas and curricula in the development of which they had no role. There is absolutely no doubt that Dewey was the leader and that his words and thoughts were given more weight than those of others, characteristics that inhere in the position as well as in the man in the position. In numerous places in the Mayhew and Edwards book, stress is placed on the importance of recognizing that teachers did differ on numerous dimensions and that one had to take these differences into account in working with teachers. Although central to Dewey's ideas, it has been strangely difficult for many people to grasp the conception that it is possible, and indeed necessary, to guide, or lead, or stimulate a teacher or child (or any other human) without requiring that the person give up his capacity and right to work through issues and problems in his way and at his pace. To act on the basis of this conception requires, among other things, being able to tolerate risk-taking, i.e., the teacher or child may not be willing or able to grasp what is at issue and one must be prepared to wait and watch and seize the next opportunity for discussion. That is to say, one respects the other person's right to learn in his own way in the context of a relationship in which one has assumed the obligation to present and defend one's own point of view. It may well be that the difficulty people have in grasping this conception is that it is not one that gives rise to a "how-to-do-it" formula.

process of implementation throughout the school, one could answer the question in two ways. One could say that few, if any, principals could *conceptualize* the problems of theory and practice as well as Dewey but certainly that should be no barrier to the principal who aspires to grapple with and master the conceptualizations. Another way of answering the question is to point out that on the basis of the Mayhew and Edwards account, as well as Dewey's own statements, one could maintain that Dewey may have been a better conceptualizer than an implementer, and he was a good implementer. Just as Freud was a better theorist and investigator than he was a therapist — in fact, his investigative curiosity seems to have adversely affected his therapeutic skills — the same may have been true (to a lesser extent) of Dewey. Principals do not have to possess John Dewey's conceptual skills, if only because John Dewey has left them his intellectual legacy. The task of the principal is that if he takes this intellectual legacy seriously, he has taken on a task of implementation that involves him in all aspects of the school, and in many aspects of the community, in ways radically different than are now true of the modal principal. He judges himself not by the absence of problems but how problems surface and get resolved; he judges himself not only with what teachers do but in the ways they think; he judges himself not only by what teachers do in their classroom but in how they relate and utilize each other; he actively seeks the participation of parents and others in the community rather than viewing them as outsiders or irritants; he distinguishes between pride about the level of children's knowledge and pride about the quality of their thinking; and in relationships between those of differing roles (e.g., principal-teacher, student-teacher, parent-principal) he knows the difference between honest give-and-take and the intellectual and personal charade that goes with the spirit of *noblesse oblige.*

The things that Dewey did in his school are in most if not all respects capable of being done by principals today. There is nothing in the role of the principal that would prevent him from doing most of these things. As I pointed out in Chapter 9, the role of the principal is defined in terms of a minimal level of performance and not in terms of any maximal level. This is not to say, of course, that it is or would be easy, or that it can be accomplished other than over an extended period of time, or that the endeavor would not bear the characteristics of struggle and battle, or that it would fall short of the mark. To say that principals are capable of doing what Dewey did — to establish the kinds of regularities that characterized his school — requires, of course, that they think the way he did. The thinking of the modal principal is quite different from what would be required to establish the desired regularities.

The reader of the Mayhew and Edwards account would be warranted in raising still another objection: "The Dewey School had relatively few children. It was much, much smaller than any of our schools today. How much of what was accomplished there was due to smallness?" This is a deceptively legitimate question. I say "deceptively" because at the same time that it raises a legitimate question it may be interpreted as implying something that is far from true. There can be no doubt that the size of our schools today makes the problem difficult and I am not simplifying the problem, but rather stating it, when I say that what is required is imagination and a characteristic that Dewey *and his theory* had: experimentation, learning from failure, and constant inquiry. Size is a problem; it is not an excuse. I have seen a number of small schools, all of which were only somewhat larger than the Dewey school, but which were characterized by every defect usually considered a consequence of bigness.

Two of these were new city elementary schools containing eight classrooms. Their size had nothing to do with educational policy but rather with the fact that existing schools in their areas were crowded and it was concluded that an additional small school would take care of the problem. These two schools remained very small for three years but, as is frequently the case, a spanking new school acts like a magnet in attracting new residents who (understandably) confuse a new building with new ideas. Each of these schools required tripling of its size within six years. Many people, within and without the school system, complained bitterly about this growth and pointed to the many problems that these schools were encountering. The fact is that all of these problems clearly existed when the schools were small. For one of these schools it would be incorrect to say that its problems were accentuated, but rather that with the increase of educational personnel and parents who had expected a quite different situation, it was made more likely that its defects would become more public.

To attribute the accomplishments of the Dewey School to its size — to look at smallness as inevitably having virtuous consequences — is to downgrade the role of ideas and conceptions. The degree to which, and the ways in which, size is a problem depends, obviously, on how one thinks about life in a school. I have seen large schools run, in the words of some principals and their admirers, like "tight ships," which is fine if one thinks about schools the way one thinks about ships. These ships ran smoothly until, in the past two years, the crew mutinied.

To Dewey size was a problem, and he viewed bigness as destructive of what his school was and hoped to be. There is nothing in his theoretical conceptions that justifies such a degree of pessimism. There is much in his conceptions to justify the conclusion that the inquiring mind of man grappling boldly with the problems confronting him can come up with conceptions that pave the way to new courses of action — and this is what Dewey demonstrated in his own life. At a time in his life when, so to speak, he "had it made" — respect from his professional community, national stature, time for reflection and writing — he immersed himself in the world of action not because he was by temperament an activist but because the testing of his ideas required it. He learned by doing. For him "doing" was not merely an extension of thinking but a productive way of rethinking and changing.

It was not my purpose in this chapter to present the Dewey School as a past educational paradise to which we should return or which we should imitate. The Dewey School was far from a total success. My primary purpose, as indicated at the outset of this chapter, was to describe the culture of a school quite different from that in the modal school today, in order to emphasize that there are alternatives from which we can choose a way of thinking and a course of action. In describing this alternative I wanted to be able to stress that this particular school, unlike the modal school of today, did not only stem from a conception of what an individual child was like, or what groups of children were like, but more than this from a conception that school was truly a social affair in which the thinking of children, teachers, parents, and principal were inextricably related and in which each had a legitimate stake and function in determining what life in the school would be.

There is one major limitation to what Dewey thought and did and this we shall take up in the next chapter. As we shall see, it concerns the problem of change in a way that will force us to return to the theme of an earlier chapter: the modal process of change in a school.

ᴄ13ᴐ

The Problem of Change

John Dewey created a school; he did not have to change an ongoing one. The problems, theoretical and practical, in creating and maintaining a setting that is not self-defeating in nature are enormous and have been barely studied. In fact, the problems have hardly been formulated (Sarason, 1969). For almost all of those who tried to apply Dewey's ideas, particularly in relation to the public schools, the problem was how to change an ongoing school so that it would reflect these ideas.[1] There is no doubt that Dewey was quite an influence on the public school, as Cremin

[1]One of the most interesting attempts to apply Dewey's ideas to a public school setting was that by Wirt in 1906 in Gary, Indiana. It was a most serious attempt and was the object of national attention. Levine and Levine (1970) have very recently reviewed the Gary story as an instance of "the problems in innovation and in institutional change." What emerges from the Levines' account, based in part on the comprehensive evaluation of the Gary system by Flexner and Bachman (1918), is that the execution of the plan left much to be desired. That is to say, it was not at all clear what the conception of the change process was, if any conception was at all explicit in the minds of Wirt and others. There was much in the Gary project that was innovative and worthwhile. In fact, many of the ideas that powered that project are being resurrected today. Unfortunately, there is no basis for optimism that its implementation today will be any more successful. I am indebted to the Levines for bringing to my attention newspaper accounts (e.g., New York Times, October 17 and December 2, 1917) of what happened when an attempt was made to implement the Gary plan in New York City. There were *pupil riots* and community unrest and demonstrations. In fact, the October, 1917, riot account has a startling ring of modernity. The Gary and New York stories will be in center stage of a book the Levines are now writing.

(1961) has so well described, but this was an influence having many of the characteristics of more recent attempts to introduce change, that is, the *content* of curricula changed, new *activities* appeared, and what people *said and talked about* took on a different content and quality — but life in the school and classroom (in the terms we have discussed earlier) did not change very much, if at all.

Although Dewey was inordinately knowledgeable of what life in schools and classrooms was like, and he wanted this to change, he never seemed to rivet on the problem of the pitfalls and obstacles that such an attempt would inevitably encounter. He was too busy demonstrating and testing his ideas in a school of his own creation. As a result, his followers, like their modern counterparts, went forward with ideas and missionary zeal as if these were enough to accomplish their goals. Good ideas and missionary zeal are sometimes enough to change the thinking and actions of individuals; they are rarely, if ever, effective in changing complicated organizations (like the school) with traditions, dynamics, and goals of their own. To change complicated settings requires, initially at least, a way of thinking not the same as the way we think about changing individuals. What I will do in this chapter is to suggest what some of the characteristics of this way of thinking might be. I have discussed some characteristics in earlier chapters and, therefore, shall restrict myself to those I consider of equal importance but that were only alluded to or not discussed at all.

THE SCOPE OF THE CHANGE

A large percentage of proposals of change are intended to affect all or most of the schools within a system. The assumption seems to be that since the change is considered as an improvement over what exists, it should be spread as wide as possible as soon as possible. The introduction of new curricula is, of course, a clear example of this. What is so strange here is that those who initiate this degree of change are quite aware of two things: that different schools in the system can be depended on differentially to respond to or implement the proposed change, and that they, the sources,

implementers of change, do not have the time adequately to oversee this degree of change. What is strange is that awareness of
these two factors seems to be unconnected with or to have no effect
on thinking about the scope of the change. This is like a psychotherapist who, after listening to a patient present many serious
personal problems affecting his life, decides that he will attack
simultaneously all of these problems even though in another part
of his head he is quite aware that the symptoms will not be equally
vulnerable to change and that within the time he spends with the
patient it will literally be impossible to deal with all of the
symptoms.

   This is not a practical problem in the sense that its solution
requires more people, the favorite remedy for poorly diagnosed
problems. Aside from the fact that there will never be "enough"
professional personnel (Chapter 10), the justification for initiating
a change in many different places at the same time is not obvious.
My own experience and reading about past experience suggest
that far from being obvious that one should go that route, the
reverse is probably true.

   I first began to think of this problem when for a number of years
a suburban school system (consisting of seven elementary schools, one
junior and one senior high) asked me to advise them about some proposed extension of psychological services. To extend these services, and
to introduce new ones, they were prepared to hire more staff. Primarily
they were asking me to consult on the substance of their present and
proposed services. I spent two days visiting with principals, groups of
teachers, supervisory personnel, etc. Throughout most of this time I
was assuming, as were those seeking changes and new services, that all
the schools would be involved. However, I had made it clear that I felt
that the services would be spread too thin, but this reservation was not
based on a consideration that, for reasons that escape me, occurred to
me toward the end of the two-day visit, i.e., it was abundantly clear that
the schools varied considerably in their views toward new or extended
psychological services and in at least two of the schools there would be
extreme difficulty. I then asked why it was necessary to introduce the
new services in all, or even most, of the schools. Why not pick one's
spots, learn from the experience, and then take up the tactics of extension? What if the schools that were not to receive service were part of
an ongoing group to discuss and evaluate what was going on in the
·schools receiving service? It was clear that these suggestions or ways of
thinking had not occurred to people, and it is interesting, as it was predictable, that an assortment of objections were serially raised. It did not

occur to me until much later that the basic question, which was never clearly formulated, was never discussed: granted that there are problems in whichever of the two ways one proceeds, which one makes it more likely that the proposed changes and services will 'take'?

This question is important in two ways: First, it states that there is at least one alternative to the accustomed way of thinking and, in fact, implies that there are more. Second, the question exposes the inadequacy of the usual conceptionalization of the school culture in that it does not in any clear way give us a basis for choosing among alternatives. I consider it an extremely important question when we are compelled to recognize that we have no secure basis for answering it.

Let us now take a variant of the "how much how quick" question. It is a variant I have observed in three different school systems in this country, and the knowledgeable reader will know that it is occurring in many more places.

In each of these cities a top administrator in a school system and the head of the local community mental health center propose that one or two "difficult" schools will be selected into which a wide variety of services will be put: services to individual children, supportive services to teachers and principal, services to families, and, in two instances, outside educational specialists brought in on a consulting basis. I shall not here be concerned with the outcomes of these projects, which ranged from what may be termed slight success to overwhelming catastrophe, because whatever I have said in previous chapters about the modal process of change in the school culture characterized these projects, unfortunately, in particularly clear ways. My point here is a restricted one and it concerns the fact that all or most of these services, involving a fair number of people, were started pretty much at the same time in the target school or schools.

Here, too, one must ask: why all at once? Unlike our earlier example, we know enough about the single school to be able to state why one should not start all at once. The more new people who flood a school, the more questions school personnel will have about role relationships, role functions, and so on. The more "experts" who come in the more likely it is that the principal will not view himself as the principal. The greater the number of outsiders who do not know the culture of the school, the more time they have to spend in learning, and during this time the amount of help they can give is small. (Of course, if they, from the begin-ning, fall into the trap of acting as if they were knowledgeable and expert, tragedy is in the offing). A predictable response on the part of school personnel is: What are they getting paid for? One could go on and on. It is one thing to say that one should not start in this way, and it is quite another thing to be able to say just where one should start, how one phases in services, and with whom. I make the assumption that with any complicated social organization not all starting points are equally effective in leading to a widespread change in that complicated setting. I regard this statement as a glimpse of the obvious but equally obvious is the fact that it is not obvious to many others who are in the business of changing schools.

The reader may ask: Well, where *do* you start? I can answer this question in three ways and none of them will be considered satisfactory. The first answer is that I am not at all sure how to answer the question. Second, it is an important theoretical ques-tion of such practical import that it deserves far more attention than it receives. I fully realize that in the real world decisions as to where one starts have to be made, and that one does not sit back and await the answers that others hopefully will someday provide. But the thrust of the second "answer" is that we have to recognize that we need better conceptualizations as guides to action than we now have.[2] The third answer is far more complicated and starts with the question: *who* should start where? The reader will notice

[2] In recent years there has been an increasing awareness of the need to study and conceptualize the change process in relation to the schools, e.g., Miles, M. B., 1964; Watson, G. (ed.), 1967; Bentzen, M. M. and Goodlad et al., 1968. The in-terested reader should consult these publications, although they involve for the most part new projects the results of which will not be known for some time. There are, of course, similarities between some of the points I have made in this book and these publications. There are important differences. Whereas I have strongly emphasized the need for descriptions of the modal process of change (and its variations) as a basis for conceptualization, as well as a control against premature theorizing, these writers (for the most part) seem to assume that we know the modal process. It is also quite clear that their way of thinking about change has been very heavily influenced by those who have studied the industrial setting, an influence that can only be justified by demonstrating that the culture of the school and industry have all that much in common so as to transfer change strategies from one setting to the other. This degree of genotypic similarity has not been demonstrated, and I do not think it can be. Related to this reservation is another one and that is that techniques that seem to have been helpful in the industrial setting — and I refer specifically to various group dynamics procedures — are not only applied in the school setting, but have come

that we have been conducting this discussion on the implicit assumption that whoever takes or is given responsibility for the change process will or must decide where to start. I would like to suggest that this assumption may be quite invalid and the beginning of trouble. For one thing it implies that it is possible for the agent of change to know and understand the targets of change (e.g., principals, teachers, parents, etc.) and their relationships to a degree sufficient to make a judgment about where to start. Rarely, if ever, is this, or could it be, the case. Furthermore, the very fact that we have a concept of "agent of change" has the effect of obscuring the necessity for the agent of change to be able to change his judgment on the basis of new and more information. I confess that I find it somewhat amusing to observe how much thought is given to developing vehicles for changing target groups and how little thought is given to vehicles that protect the agent of change from not changing in his understanding of and approach to that particular instance of change. I would suggest that where one starts has to be a problem that is presented to and discussed with the target groups — not as a matter of empty courtesy or ritualistic adherence to some vague democratic ethos but because *it gives one a more realistic picture of what one is dealing with. An obvious consequence of this is that in different settings one may very well answer the question of where to start rather differently,* a consequence that those who need to follow a recipe will find unsatisfactory because there is no one place to start. Still another consequence is that one may decide, indeed there are times one should decide, *to start nowhere,* that is, the minimal conditions required for that particular change to take hold, regardless of where one starts, are not present. The reader should note that the decision not to proceed with a particular change, far from being an evasion, forces one to consider *what other kinds*

---

to be viewed by many people (not the authors cited above) as panaceas. This is regrettable on three counts: the techniques have come to be viewed as ends in themselves (nowadays everyone, it seems, is in or is urged to participate in some kind of sensitivity training group); they place such an emphasis on "communication" and "interpersonal relations" as to convey the impression that they are the most important source (etiologically speaking) of problems in the school culture, whereas they are, in my opinion, far more symptoms than cause (in contrast, for example to dilemmas of role, the effects of routine and tradition, life in the classroom, irrelevant preparation, and the usual ways in which teaching and learning are conceptualized); finally, overselling these techniques does a disservice to that which is valid and helpful in their limited use.

of changes have to take place before the minimal conditions can be said to exist.

Any conceptualization of the change process must deal with two questions: what kind and depth of knowledge must the agent of change have of the target groups in the setting, and how does he obtain it, that is, how do we protect him against the fact that he is, like the rest of us when we do not have explicit guidelines, a rather poor gatherer and processor of information? Freud understood this problem well in regard to a particular two-person interaction. We have no such degree of understanding when we are dealing with the interaction between an agent of change (which may be one person or a small group) and a complicated social organization like a school.

TIME PERSPECTIVE AND
THE CHANGE PROCESS

The reader will agree that it would be strange and silly if someone were to ask a first-grade teacher why she cannot teach her pupils to read in one day. We would consider the questioner quite stupid. But what if he persists and the teacher has to give him some kind of answer? We know, of course, the outlines of what the teacher would talk about, for example, the nature of the learning process, maturational factors, perceptual readiness, motivation, and so on. Essentially the teacher's time perspective is determined by the way she conceives of the nature of the processes involved.

Let us take the instance of a psychoanalyst who has just taken on a new patient in treatment. In taking this step the analyst has agreed to see the patient four or five days a week *for a period of years.* Many people, including the beginning patient, cannot comprehend why so much time is needed to help someone in personal distress. If one asks this of the analyst he would, like the teacher, describe a set of related conceptions, which, in light of certain goals, give rise to problems and tactics that require one to take a rather long time perspective. Given his way of thinking, the analyst sees nothing strange in having such a time perspective. Other types of psychotherapies, involving different conceptions and having other (or even similar) goals, give rise to different time perspectives. It is precisely because psychotherapies differ in their underlying conceptions of what people are and how they change that so much controversy has existed about how long it takes to accomplish what with what degree of permanence.

Any conception of the change process in regard to schools, explicitly or implicitly, involves a time perspective. In light of our discussion in this and earlier chapters it should come as no surprise that the time perspective of those who initiated or oversaw the change processes (in the numerous instances I have observed) was as ill-considered as their understanding of the school culture was incomplete. But this does not get to the heart of the matter: even if one took account of the understanding of the school culture that these change agents had, their time perspective was most unrealistic, *if only because time perspective was not seriously viewed as a problem.*

Let us assume that the agents of change have worked out in a systematic fashion the relationship between their conceptions of the setting and a time perspective by which the intended change should be judged. A second aspect of the time perspective problem then arises: comparing the time perspective of the agents of change with that of those who are the targets, and that of those who will, in one way or another, participate in the process. This comparison is crucial because if, as is usually the case, the differences in time perspective are great, the seeds of conflict and disillusionment are already in the soil. In practice, the desire of the agents of change to get started — not only because of internal and external pressures but also because of the awareness, sometimes dim, that the road ahead will not be smooth — results in bypassing the different aspects of the time perspective problem, a bypass that may have no immediate adverse consequences but can be counted on to produce delayed, and sometimes fatal, difficulties. When I have discussed this with agents of change whose particular projects have ended in failure, partial or complete, one of the most frequently stated "causes" of difficulty was that *other people* were unrealistically impatient.

IMPLEMENTED AND NON-IMPLEMENTED CHANGE PROPOSALS

Anyone interested in the change process in schools, be it from a descriptive, or practical, or theoretical viewpoint, would do well at some point to give attention to proposals for change that are never implemented. Elsewhere (Sarason, 1967) I have put the problem in this way:

> Some of the most interesting and important aspects of the processes of change are revealed before the point of implementation of proposals for change. The importance of these aspects resides not only in how they affect implementation *but in the degree to which they result in no implementation at all.* It is not enough for the person interested in processes of change in various types of organizations or social systems to focus on ongoing or planned changes, although there is no question that such a focus can be a productive one. It is my contention, however, that an equally important part of the problem is the frequency of, and the contexts that surround, proposals for change that either do not get a hearing or never reach the stage of implementation. I have no doubt that these instances are far more frequent than those that reach the stage of implementation. Organizations — such as a university department, a professional school, a social agency — vary tremendously among and between themselves in the degree to which proposals and ideas for change never reach the stage of discussion or implementation.

> In recent months I have taken to asking members of various types of organizations what their estimate was of the relationship between proposals made and proposals implemented. The most frequent response was embarrassed silence. In some instances the embarrassment stemmed from the feeling that the question touched on something which, if pursued, would be quite revealing of that organization, and the revelation would not be very pleasant. In other instances, the embarrassment was a consequence of the realization that the individual had never been aware of what was implied in the question, although I tried to ask the question without stating what I thought its implications were.

> The significance of the question I have been putting to individuals may be gleaned in the following opinion: the greater the discrepancy between the frequency of proposals for change that are never implemented, and the number of proposals that are implemented, the more likely that the implemented changes over time will increasingly lose whatever innovative characteristics they may have had or were intended. In other words, the more things change on the surface the more conditions remain basically the same.

> The basis for this opinion brings us back to one of the major interests of the Psycho-Educational Clinic, i.e., the culture of the school and the processes of change. It has been in relation to our work in various school systems that we have become acutely aware

of how implemented changes quickly lose their innovative intent. Elsewhere I have indicated that one of the major reasons for this self-defeating process is the tendency for change proposals to emanate from on high without taking into account the feelings and opinions of those who must implement the changes, i.e., the teachers. What I emphasized was the interpersonal turmoil that such tendencies engender and its effect on the content and goals of change. My comments, however, were in relation to the history and consequences of a single proposal for change (e.g., new math, bussing, etc.) and neglected what I now think is the more general characteristic of the system: the marked discrepancy between the number of proposals to change the system and the number of proposals actually implemented. Put in another way: the fate of any single proposal for change will be determined in part by the number of changes that have been proposed but never implemented. If this is true, my observations suggest that it is because those who have to implement any single proposal for change react to it in terms of their knowledge of and experiences with other proposals (implemented or not) for change in the system. If they are aware, rightly or wrongly, that there is a discrepancy between proposals made and implemented, and particularly if this awareness is associated with feelings of dissatisfaction, it often affects the implementation of the single proposal for change in a way so as to fulfill the prophecy that the more things change the more they remain the same. The fate of a single proposal for change cannot be understood apart from all other proposals for change if only because those who do the implementing do not understand or react to it in that way — and any theory of change and innovation must face this inescapable fact.[3]

I came to this problem the hard way. The reader will recall that in Chapter 8 I presented the standard talk I always gave to the entire faculty of a school with which our clinic would be working. This meeting almost always took place in the June before the September we would start. Elsewhere (Sarason et al., 1966) we describe in some detail the "port of entry" problem, that is, the difficulties we had in being accepted in a school. It was not until we were in the school for some time (and I am referring primarily to urban schools) that I learned that part of our difficulties stemmed from three reactions to my talk. The first reaction was in the nature of "here we go again." That is to say, over the years

[3]S. B. Sarason "Toward a Psychological Change and Innovation." *American Psychologist* XXII (1967), p. 227.

they had been told or had heard of proposals to bring in new services but nothing ever seemed to happen. The second reaction, somewhat contradictory to the first, was that in the past people had shown up to render some kind of help but somehow or other they managed to disappear; or their appearances were so infrequent as to be valueless. They fully expected that we would disappear, particularly when we saw the extent of the problems in these schools. (Truth to say, there were many times we wanted to disappear.) The inescapable fact is that we were ignorant of the fact that we were perceived as transients on whom one could not or should not depend. (There were, of course, other considerations in their reaction.) We were not only perceived as particular kinds of individuals or personalities but as representatives of a class of events with which they felt unfortunately familiar.

The third reaction primarily characterized principals and some of the older teachers, and it concerned their strong feeling of dissatisfaction that whatever proposals they had made to improve their schools rarely reached the discussion stage and, more rarely, were implemented. Since they felt that way about *their* proposals, they did not view us too kindly because we represented *someone else's* ideas about what needed to be done.

There are two general points that deserve emphasis. The first is that when a change will involve a large part of a school system, the fate of the change will in some measure be a function of the discrepancy in that system between proposals made and proposals implemented, particularly if this discrepancy is something of which the agents of change are not aware. The second point is that the fate of a change that is directed, let us say, to a particular school will in part be a function of the history in that school between proposals made and proposals implemented. It may be that all I am saying is that prehistory is important. If true, I would then have to say that in the modal process of change in the school what is important is not recognized.

THE UNIVERSE OF ALTERNATIVES

In numerous places in this book I have attemped to demonstrate that faced with any problem or practice there are different ways in which we can think about them, an obvious enough point that should not obscure the empirical fact that our thinking does not, except rarely, reflect the obvious. Why this is so is less important here than the fact that it is so. What is crucial for our purposes is that any theory of the change process must confront and deal with this issue, by which I mean that it must provide a basis that controls against the tendency to think as if a universe of alternatives did not exist. Where this control does not exist it is too easy to accept what is with what could be. In discussing this point in Chapter 2 I mentioned the work of Garner (1966) on perception of auditory and visual patterns, in which he clearly demonstrates that our understanding of responses to patterns is in part a function of all possible related patterns that can be generated and to which an individual may be exposed. Although on the surface the perception of patterns is quite different than the problems we have discussed, the principle he demonstrates has clear significance for us because it states that what is before us is but one instance of a large number that potentially could be before us. Garner's studies, as he recognized, dealt with patterns with a finite number of possibilities, in addition to which he could choose patterns so as to manipulate the number of possibilities that could be generated. With the different problems we have discussed in this book we do not have a finite number of possibilities, and our ability to manipulate situations of any complexity is small indeed. It is precisely because we are not dealing with a finite, easily determined university of alternatives that it is so essential that we develop formal means that will protect us against undue constriction of possible ways of thinking. It is not terribly helpful to tell or encourage people to think systematically about the universe of alternatives relevant to a particular problem or practice. It is like telling people to be good: it strikes a responsive chord but the sound does not last very long.

I am unprepared to pursue further the necessity for a theory of change to deal with the universe of alternatives in thinking, although the reader may be assured that I have given, unsuccessfully, a good deal of thought to the problem.[4] But in my thinking about the problem, particularly as that thinking has taken place in practical efforts related

---

[4]Simon (1947, 1957) has dealt at length with similar kinds of questions in relation to his analyses of administrative man and economic man. He states, "Rationality requires a choice among all possible alternative behaviors. In actual

to the creation of complicated settings (Sarason, 1970), I have tentatively concluded that a small group of people focusing together *only* on the problem of the universe of alternatives applicable to a particular problem or practice is far more productive than what any one of them could come up with. I do not mean a small group in which each member indulges his capacity to free-associate, or where one's conviction about or predilection for particular types of alternatives is a relevant consideration, but one in which alternatives, *independent of how one may regard them,* is what individuals have to come up with. As I review these experiences I intuitively feel that it should be possible to develop guidelines that would allow for systematic exploration of the particular universe of alternatives. I might emphasize that one's affection for particular alternatives is the most effective barrier to coming up with alternatives.

But we have only discussed the universe of alternatives in regard to ways of thinking about a problem or practice, for example, what are the different ways in which parents can participate in classroom activities, what are the different ways in which pupils can participate in preparing examinations, what are the different ways in which a principal can be prepared for his position, what are alternative ways of de-routinizing the school day and year, what are the different ways a teacher can generate and utilize question-asking behavior in children, what are the different ways in which a neighborhood or community can exercise "control" over schools, and so on? The number of problems is probably as great as the alternatives to any one of them. *But complexity of the problem increases dramatically when one realizes that each alternative confronts one with a universe of alternatives of action.*

It is a truism in research, honored as often in the breach as not, that one's knowledge of methods and techniques should not determine the problems one studies. The nature and formulation of a problem is the primary determinant of the methods to be employed, or if appropriate methods are not available they have to be developed. The way I have discussed the concept of the universe of alternatives in relation to the change process may present difficulties to those wedded to a particular way of doing things

---

behavior, only a few of all these possible alternatives ever come to mind" (1947, p. 81). At another time he states, "The capacity of the human mind for formulating and solving complex problems is very small compared with the size of the problems whose solution is required for objectively rational behavior in the real world — or even for a reasonable approximation to such objective rationality" (1957, p. 198).

because it is clear that the concept will require a rather different methodology. Some readers may feel overwhelmed by the complexity I have attempted to describe; others may feel annoyed at what seems to them to be an unnecessary or unclear complexity. My answer to these reactions is in three parts. The modal process of change I have described, as well as its underlying assumptions, has been singularly unproductive of its intended outcomes, an understatement that in some quarters will be viewed as charitable in the extreme. What is required are new conceptualizations or ways of thinking that not only account for our failures but give rise to new modes of action. The problem *is* complex and at such a level that when we are offered simple or single solutions (like more money, community control, decentralization, Headstart, etc.) we have to learn to distinguish between good intentions and unfortunate ignorance. It is not that these single or simple solutions are in themselves wrong or inadvisable but rather that they are viewed as ends, which if reached will in some mystical way change the quality of life in the classroom and school.[5] The Headstart program, for example, seemed to be based, first, on the awareness that ghetto schools were antithetical to the educational development of its pupils, and, second, on the assumption that if these children could be worked with before they started school they would better be able to cope with it. (Don't lower the bridge, raise the river!) It has, unfortunately, become clear that this strategy of avoiding coming to grips with the realities of the culture of these schools was misguided. I take no pride, and I certainly take no pleasure, in the fact that when Headstart was started I predicted, on the basis of my experience in ghetto schools, that a small

[5] Decentralization of our large urban school systems is considered by many people as a solution to the ills of the school, although why this should be so is mystifying. But it has become a kind of slogan or rallying point, and, in the process, the fantastic complexity of achieving intended outcomes in schools and classrooms, for which decentralization may be the first and *easiest* step, goes unrecognized or undiscussed. For example, Rogers' (1968) detailed description of the attempts to desegregate the New York City schools has been used by some to argue for decentralization as a solution to a sorry mess, even though Rogers toward the end of his book makes it clear that the act of decentralization in itself guarantees nothing. As Kaufman (1969) succinctly states in his review of Rogers' book: "Even decentralization, while it may lessen some tensions for a while, is by no means a permanent resolution of the underlying difficulties, as Professor Rogers observes . . . . Manipulating local administrative machinery is at best only a palliative (though even palliatives are important to those who suffer)." Cohen's (1969) discussion of decentralization is also recommended to the reader.

number of children would benefit, most would not, and some might even be harmed. Why transplanted blossoms should be expected to flower in unfertile soils escapes me. In the context of political and social movements it is inevitable that one often has to take stands for or against simple solutions, especially as in the case of education where these solutions reflect so many other social problems. But there are ways of taking stands for simple solutions which do not absolve us of the responsibility of being realistic and critical.

14

The Basis for Hope

Of the major reactions people have had about schools, two require mention here. The first of these may be characterized by one word: hopelessness. As one person said to me: "Our urban school systems are like New York City. They are essentially ungovernable and unchangeable." If one asks for justification of such an extreme response, one hears a catalogue of instances and events, all of which confirm that man's capacity to do and tolerate stupid things is vast indeed. As I see it, the sole virtue of this reaction is that it permits one to give up the intellectual struggle to understand why the situation developed the way it has, and to avoid the turmoil and conflict that inevitably confronts one in the world of action. There are few things, if any, that are better than hopelessness for demonstrating the dynamics of the self-fulfilling prophecy.

The second reaction, and one I clearly share, starts with the recognition that we have no good basis for comfort in regard either to the adequacy of our schools or to the beneficial effects of the major efforts to change them. This is not a recognition colored exclusively by the language of an individual psychology. That is to say, it is not a recognition that sees the problem primarily in terms of personality characteristics, motivation, resistances, the presence or absence of creative or imaginative individuals, or any other dimension along which individuals vary. It is rather a recognition that the problem inheres in the fact that history and tradition have given rise to roles and relationships, to interlocking ideas, practices, values, and expectations that are the "givens" not requiring thought or deliberation. These "givens" (like other categories of thought) are far less the products of the characteristics of individuals than they are a reflection of what we call the culture and its traditions. I illustrated this point in an earlier chapter when I described the reaction of school personnel to two questions. First, why should there be physical education programs in the schools? Second, is it necessary for each school to have a principal? The fact that for so many teachers (and others) it was inconceivable that a school would not or should not have a principal or a physical education program says far more about the school culture and its traditions than it does about teachers as individuals.

One of the most difficult obstacles to recognizing that the major problems in our schools inhere far less in the characteristics of individuals than it does in its cultural and system characteristics is that one cannot *see* culture or system the way one sees individuals. Culture and system are not concrete, tangible, visible things in the way individuals are. In many respects it is easier to think about an individual teacher or an individual principal than it is to think, for example, about the roles of teacher and principal and their relationships independent of individual personalities. It is only in recent years that we have become aware of how little we know about schools as functioning organizations or systems. For example, in a very thoughtful review of the literature relevant to the school as a complex organization Bidwell (1965) begins in this way:

> Reviewing the sociological literature on education from 1945 to 1955, Gross (1956) commented that a systematic study of the school as an organization had yet to be made. His comment is still true. Few students of organizations have turned their attention to schools, and few students of schools have been sensitive to their organizational attributes. To understand what schools are like as organizations — what their characteristic structures, processes, and functional problems are — we now must rely on empirical work, much of which either was not explicitly directed toward these questions or was narrowly focussed on some subsystem, process, or activity within the school, without being informed by a more general conception of the school as an organization.[1]

[1]C. E. Bidwell, "The School as a Formal Organization," in J. G. March (ed.),

After reviewing the literature Bidwell concludes his discussion in this way:

> The attempt here has been to suggest some possible dimensions of a framework for studying schools as organizations. The ideas advanced await new empirical evidence. Hopefully, this evidence will come from research including many more studies than presently exist concerned with the actual functioning of schools and school systems. Studies using direct observation, informants, and the analysis of documents are especially needed. Ratings of others' behavior or judgmental nominations, which to date have been the principal sources of material on school operations, are weak substitutes for phenomenological data. Moreover, the attitudes of school personnel, about which we now are best informed, constitute only a portion of the complex of variables which bear on the operation of school organizations.[2]

The plea that Bidwell makes is identical to one that I have made throughout this book.[3] Far less important than any identity between what Bidwell has said and what I have attempted is the fact that there is growing awareness that we know far less about the *"actual* functioning of schools and school systems" than we have realized. If this is true, it suggests that our past efforts to change and improve our schools have been less than successful in part because we *thought* we knew what we needed to know about the actual functioning of these complex organizations. In short, the problem has resided not only "out there" in the schools, but in the ways in which we have been accustomed to thinking about what it was that needed to be changed, and these ways of thinking prevented us from recognizing what we did not know but needed

---

Handbook of Organization (Chicago: Rand McNally & Company, 1965). By permission of Rand McNally & Company.

[2] *Ibid.*

[3] Our lack of knowledge about the actual functioning of schools is by no means peculiar to these parts of the educational scene. For example, in a four-paragraph comment on university governance (Saturday Review, January, 1970) Logan Wilson states: "I don't know of a single empirical study of a campus that delineates just how decisions are now made. In many institutions it is a kind of shell game, and I suspect that this is a source of frustration to many students who make recommendations and then are mystified about what happens to them." This simple, clear, and justified statement should give pause to those who believe that the different efforts to change the university in one way or another are really directed to the way things are.

to know. If at least part of the problem has been a consequence of the ways we have been thinking, one is not justified in concluding that we are dealing with a hopeless situation. More than that, however, it serves to remind us that what happens "out there" is not only a reflection of the objective nature of "out there" but the way in which we think about what is "out there." In situations of failure or crisis it is much easier to project blame outward than it is to implicate our ways of thinking and their consequences for our actions.

It was because of these kinds of considerations that the early chapters of this book were devoted to the critics of our schools and those who assume the responsibility for changing some aspect of the schools. In those discussions I was essentially asking three questions that had direct bearing on their ways of thinking. The first question concerned the extent of their knowledge or experience about the actual functioning of schools and school systems. The second question was the extent to which the school was viewed as an organization possessing a unique culture and was, therefore, different from the setting or organization from which the critic comes. The point I emphasized in this connection (using the university setting as an example) was that the invalid assumption about the uniqueness of the school culture not only prevented the critic from seeing communalities between his and the school culture but almost guaranteed that his efforts to change the schools would fail. The likely consequence would be that the failure would be explained only as a function of the school and not in terms of his ways of thinking and limitations in knowledge. The third question, and one derived from the first two, was in two parts: What were the critic's or change agent's implicit or explicit conceptions about how one effectively introduces and maintains a change in the school culture? What knowledge did the critic have of the modal process by which a change is initiated and accommodated in the school culture? It was in light of these questions, as well as of the aim to describe some aspects of the actual functioning of schools, that I chose to discuss in detail the introduction of the new math in a particular school system.

In reading the account of the introduction of the new math, some readers may have wondered about describing the process as "modal." At the time this book was being completed, McIntyre's (1969) monograph appeared, and it confirms most of what I described and concluded. His account of his experiences in introducing a new service (not a new curriculum) into two highly similar schools in a small homogeneous town is one of the most detailed accounts we have of the change process, and it underscores the wisdom of Bidwell's suggestion that what is needed are descriptions of the actual functioning of schools as complex organizations. His detailed, dispassionate, frank, and moving account makes several major points. The first of these points centers on the too frequent tendency to underestimate the complexity of the school system as a social system, and how this adversely affects what one hopes to accomplish; that is, part of the problem resides in the thinking of those who wish to innovate in some way. Second, that the major obstacles he encountered on what turned out to be the road to failure resided not only in McIntyre's lack of knowledge of the actual functioning of schools but in the structure and traditions of schools; the major obstacles did not reside in the perversities or personalities of individuals although these factors are always present.

> In trying to understand such a complicated human network as a school system, it is insufficient to characterize its organizational structure as more or less authoritarian. There can be many variations in organizational structure, and these variations are important in terms of the pattern of human functioning. Likewise, similar organizational structures can be inhabited by different kinds of people, and this too is important. The interaction between structure and individuals must be our focus. Furthermore, to make matters even more complicated, *it is precisely this kind of interaction, occurring over long periods of time, that results in something we can call a subculture, which is held together by a force not much different and no less powerful than the feelings of morality that bind our larger Western culture.*
>
> In analyzing the influence of organizational structure on patterns of functioning, I think we have to become concerned with two kinds of influence. One is the current cross-sectional effect that structure has on the action alternatives available to individuals within the structure. The other is a longitudinal effect that derives from individuals living within a particular structure over a length of time, wherein action alternatives become available or unavailable to the individuals more as a result of felt tradition than a practical assessment of possibilities. The distinction is important because each involves vastly different attitudes and intel-

lectual processes on the part of the individuals being influenced. The former involves a relatively pragmatic, objective assessment of current structural characteristics as they affect actions and consequences, and is done presumably in much the same way a businessman evaluates a business proposition. The latter, involving as it does the weight of tradition as it affects one's feelings toward the acceptability of certain kinds of alternatives, has a way of generalizing above and beyond the current situation to include whole classes of actions and alternatives which are then accepted or rejected almost automatically, and comes to look very much like that kind of morality (inherent rightness or wrongness of particular courses of action) that holds together and gives characteristic form to cultural and subcultural systems.

For example, teachers may have been prevented initially from discussing classroom difficulties with their principals due to the school's organizational structure. Since it is frequently a principal's responsibility to evaluate the performance of teachers and to judge their eligibility for rehiring, for tenure, for pay increases based on number of "successful" teaching years, and to recommend teachers for new jobs, it could then be very risky for teachers to discuss real problems with a principal. The first few times a teacher must have to think a problem through every time it occurs. Over time, however, the accumulative weight of such decisions results in the automatic character of tradition in which it could become almost morally unthinkable for teachers to discuss openly their classroom problems with a principal, or anyone else in authority. Such traditions can become relatively autonomous of the real situations that created them, can be perpetuated in the same way that other cultural traditions are perpetuated, and can become something newcomers must learn or run the risk of becoming outcasts. It could generate suspicion of anyone perceived as having higher authority, such as a psychological consultant. To reverse such a tradition would require much more than simply altering the circumstances that created it. Traditions become built-in ways of thinking and acting for which alternatives diminish rather than increase.[4]

When one reads McIntyre's descriptions and gets the feel for the anxiety he experienced and the interpersonal conflicts and frustrations he encountered, it is remarkable that his final conceptualizations center not on individuals and their personalities but

[4]D. McIntyre, "Two Schools, One Psychologist," in Kaplan, F., and Sarason, S. B., eds., *The Psycho-Educational Clinic: Papers and Research Studies* (Boston: Department of Mental Health, Commonwealth of Massachusetts, 1969).

rather on the subtle and massive effects of culture and tradition on ways of thinking, patterns of relationships, and the awareness of alternatives. Although he does not discuss it, when one finishes his monograph one may infer that if he could start anew he would proceed differently than he did because of his deeper understanding of how a school system actually functions— and therein resides the basis of hope. Far from ending on a note of hopelessness he ends on a level of conceptual understanding that, if taken seriously and further developed by others, may well lead to more appropriate and effective efforts at change.

In stressing the importance of determining the actual functioning of the complex organization of the school (or the greater complexity of a school system) one has to face squarely two major problems: one cannot study everything, and the human observer is far from a neutral instrument. It was these considerations that led us to a discussion of how one might look at the school and describe its actual behavioral and programmatic regularities, which could serve as the criteria by which one determines how effectual one's efforts at change have been. It has been all too frequent in the past that the criteria for determining change have been either so vague or value laden or unduly complex that they have permitted the glossing over of the question of evaluation — or more frequent, they guarantee that the final criterion will be the personal opinion held even before the effort at change was attempted. By illustrating and emphasizing behavioral and programmatic regularities, and contending that any meaningful effort at change involves a change in one or more of these regularities, I was in essence suggesting that future efforts at change, far from being exercises in futility, can be far more effective than they have been in the past. But there was an implication to our discussion that is illustrated by the following story, which may or may not be apocryphal. An individual became interested in the field of genetics and was most impressed by how much more progress that field had made in the past decade or so compared to previous ones. Upon meeting an eminent geneticist the individual took the opportunity to ask him how he would account for the accelerated rate of knowledge. The geneticist is supposed to have replied: "We began to ask the easy questions." I regard the question of behavioral and programmatic regularities as a type of "easy" question the answers to which may take us far.

There are aspects of the school culture about which I have said nothing or to which I have made only allusions. For example, I have not discussed the board of education: the ways in which its members are chosen, its powers (formal and informal), the ways in which policy is formulated, its sources of knowledge about the system, and the range of activities and practices it does influence or is capable of influencing. The role of superintendent of schools has also been absent from our discussion, as is also the case with the many different types of upper-echelon administrators who are usually located "downtown."

The knowledgeable reader will know that important aspects of the school can only be comprehended by examining the formal and informal relationships between a school system and the state department of education, a set of relationships that leads one into the legislative process and, of course, politics in the narrow sense. Finally, I have only briefly discussed the purposes and adequacy of the many different types of training programs in our colleges and universities from which educational personnel come. But I do not note these aspects of the school culture only to emphasize the complexity of the school culture or my limitations in knowledge about and experience with them. I mention them in order to stress two points. The first is one that I discussed earlier in the book: how one describes and experiences the school culture is largely determined by one's relationship to it. One might say that the school culture is in the nature of an ink-blot, which, although it does have certain objective characteristics (e.g., color, size), can be experienced and responded to in different ways by different people; there may be communalities in response to the ink-blot but to the clinician it is the source of variation of response that he seeks to understand. The second point is a consequence of the first: one's relationship to or place in the culture influences one's conception either of how the culture changes or of how it could be changed. The nature of the influence is by no means obvious. For example, there is the conception of system change that emphasizes the importance of changing the behavior or attitudes of the highest echelons of authority and responsibility. It may seem strange to some when I say that in my experience this conception is held with increasing certainty and frequency as one goes from the top to the bottom of the system. The opposite tends to be the case with the conception that emphasizes administrative-structural or power changes as a way of achieving goals of change. There is, of course, the conception of change that puts the greatest emphasis on the importance of altering, in one way or another, the base of the pyramidally organized system, that is, the teachers. In recent years, and particularly in our urban settings, this conception has been advocated by various community groups. (It is also held, in my experience, by those at the top of the pyramid — but it is a view they only express privately.) The proponents of these and other conceptions of change tend, unfortunately, to miss the point that their particular conception may not be logically adequate to all goals of change. It is not a matter of whether one conception is in some abstract sense "right" and all others are "wrong." Any meaningful attempt to change the school culture requires an over-arching conception that encompasses these other conceptions in a way that prevents one from oversimplifying the complexity of the goals to be achieved, and from recognizing that these complex goals require the simultaneous use of different tactics or procedures.

The focus I have adopted in this book reflects a value judgment that among all the aspects of the school culture that are or may be the objects of change, none is as important as the quality of life and thinking in the classroom and that the roles of teacher and principal are obviously crucial.[5] In making this judgment it is not necessary that I question the legitimacy of any attempt to change any other aspect of the school culture. It seems clear enough that on the verbal and action levels most attempts to change anything in the school culture have as their direct or indirect goal the changing of some aspect of life in the classroom. That these efforts

[5]One of the most interesting (and hopeful) aspects of McIntyre's monograph is suggested by its title "Two Schools, One Psychologist." What gave rise to this monograph was McIntyre's puzzlement about how strikingly different his experiences were in two highly similar schools in the same small system. What emerges clearly is how important the differences between the two principals were in determining not only the quality of McIntyre's experience but that of teachers and children as well. His account supports the contention that any effort to change any of the aspects of the classroom that does not deal directly with the problem of change in the principal, is unlikely to be other than minimally successful. Although his account demonstrates well the importance of the role of the principal in the change process, he goes to some lengths to describe the importance of other roles as well. The fact remains, however, that in the many efforts to introduce change in the life of classrooms that I have observed, the problem of change in the principal was either never raised, or if it was raised it was bypassed or so indirectly faced and handled as to be ineffective (and later self-defeating).

have generally failed is not attributable simply to faulty technique or to a particular group but rather to the ways in which we are accustomed to look at and think about life in the classroom. What I have tried to do in this book is to discuss ways of looking and thinking about life in school that would lessen the likelihood that efforts at change will have the all too familiar consequences of substituting one set of books for another, one type of ritual for another, maintaining the confusion between thinking and the acquisition of knowledge, between overt conformity and internal satisfaction, perpetuating the false assumption that the teacher and the pupil require different conditions for productive learning, and finally, obscuring the fact that in practice the most frequent way in which children are expected to learn individual responsibility and social reciprocity is by *not* being exposed to such experiences. If the more things change the more they remain the same, it is because our ways of looking and thinking have not changed. This should not be surprising when one recognizes that the agents of change from outside the school culture are too frequently ignorant of the culture in which the change is to be embedded, or if they are part of the culture, they are themselves victims of that very fact. Freud was only the most recent in a line of great philosophers who saw clearly that before one intrudes into the lives and settings of others one had better know the sources of one's own way of looking and thinking. Objectivity in regard to the school culture, or that degree of it which man is capable of achieving, is not won by wishing or good intentions; it is won, to the degree that it can be won, by a willing struggle in which the culture, often our ally, becomes our adversary. Recognizing the adversary gives one a basis for asserting that the problem is neither hopeless nor insoluble.

⌒ Bibliography ⌒

AUSUBEL, D. P., "Crucial Psychological Issues in the Objectives, Organization, and Evaluation of Curriculum Reform Movements." *Psychology in the Schools,* IV (1967), 111-120.

BARKER, R. G., *Ecological Psychology.* Stanford: Stanford University Press, 1968

BARKER, R. G., and GUMP, P. V., *Big School, Small School.* Stanford: Stanford University Press, 1964.

BEACH, F. A., "The Snark Was a Boojum." *American Psychologist,* V (1950), 115-124.

BENTZEN, M. M., GOODLAD, J. I., LAHADERNE, H. M., MYERS, D. A., NOVOTNEY, J. M., SINCLAIR, R. L., SPITZER, L. K., and TYE, K. A., *The Principal and the Challenge of Change.* Los Angeles: Institute for Development of Educational Activities, 1100 South Glendon Avenue, 1968.

BIDWELL, C. E., "The School as a Formal Organization." In J. G. March (ed.), *Handbook of Organizations.* Chicago: Rand McNally, 1965.

BOOTH, P., New York Times Book Review Section (June 22, 1969).

BRUNER, J. S., *Toward a Theory of Instruction.* Cambridge, Mass.: Harvard University Press, 1966.

COHEN, D. K., "The Price of Community Control." *Commentary* (July, 1969).

CONANT, J. B., *The Education of Teachers.* New York: McGraw-Hill, Inc., 1963.

CORWIN, R. G., *A Sociology of Education.* New York: Appleton-Century-Crofts, 1965.

CREMIN, L. A., *The Transformation of the School.* New York: Alfred A. Knopf, Inc., 1961.

DE TOCQUEVILLE, A., *Democracy in America.* New York: New American Library (Mentor Books), 1956.

EPSTEIN, J., Book Review: New York Review Of Books (December, 1964) Vol. 3.

FEHR, H. F., "Sense and Nonsense in a Modern School Mathematics Program." *The Arithmetic Teacher,* XIII (1966) 83-91.

FLEXNER, A., and BACHMAN, T., *The Gary Schools: A General Account.* New York: General Education Board, 1918.

FRIEDMAN, N., *The Social Nature of Psychological Research.* New York: Basic Books, Inc., 1967.

GARNER, W. R., *Uncertainty and Structure as Psychological Concepts.* New York: John Wiley, 1966.

GOLDHAMMER, K., SUTTLE, J. E., BECKER, G. L., and ALDRIDGE, W. D., *Issues and Problems in Contemporary Educational Administration.* Eugene, Oregon: Center for Advanced Study of Educational Administration, University of Oregon Press, 1967.

GOODLAD, J. I., "The Schools and Education." *Saturday Review* (April 19, 1969).

GREEN, T. F., *Work, Leisure, and the American Schools.* New York: Random House, Inc., 1968.

GREENBERG, D. S., *The Politics of Pure Science.* New York: New American Library, 1967.

GROSS, N., "Sociology of Education, 1944-55." In H. L. Zetterberg (ed.), *Sociology in the United States of America: A Trend Report.* Paris: UNESCO, 1956.

GROSS, N., and HERRIOTT, R. E., *Staff Leadership in Public Schools.* New York: John Wiley, & Sons, Inc., 1965.

GUMP, P. V., and KOUNIN, J. S., "Issues Raised by Ecological and 'Classical' Research Efforts." Paper read at 1959 meeting of the Society for Research in Child Development.

HENRY, J., *Culture Against Man.* New York: Random House, Inc., 1963.

HILL, K., and SARASON, S. B. "A Further Longitudinal Study of the Relation of test Anxiety and Defensiveness Test and School Performance over the Elementary School Years." *Monographs of the Society for Research in Child Development,* XXXI (1966) No. 2.

HOLT, J., *How Children Fail.* New York: Pitman Publishing Corporation, 1964.

HOOK, S., *Reason, Social Myths and Democracy.* New York: Harper Torchbooks, 1966.

JACKSON, P. W., *Life in Classrooms*. New York: Holt, Rinehart, and Winston, Inc., 1968.

JONES, R. M., *Fantasy and Feeling in Education*. New York: New York University Press, 1968.

KAUFMAN, H., Book Review. *Trans-action*, VI (April, 1969), No. 6, 58-61.

KELLY, J. G., "Towards an Ecological Conception of Preventive Interventions." In "Research Contributions from Psychology to Conceptions of Community Mental Health" (Carter, J. W., ed.), *Community Mental Journal Monograph*, (1968).

KOHL, H., *36 Children*. New York: New American Library, 1967.

KOUNIN, J. S., "Observation and Analysis of Classroom Management." Paper read at 1967 meeting of the American Educational Research Association.

KOUNIN, J. S., FRIESEN, W. V., and NORTON, A. E., "Managing Emotionally Disturbed Children in Regular Classrooms." *Journal of Educational Psychology*, LVII (1966), 1-13.

KOUNIN, J. S., GUMP, P. V., and RYAN, J. J. "Explorations in Classroom Management." *Journal of Teacher Education*, XII (1961), 235-246.

KOZOL, J., *Death at an Early Age*. Boston: Houghton Mifflin Company, 1967.

LAUTER, P., "The Short, Happy Life of the Adams-Morgan Community School Project." *Harvard Educational Review*, XXXVIII (1968), 235-262.

LEVINE, A. G., "Marital and Occupational Plans of Women in Professional Schools: Law, Medicine, Nursing, Teaching." Doctoral Dissertation, Yale University, 1968.

LEVINE, M., and LEVINE, A., *A Social History of Helping Services: Clinic, Court, School and Community*. New York: Appleton-Century-Crofts, 1970.

MCINTYRE, D., "Two Schools, One Psychologist." In *The Psycho-Educational Clinic: Papers and Research Studies* (Kaplan, F., and Sarason, S. B. eds.) Boston: Department of Mental Health, Commonwealth of Massachusetts, 1969.

MAYHEW, K. C., and EDWARDS, A. C., *The Dewey School*. New York: Atherton Press, 1966.

MILES, M. B. (ed.), *Innovation in Education*. New York: Bureau of Publications, Teachers College, Columbia University, 1964.

MILLS, C. W., *The Sociological Imagination*. New York: Grove Press, 1959.

ROGERS, D., *110 Livingston Street: Politics and Bureaucracy in the New York City School System.* New York: Random House, Inc., 1968.

ROSENTHAL, R., *Experimenter Effects in Behavioral Research.* New York: Appleton-Century-Crofts, 1966.

ROUSH, G. J., "What Will Become of the Past?" *Daedulus* (Summer, 1969), 641-653.

SARASON, S. B., "Towards a Psychology of Change and Innovation." *American Psychologist,* XXII (1967), 227-233.

SARASON, S. B., "The Creation of Settings." In *The Yale Psycho-Educational Clinic: Collected Papers and Studies* (Sarason, S. B., and Kaplan, F., eds.). Boston: Massachusetts State Department of Mental Health (Monograph Series), 1969.

SARASON, S. B., DAVIDSON, K., and BLATT, B., *The Preparation of Teachers. An Unstudied Problem in Education.* New York: John Wiley, 1962.

SARASON, S. B., DAVIDSON, K., LIGHTHALL, F., WAITE, R., and RUEBUSH, B., *Anxiety in Elementary School Children.* New York: John Wiley & Sons, Inc., 1960.

SARASON, S. B., and DORIS, J., *Psychological Problems in Mental Deficiency,* 4th ed. New York: Harper & Row, Publishers, 1968.

SARASON, S. B., HILL, K., and ZIMBARDO, P., "A Longitudinal Study of the Relation of Test Anxiety to Performance on Intelligence and Achievement Tests." *Monographs of the Society for Research in Child Development,* 1964, No. 98.

SARASON, E. K., and SARASON, S. B., "Some Observations on the Teaching of the New Math." In *The Yale Psycho-Educational Clinic: Collected Papers and Studies.* (Sarason, S. B., and Kaplan, F., eds.) Boston: Massachusetts State Department of Mental Health (Monograph Series), 1969.

SARASON, S. B., LEVINE, M., GOLDENBERG, I. I., CHERLIN, D. L., and BENNETT, E., *Psychology in Community Settings.* New York: John Wiley, & Sons, Inc., 1966.

SCHWEBEL, A., "Physical and Social Distancing in Teacher-Pupil Relationships." Doctoral Dissertation, Yale University, 1969.

SIMON, H. A., *Administrative Behavior.* New York: The Macmillan Company, 1947.

SIMON, H. A., *Models of Man.* New York: John Wiley & Sons, Inc., 1957.

SPINDLER, G. D. (ed.) *Education and Culture.* New York: Holt, Rinehart and Winston, Inc., 1963.

STEPHENS, J. M., *The Process of Schooling. A Psychological Examination.* New York: Holt, Rinehart and Winston, Inc., 1967.

SUSSKIND, E. C., "Questioning and Curiosity in the Elementary School Classroom." Doctoral Dissertation, Yale University, 1969.

TAYLOR, D. W. (Chairman) "Education for Research in Psychology." *American Psychologist*, XIV (1959), 167-179.

USDAN, M. D., "The School Administrator: Modern Renaissance Man." *The Record* (Teachers College, Columbia), LXIX (1968), 641-648.

WALLER, W., *The Sociology of Teaching.* New York: John Wiley & Sons, Inc., 1932.

WALLIN, J. E. W., *The Odyssey of a Psychologist.* Wilmington, Delaware: published by the author, 1955.

WATSON, G. (ed.), *Change in School Systems.* Washington, D.C.: National Training Laboratories, National Education Association, 1967.

WATSON, G. (ed.), *Concepts for Social Change.* Washington, D.C.: National Training Laboratories, National Education Association, 1967.

WATSON, J. D., *The Double Helix.* New York: Atheneum Publishers, 1968.

WEINBERG, A. M., "But is the Teacher also a Citizen?" *Science* (August 6, 1965), 601-606.

WERTHEIMER, M., *Productive Thinking.* New York: Harper & Row Publishers, 1945.

WHITEHEAD, A. N., *The Aims of Education.* New York: Mentor, 1929 (paperback).

ZAX, M., and COWEN, E. L., "Early Identification and Prevention of Emotional Disturbance in a Public School." In Cowen, E. L., Gardner, E. A., and Zax, M. (eds.) *Emergent Approaches to Mental Health Problems.* New York: Appleton-Century-Crofts, 1967.

⌢Index⌢

243